The Fort Parker
Comanche Raid
& Its Aftermath, Texas 1836

The Fort Parker Comanche Raid

& Its Aftermath, Texas 1836

Louis Gelert

LEONAUR

The Fort Parker Comanche Raid
& Its Aftermath, Texas 1836
by Louis Gelert

FIRST EDITION

Leonaur is an imprint of Oakpast Ltd

Copyright in this form © 2016 Oakpast Ltd

ISBN: 978-1-78282-525-8 (hardcover)
ISBN: 978-1-78282-526-5 (softcover)

http://www.leonaur.com

Publisher's Notes

Contents

The Raid on Fort Parker, 1836

A. J. Sowell

Early in the fall of 1835, a small colony of whites, known as Austin Colony (now Grimes County), arrived and settled at a point about two and a half miles north of the present county seat. The following persons composed the colony: Silas M. Parker, John Parker, James Parker, L. T. M. Plummer, Benjamin Parker, Elisha Anglin and his son, Abraham, Samuel Frost and family, Seth H. Bates and son, Geo. E. Dwight, J. Nickson and the heroic Mrs. Plummer. The early outlook for this little band of brave and industrious people were first of the most pleasing and encouraging nature, indeed they were all happy upon the realization of long anticipated hopes for they were seeking, what apparently laid at their feet, rich and productive soil, broad and flourishing pasturage, good timber, excellent water, and abundant game; but, alas! these pleasing realisations were soon to be over-clouded by the dark and frustrating clouds of adversity, warfare and death.

The sad sequel of this little band has been verbally related to the author of this sketch (Maggie Abercrombie) by one of the old settlers, above mentioned, who is still alive, (1884), but too decrepit and old to write. From his conversation is gathered the following data: The first evidence of trouble that appeared to the people was caused by a small party of settlers from Colorado, who, not being content to pursue their avocations peaceably and honestly, attempted to infringe upon the rights of a tribe of Tehaucano Indians, who had a small village upon the hills of the same name (Tehaucano), situated in the northern part of the county. These Colorado settlers repeatedly molested and annoyed the Indians by attempting to steal their horses.

The Indians had manifested a civil disposition until these annoyances provoked their resentment and revenge, and in the instances alluded to, they repulsed the white Colorado settlers, killing Williams, the leader, and wounding Huldaman, a small boy. From this unfortunate event, the Indians exhibited no little degree of malice and revenge, and would frequently glide into the white settlements at midnight and steal their stock and cattle. They appeared perfectly defiant in their village, which stands on one of the highest hills in central Texas, and over- looks the broad green prairies for miles and miles around. They seemed to believe these hills, like Caesar, did the hills of Rome, a formidable fortification against any and all intrusion, and would often in day time commit fearful crimes, and immediately repair to their quarters on the hills.

No sooner had the settlers begun to take the preliminary steps for shelter and comfort, than did the alarming indications of molestation become more manifest, and the propriety of defence manifest itself. They therefore soon erected that rude fortification known to the darker pages of Texas history as "Fort Parker," and which shall ever live in the hearts of the countrymen, as does the recollections of San Jacinto and the Alamo. Of these trials, scenes and dangers one of the old survivors has written as follows:—

> After our log fort had been erected, we pursued our avocations with better satisfaction than before, and not until May, the succeeding year, did we suffer any very great depredations from the Indians. During this month the fearful and cowardly massacre of Fort Parker was enacted. It was no day for the awful deeds committed, for nature had ushered into light a May day as gentle and as serene as the soft light of the dawning sun that stole carelessly over our sleeping farms. At an early hour, and while a few of our more delicate ones were still engaged in slumber, we noticed upon an eminent point on the prairie, not exceeding four hundred yards from the fort, a body of restless Indians. This unexpected spectacle created the usual result among the women and children, and while the men were naturally surprised they knew that discipline, composure and fortitude, were their imperative duty and safeguard. A white flag was conspicuously hoisted by the Indians as an indication of peace. Very soon afterwards, a warrior from their camp approached the fort and in a civil manner offered to make a treaty. To this. Captain Benjamin Parker, commander of the fort, responded.
>
> After a short interview he returned and notified the inmates that he believed the Indians intended to fight. He, however,

returned to the hostile camp, which was no sooner reached, than he was a mangled corpse, literally chopped into pieces by the bloodthirsty demons. They immediately began their hideous war-whoop, and with wild, infuriated yells, charged upon the fort. Fortunately, several of the inmates had left the stockade by this time, while others were endeavouring to escape. Mrs. Nixon, a brave little woman, heroically made her way through an exposed field, where she notified her father, husband and brother, of the imminent danger that threatened them.

Mr. John Parker and wife, with Mrs. Kellogg, had gotten a mile or more away when they were overtaken, the old man killed and scalped, his wife speared and left for dead, and Mrs Kellogg made captive. Samuel M. Frost and his son were brutally killed, also Silas M. Parker. Mrs. Plummer in trying to escape by flight, was knocked down by a huge Indian, and with her child, seventeen months old, made prisoners. Cynthia Ann and John, two children of Silas Parker, were also captured. The survivors met a few days afterwards, when it was discovered that only eighteen of the original number of their party were present.

The alarm spread through the settlements like wild fire, and a small body of men soon repaired to the fort, but seeing no line of defence against the great number of Indians which approximated near eight hundred, they, after close concealment in ambush, retreated to their respective homes, and in a short time all moved away to Fort Houston, about three miles distant from the present city of Palestine.

The wounded wife of John Parker, covered with blood and scarcely able to walk, was found after night by a party of three or four, by whom she was conveyed to the Fort Houston settlement. She did not survive a great while. Soon afterwards a party repaired to Fort Parker and buried the remains of the dead. Mrs. Kellogg was, a few months afterwards, purchased by General Sam Houston from some friendly Delaware Indians, who held her at one hundred and fifty dollars ransom. Mrs. Plummer was also purchased from her captors by Colonel Donnahue, and after weeks of suffering and trial, reached Santa Fe. She was a captive over two years, and had many thrilling adventures.

Mr. R. F. Mattison writes of Mrs. Plummer's adventures and of "old Fort Parker," as follows:—

Mrs. Plummer, whose captivity and sufferings among the Comanche Indians we are now about to relate, was the daughter of Rev. James W. Parker, the captain of a small company of rangers, and the commander of Fort Parker. When the fort fell into the hands of the Indians, by means of a ruse to which they resorted, she attempted to escape, carrying in her arms her little son, James Pratt, only eighteen months old. Nothing could give us a more exalted estimation of female courage and fortitude, than the act of this frail, delicate little woman, who was willing to risk her life that she might save her infant child; while with the heartrending screams of friends were mingled with the terrible yells of the brutal and savage foe, she ventured out alone, risking all to save her dear one; with no shield, no protection, save the burning eye; of God and the feeble prayers that were ascending to Him. With the infant pressed close to her bosom, she rushes across the field in the direction of adjoining timber. She strains every nerve and speeds onward, urged only by fear and affection.

It was not, however, in the providence of God, that Mrs. Plummer and her child should meet death heroically or escape. A huge, savage warrior, painted and begrimed with dust and blood, discovers and pursues her with a savage yell of triumph. Though fear lent swiftness to her feet, she is not fleet enough to leave him behind. He overtakes her, clutches a hoe left in the field, fells her to the ground and seizing her by the hair of the head, drags her, still clinging to her boy, though stunned and unconscious, past the fort and into presence of the main body of Indians. She awakes to consciousness only to see her child torn from her bosom and hear the groans and cries of her wounded and dying friends.

Her anxiety was increased and her suspense rendered almost intolerable by seeing the dead and mutilated body of her uncle, Benjamin Parker, the reeking scalp of the aged grandfather, Rev. John Parker, and many other signs of the butchery now going on in and near the fort, where all was hushed in the silence of death, except the fiendish yells of triumph from the treacherous Indians. It was not till then she was made aware of her captivity. Mrs. Plummer was not allowed to speak to her relations, not even to her own little boy, James Pratt. She and the rest were beaten with clubs by the Indian braves and lashed with rawhide thongs by the squaws.

After leaving the fort the two tribes, Comanches and Kiowas, remained and travelled together until midnight. They halted on an open prairie, staked out their horses, placed their pickets, and pitched their camp. Bringing all their prisoners together for the first time, they tied their hands behind them with rawhide thongs so tightly as to cut the flesh, tied their feet close together, and threw them upon their faces. Then the braves gathered around with their yet bloody dripping scalps, commenced their usual war dance. They danced, screamed, yelled, stamping upon their prisoners, beating them with bows until their own blood came near strangling them.

The remainder of the night these frail women suffered and had to listen to the cries and groans of three tender children. Add to this heart-sickening scene, one more heartless and cruel still. The infant of Mrs. Plummer, born during her captivity, and while only six weeks old, was torn madly from her bosom by six giant Indians, one of them clutched the little prattling innocent by the throat, and like a hungry beast with defenceless prey, he held it out in his iron grasp until all evidence of life seemed extinct. Mrs. Plummer's feeble efforts to save her child were utterly fruitless. They tossed it high in the air and repeatedly let it fall on rocks and frozen earth.

Supposing the child dead they returned it to its mother but discovering traces of lingering life they again, by force, tore it angrily from her, tied plaited ropes around its neck, and threw its unprotected body into hedges of prickly pear. They would repeatedly pull it through these lacerating rushes with demoniac yells. Finally, they tied the rope attached to its neck to the pommel of a saddle and rode triumphantly around a circuit until it was not only dead but literally torn to shreds. All that remained of that once beautiful babe was then tossed into the lap of its poor distracted mother. This truly-drawn picture portrays some of the dark deeds of woe and strife that betel this little band.

Mrs. Plummer also said that In one of her rambles, after she had been with the Indians some time, she discovered a cave in the mountains and, in company with an old squaw that guarded her, she explored it and found a large diamond, but when she was ransomed the

Indians stole it from her and she was compelled to leave it. She said also here in these mountains she saw a bush which had thorns on it resembling fish hooks which the Indians used to catch fish with, and she herself has often caught trout with them in the little mountain streams.

In the year 1838 another colony arrived near Fort Parker, with a view of locating, etc., but in this purpose they were disappointed, for the Indians had lost none of their troublesome and treacherous spirit, and in the year 1839 they were again compelled to flee the Indian annoyances, not, however, without having improved considerable land, built several log houses, and selected their town site, which was donated to them in a five hundred acre tract of land, by Mr. Herrin, who lived near Nacogdoches.

Limestone County was organised permanently two years afterwards, 1846; that is two years after the return of some of the families, in 1844.

The James Parker Account

James Parker

In presenting this little book to the public, our aim and desire is to impress or refresh the minds of the people of the hardships and suffering the pioneer settlers of Texas had to endure in opening the way for the blessings and civilization the people of Texas now enjoy. We realize the fact, that half has never yet been told, no doubt it never will all be told. Our grandfather has only given a brief sketch of his travels and trials while seeking to rescue his daughter and grandson from captivity by the redmen; also his niece, Cynthia Ann Parker, that was captured at the Parker Fort massacre on the Navasota River; and it is not our desire to rekindle the *ill* feelings between the redmen and the paleface men, that existed between the two tribes at that time. We would much rather strengthen, amity confidence and good will between the tribes.

Who knows what suffering and grief those people endured with the captivity of the little girl, Cynthia Ann Parker, who in later years became the wife of a favourite Comanche Chief. Then in the due course of time became the *mother* of the noted Chief Quanah Parker, who in later years, by his great influence over the redmen, persuaded and prevented the redmen from waging a cruel war on the paleface. On one occasion the redmen declared war on the paleface; Quanah alone opposed the war and they held another council and because of the paleface blood in his veins they declared him a traitor to the redmen, and condemned him to be put to death. He told them:

The paleface have many braves; we have only a few braves; our braves will all be killed by the many paleface braves; save our braves, raise more braves, and become a great nation like the paleface.

Quanah Parker, Chief of Comanche Indians

Yet they declared he must die:

> I am willing to die for my braves, give me a fair chance; fight
> me singly, one at a time; do not take advantage and double on
> me, and I will fight you to the death to save my braves.

In this one act, he no doubt averted war and preserved many lives
of both tribes, as well as much suffering and distress. Is it the unseen
hand of providence? Who knows, who can say, of a truth, it is, or is not.

In offering this little narrative to the public, we are sorry the first
10 pages are incomplete, having been torn and destroyed. Hoping
the public will give this little narrative a liberal patronage and careful
consideration, of its contents, and think if we of today do not owe to
the memory of all of the pioneers who blazed the way in this great
State, for our present enjoyment and blessings; we say all, not only
those mentioned in this little book, but all who helped in the struggle
in those perilous times, a gratitude of which language is not at our
command to express.

Respectfully,

Mrs. Jane Kennedy,	Granddaughter of J. W. Parker.
Mrs. Rachel Lofton,	Great-granddaughter.
Mrs. Susie Hendrix,	Granddaughter.

CAPTURE OF FORT PARKER

On the 19th day of May, 1836, Parker's Fort, under my command,
was captured by a band of the Comanche and other tribes of Indians,
under the following circumstances. A few days previous to the day
above named, I had disbanded the troops under my command, as there
appeared to be but little danger of an attack, and the government was
not in a condition to bear the expense of supporting troops, unless the
circumstances were of such a nature as to imperiously demand it. On
the morning of the day before mentioned, myself, two of my sons-
in-law, and my oldest son, had repaired to the farm, a short distance
from the fort, to finish laying by our crop of corn; leaving in the fort,
my father, (Elder John Parker,) my two brothers, Benjamin and Silas,
and family, my wife and six children, including Mrs. Plummer, whose
narrative is annexed to this book, Mrs. Nixon, my mother-in-law, Mrs.
Duty, Mr. Frost and family, my sister-in-law, Mrs. Kellogg, Mr. Dwight
and his family; making in all thirty-four, eighteen of whom were children.

About an hour after I left the fort, a band of Indians approached it, bearing a *white flag*; and when my brother Benjamin went out to meet them, he was told their object was peace, and that they had come to make a treaty with the whites. This treacherous *ruse* was too successful. It threw those in the fort so much off their guard that it was not until the enemy had almost entirely surrounded them and had manifested their hostile intentions by killing my brother Benjamin, who was in their hands, that any attempt was made either to resist or escape. (See *Narrative of Rachel Plummer* at the end for particulars of what then occurred).

Before this, however, my daughter, Mrs. Nixon, becoming alarmed, had left the fort, and ran to the field to alarm us. Before she reached us we heard her screams, and ran immediately to meet her. She, in most breathless anxiety, informed us of what was going on at the fort, and we all immediately started for the fort. We had not proceeded more than a few hundred yards before we met my wife and children, who confirmed what my daughter had told us. It was immediately agreed upon by us that I should take my wife and children to a place of concealment, that Mr. Plummer should proceed to alarm some neighbours about half a mile off, and that Mr. Nixon should go on to the fort. I proceeded to place my family in a place of safety, which I did by directing my course to the River Navasott, about half a mile distant, which I succeeded in crossing with my wife and children. Having placed them where I thought they would be safe, I retraced my steps for the purpose of reaching the fort as soon as possible.

On re-crossing the river, I met Mrs. Frost and her family, in the care of Mr. Dwight, who had also escaped from the fort, and Mr. Dwight informed me that he had been overtaken by Mr. Nixon, who informed him that he had been to the fort, and that all was lost; either killed or taken prisoners! As Mr. Nixon approached the fort, he discovered a company of Indians who were dragging off my brother Silas' wife and children, four in number, as prisoners. With a bravery scarcely paralleled in any warfare, he drew his gun to his shoulder and rushed upon the enemy, some forty or fifty in number, and although he did not fire, (which under the circumstances would have been not only useless but very hazardous,) succeeded by his daring boldness and determined appearance, in effecting the rescue of the mother and two of her children; while the Indians succeeded in carrying off the other two children, one of whom is yet a prisoner among them, and whose release I hope, in the Providence of God, to be able to effect, by the means this humble narrative may place in my hands.

16

My father, mother-in-law, and Mrs. Kellogg, my sister-in-law, made their escape from the fort, and had proceeded about three-fourths of a mile, when they were overtaken by the enemy and stripped of their clothing, and the two first named were murdered—my father being shot through with an arrow, and scalped—my mother-in-law being stabbed with a knife, and left as dead; while my sister-in-law, Mrs. Kellogg, was taken off as a prisoner. Mr. Frost and his son Robert were slain in the fort, from whence was taken Mrs. Plummer and her child, about 18 months old, as prisoners. Thus were five slain, one badly wounded, and five taken prisoners, and twenty-three made their escape.

Mr. Plummer having succeeded in alarming the neighbours, he, in company with some fifteen others, returned to the fort just as the Indians, after having stripped it of every thing, destroyed the cattle, and secured the horses, were leaving it. The Indians being seven or eight hundred strong, they did not attack or attempt to follow them; but retreated to the woods, where they concealed themselves until the next day, when they proceeded to another settlement about sixty miles east of the fort, near Fort Houston.

Mr. Nixon, after having gallantly released the prisoners, as mentioned, and having placed them in the care of Mr. Plummer and his company, turned his attention to myself and those with me. In passing through the river bottom, we often came to sandy places where we could be tracked. If there was necessity for flight, I thought there was also necessity for precaution, and accordingly when I came to those sandy places, I made all the company pass over them by walking backwards, in order that our tracks would present the appearance of our having gone in a contrary direction from the one we were pursuing, and thus deceive the Indians, should they attempt to follow our trail. This ruse deceived Mr. Nixon, who after a fruitless search of two days to find us, gave us up, supposing that we also had fallen into the hands of the savages.

Whilst he was thus wandering about, undetermined what to do, he accidentally found Mrs. Duty, who had been stabbed in the right breast with a large knife, which did not enter the chest, but passed off near her ribs. He was passing near her after dark and heard her groans, and on approaching her, found her in a dying and most pitiable condition. It had been twelve or fourteen hours since she was stabbed, and faint with the loss of blood, stripped of every vestige of clothing, she lay mangled and bleeding on the cold ground, in a dark and howling wilderness, while her life-blood was fast ebbing from her wound. He at first attempted to remove her, but she fainted in his arms; and his only means of reviving her, was by bringing water to her in his shoe. This he repeated several times, and finally, after great exertion, succeeded in getting her to a neighbouring house, though it was deserted. Before the morning, he succeeded in finding the company raised by Mr. Plummer, when all the attention was rendered her their situation afforded, and her wounds dressed. She was taken along by the company that went to the settlement near Fort Houston, where she recovered, but has subsequently died.

Mr. Plummer, in searching for his wife and child, was separated from this company, and wandered through the country, and finally made his way to Tinning's settlement, on the Navasott, which he reached soon after my arrival there.

I must, however, ask the reader to go back and accompany myself, my family, Mrs. Frost and her family, and Mr. Dwight and his family, making in all 18 persons, from the time we crossed the Navasott, near Fort Parker, until we reached this settlement, a distance of 90 miles, the way we were compelled to travel it.

I must leave it to the mind of the reader to conjecture, if it can, for it is beyond the ability of my pen to describe the feelings that filled the breasts of myself and my almost helpless companions in sorrow and suffering. There we were in the howling wilderness, barefooted and bareheaded—a savage and relentless foe on the one hand; on the other, a trackless and uninhabited country literally covered with venomous reptiles and ravenous beasts—destitute of one mouthful of food, and the means of procuring it—our fathers, mothers, and children, having all, except those composing our company, just fallen a prey, as we supposed, to savage barbarity; and fearfully expecting at every step to share their fate ourselves—all, all rushed upon our minds like a blighting sirocco—it made the soul sick—despair seized upon the heart, and reason well-nigh deserted her throne.

I have stated that our company consisted of 18 persons. Of this number, 12 were children from 1 to 12 years of age. I desired, after night had come on, to return to the fort, to see if I could procure some food and information of what had become of those who were with us—whether they were slain, or had made their escape—but my companions said they would rather risk starving than I should leave them, fearing I would fall into the hands of the enemy, in which event, they knew they would perish in the wilderness, as they were all alike ignorant of the course to pursue to reach a settlement, and of the proper precaution to avoid falling into the hands of the enemy. I therefore determined to start for the settlement.

As it was prudent that we should travel at night and remain concealed in the day, I directed the women and children to conceal themselves in the briars, and I climbed a tall tree, by which I was enabled to reconnoitre the fort. All was silent as death. I in vain strained my eyes to see some living object, and listened to hear some human voice about the fort. Descending from the tree, I took one of my children on my shoulder, and led another; the other grown persons followed my example, and we started through the thickly entangled briars and underbush in the direction of the settlement. My wife was in very delicate health. Mrs. Frost's grief at the loss of her husband and son was inconsolable; and all being barefooted, except my wife and Mrs. Frost, our progress was very slow. Many of the children had nothing on but a shirt; and their sufferings from the briars tearing their flesh and wounding their feet, was almost beyond endurance.

We travelled until about three o'clock in the morning, when the women and children being worn out by fatigue and hunger, we lay down upon the grass and slept until the dawn of day, when we again resumed our weary journey. Here we left the river bottom, in order to avoid the briars; but from the many tracks of Indians and horses on the high lands, it was evident that the Indians were hunting us; and like the fox in the fable, we were again compelled to take to the river bottom; for though the brambles did indeed tear our flesh, yet they preserved our lives from danger. Repeatedly, yes, in some places, every few steps, did I see the briars tear the legs of the little children until the blood trickled down so that they could have been tracked by it.

It was now the night of the second day, and all, especially the children and the women giving suck, began to suffer intensely with hunger. We were now immediately on the bank of the river, and through the mercy of Providence, a skunk (or polecat,) came in our way. I immediately pursued it, and after much trouble, I succeeded in catching it as it jumped into the river; and the only way I could kill it, was by holding it under the water until it was drowned. Having fortunately brought with us the means for striking fire, we soon had it cooked and equally divided amongst our company; and the portion to each was small, indeed. This was all we had to eat until the fourth day in the evening, when we were so fortunate as to capture another skunk and two small terrapins, which were also cooked and divided.

The fifth day, in the evening, I found that the women and children were too much exhausted from hunger and fatigue, and their feet so sore, that it was impossible for them to travel any farther. After holding a consultation, it was agreed upon that I should go on to the settlement, it being now about 35 miles distant, and that Mr. Wright should remain with the company. Accordingly, the next morning, I started for the settlement, which I reached early in the afternoon.

I have often looked back and been astonished at this extraordinary feat. In the last six days I had not eaten one mouthful of food, (for while the others had partaken of the animals before mentioned, I had given my share to the children,) and yet I walked thirty-five miles in about eight hours. But the thought of the unfortunate sufferers I had left behind instilled in me that strength and perseverance known only to those who may have been placed in a similar situation. God, in his bountiful mercy, strengthened and upheld me in this trying hour of need, and to Him do I most humbly give all the praise and glory.

The first house I met with was Capt. Carter's, who received me kindly, and promptly offered me all the aid in his power. He soon had five horses prepared, and himself and Jeremiah Courtney accompanied me to meet our little company of sufferers. Just at dark, we met them, and placing the women and children upon the horses, we arrived at Capt. Carter's about midnight. Here we received all that kind attention and relief which our wretched condition demanded, and that benevolent and sympathetic hearts could bestow.

We arrived at Capt. Carter's on the 25th of May. On the following day, my son-in-law, Mr. Plummer, arrived there also; he having given us up as lost, and started for the same settlement at which we arrived.

On the 27th, I started an express to the officers of the government for assistance. Maj. John W. Moody bore the express, and five hundred troops were promptly ordered to our relief. These troops had proceeded as far as Washington, when they received the intelligence that the defeated army of Santa Anna was returning upon the western frontier, (this, however, turned out to be untrue), and they were ordered to meet them. Thus was my design of returning immediately to the fort, and of pursuing the Indians and releasing the prisoners, frustrated. To go alone was useless, and to raise a company was impossible, as every person capable of serving was already in the Texas Army.

By this time, my other son-in-law, Nixon, having arrived safely at the settlement of Fort Houston, about 150 miles distant from where we were, whither he had conducted those who had made their escape, among whom was Mrs. Duty, who was now fast recovering from her wound. Hearing that we had arrived at Capt. Carter's, he came to us; and from him we learned the particulars, as to the number killed and taken prisoners. This was the first certain intelligence Mrs. Frost had of the death of her husband and son.

Thinking that my family would not be entirely safe from the Indians in a situation so far out on the frontier as the residence of Capt. Carter, I removed them farther back into the interior, in Grimes' Settlement. (To the Hon. Judge Grimes, A. Montgomery, and others, I shall ever feel grateful for their kindness to my distressed family). Here I procured a house, or, rather, a part of one, for there was another family living in it. The house was small, and had nothing but a dirt floor. I was entirely without money, or any means of procuring the necessities, much less, the comforts of life. Nor were they to be procured if I had the means, for they were not in that section of the country, so, making a virtue of necessity, I made the best arrangements I was able for the comfort of my family, preparatory to returning to the fort. I made a kind of scaffold in one corner of the cabin by driving four forks into the ground, across which, I laid some slab boards; upon these boards, was laid some straw, which was to serve as a bed.

Just as I had completed my arrangement for starting back to the fort, all of my family were taken sick with the measles; but, leaving them to the charity of the neighbours and to the mercy of Providence, I set off, accompanied by thirteen others. On our arrival at the fort, on the 19th of June—exactly one month from the time we left—we found the houses still standing, but the crops were entirely destroyed, the horses stolen, nearly all the cattle killed, and not a single article of household furniture left.

We remained at the fort three days; during which time, I was enabled to gather the bones of my father and two brothers, and those of Mr. Frost and his son; their flesh having been devoured by wild beasts.

We made a rough box, into which we deposited their remains, (except those of my youngest brother, which I preserved, as he and I had entered into an agreement, that whichever survived, should see that his brother's body was not buried,) and having dug a grave, they were buried. As I assisted in performing this last sad service to their remains, I, in the bitter anguish of my soul, exclaimed, "rest my father and rest my brothers—rest—would to God I were with you."

Finding that we could make no discoveries as to the route the Indians had taken with the prisoners, we determined to return to the settlement; so gathering as many of our cattle as we could find, we started back. On my arrival in the neighbourhood of my family, I met Dr. Adams, who was attending my wife. He informed me that my wife, as he thought, must die. As if it were revealed from heaven, I felt she would not die; and so I told the doctor, asking him, at the same time, the privilege of using his medicines, which he freely granted. I was confident that my wife's disease was as much of the mind as of the body, and directed my course accordingly. On my coming in the presence of my wife, I was horror-stricken. There she lay on a pallet of straw literally reduced to skin and bones; she was entirely bereft of reason, and appeared to have lost all sense of pain. Oh God! how my soul was pierced when she gazed upon me with her ghastly eyes! By her side lay my youngest child, having more the appearance of a corpse than a living being. Breathing a prayer to God for his merciful intercession, I applied the medicines as my best judgment dictated, and after seven days of unceasing watching and painful suspense, I was made to rejoice, through the mercy of God, in beholding my wife again restored to reason, and evidently convalescent. She finally recovered, as also did my child.

My Removal to My Present Residence

Soon after the recovery of my family, I removed to Jessy Parker's, about 50 miles distant. And here I must express the grateful feelings I shall ever entertain for the kindnesses extended to myself and family by this most generous hearted man, who though of the same name, but no way related to me, yet the many favours he bestowed on us, proved his whole-souled generosity and Christian feeling. In the neighbourhood of Mr. Parker I purchased a tract of land of Benson Risinghoover, upon which I built me a temporary camp; and having fixed my family as comfortably as I could, on the 11th of July I started to see Gen. Houston.

All I desired, was, that he should grant me a company of men. On my arrival at Col. Sublett's, near San Augustine, where Gen. Houston was confined at the time, from the wound he received at the battle of San Jacinto; and having laid my plans before him for retaking the prisoners, he decided against it, and insisted that a treaty with the Indians would be the most effective and expeditious means of releasing the prisoners. I contended that such a thing as a treaty being formed with hostile Indians until they were whipped, and well whipped, had never been known; and the more thorough the chastisement, the more lasting the treaty. All argument failed, however, and with a heavy heart and perplexed mind, I retraced my steps to the humble abode of my afflicted family. I then thought that Gen. Houston betrayed too great an indifference to the matter; though this impression, no doubt, grew out of the great anxiety felt on my part.

I arrived at home on the 12th of August, and on the 13th, I went to see Col. Nathaniel Robbins, to enlist his influence in our behalf. He accompanied me to Nacogdoches, whence Gen. Houston had gone; and we again endeavoured to persuade him to order an expedition against the Comanches; but with no success.

Feeling that Gen. Houston might think that we were seeking the glory of the expedition, which would, if gotten up, be among his divisions, we informed him that we did not desire the honours, but preferred taking our stations in the ranks. The general, however, was inexorable, and still insisted upon the advisability of a treaty.

Col. Robbins, as much chagrined at our want of success as myself, returned home—and here I must remark of this good man, who now sleeps with his fathers, that for nobleness of soul, true philanthropy, and high-toned gentlemanly deportment, his equal were few, and superiors he had none.

I then determined to visit Col. Richard Sparks, with the plan in view, that had induced me to call on Col. Robbins; however, it did no good, and I returned again to Nacogdoches, where I arrived on the 20th of August. Here I was rejoiced to meet with my sister-in-law, Mrs. Kellogg, who had been purchased by some Delaware Indians, and brought in. The consideration claimed by the Indians for their services, was $150, which Gen. Houston generously paid, as I was penniless.

I immediately started, with Mrs. Kellogg, accompanied by Mr. Milligan and several other gentlemen, for home, a distance of 140 miles. On the 22nd, we fell in with a Mr. Smith, who had just discovered two Indians stealing horses. He had shot one a few hundred yards from the road, and we turned off to see the dead Indian. On reaching the spot where he lay, we found that Mr. Smith had partially missed his aim, for the ball had merely grazed his forehead. Mrs. Kellogg immediately recognized the Indian, as not only being one of the band that had captured Fort Parker, but the very one that had shot and scalped my father; in confirmation of which, she said, if he was the same, he had a scar on each arm, as if cut with a knife. I immediately examined him, and found, with mingled feelings of joy, sorrow, and revenge, the scars as described:—joy at the opportunity of avenging the butchery of my father, and sorrow at the recollection of it.

The Indian hearing a familiar female voice, raised his head, and gazing with looks of surprise and doubt upon Mrs. Kellogg, he at length appeared to recognise her, and muttering something I did not understand, fell back, pretending to be dead. He had left her a prisoner in his town, when he and several others of his tribe started on this trip of murder and plunder—hence, his marked surprise on seeing her at liberty and with her friends. What followed, it is unnecessary to relate—suffice it to say, that it was the unanimous verdict of the company, that he would never kill and scalp another white man.

On the 6th of September, we arrived at home, joyous was the meeting of my wife and her sister. Mrs. Kellogg could give us no intelligence of any of the other prisoners, as the party of Indians that captured the Fort, dispersed in a few days after—the Ketchaws taking her, one tribe of the Comanches taking my daughter and her child, and another tribe of the same nation, taking my nephew and niece, the children of my brother Silas.

After much consideration and consultation with my friends as to the best course to pursue, I determined to go to Coffee's trading house on Red River, about 700 miles distant, to see if I could hear any thing of the prisoners, or make any arrangements to have them purchased and brought in.

Accordingly, on the 15th of September, I started, and on the 27th, arrived at Jonesborough, on Red River, where I was treated with much kindness by Maj. L. W. Tinnin, Col. John Fowler, and many others. The gentlemen named, offered to loan me money; but as I had no use for money where I was going, I declined accepting it. To Mr. Johnson, of that place, I am indebted for many kindnesses, for which I offered him a remuneration, but he would not accept it. My horse having given out, I left him at Mr. Johnson's, of whom I purchased another, and proceeded on to Coffee's establishment.

On the 2nd day of October, I heard that a woman had been brought in to Capt. Pace's, on Blue River, who I thought, from the description, was my daughter. I immediately determined to go to Pace's, distant about 80 miles, the way I was compelled to travel. Not being able to get my horse across Red River, I left him with Mr. Fitzgerald, with directions, that should I not return to his house within ten days, he should let my family know that I was dead, as I had determined to return within that time, if alive. Having, with the assistance of Mr. Stewart, made a raft, I crossed Red River. I could obtain no reliable information as to the course I should pursue, and there being no road, or even trace, I directed my course according to the best information I could obtain.

Mrs. Fitzgerald had furnished me with some meat and bread, which I lost before I had gone far, as I had great difficulty in passing through the swamps and thickets of the river bottom. I had prepared myself with a pocket compass by which I was enabled to direct my course. I walked as far as I could the first day, and at night found myself on a prairie. Being much fatigued I lay down upon the grass to sleep—but the thought that I was so near my child, it drove sleep from my eyes. I would sometimes doze for a few moments, but would soon arouse with an effort to embrace the object of my care and pursuit. I would have travelled all night, but I could not see the points of my compass, and the night being cloudy, I could not have kept my course.

The next morning, I started as soon as it was light enough to see my compass, and notwithstanding my feet were blistered and I had recovered but little from my fatigue of the previous day, I must have travelled forty miles before dark. At night, being yet on this prairie, and the ground being wet, I found it would be impossible to sleep without fire; so having found a few scrubby saplings, I broke off some brush and kindled a fire. It now commenced thundering and threatened a storm, which soon came on. The rain fell in torrents whilst the almost unceasing flashes of lightning and deafening thunder, made me feel, in my lonely condition, as if "the war of elements, the wreck of matter, and the crush of worlds," was about to be consummated.

By the flashes of lightning, I could see far around me, and the prairie presented the appearance of one unbroken sheet of water. Where I stood, the water was at least two feet deep. I had two small pistols, which I kept dry by wrapping my shirt around them and placing one under each arm. To this timely precaution, I undoubtedly owe the preservation of my life. About two o'clock in the morning, the wind changed to the North, and in less than one hour my clothes were frozen upon me, and I felt that I could not live until morning. Though unable to direct my course in the dark, I was compelled to keep in motion, or freeze to death, so I promenaded a space of forty or fifty yards, in the water a foot deep, until morning. During this time the snow fell fast, but melted as it fell.

As soon as it was light I pursued my journey, with little hope of being alive at night, or ever again beholding the face of a human being. About 9 o'clock, I saw a body of timber to the Southeast, whither I directed my steps. My progress was very slow and difficult, as the grass being about two feet high, was matted together by the ice. On reaching the woods, I seated myself upon a log to rest. I had sat there but a few minutes when I found it very difficult to keep from going to sleep. This was produced by the extreme cold; my feet and hands had lost all sense of pain, and I knew I was fast freezing to death. I attempted to rise, but could not. There was a small tree within my reach, and taking hold of it I succeeded in rising to my feet. In the short time I had been still, my limbs had become so stiffened, that I could not walk. I was afraid to let go the tree, for fear I should fall, in which case I knew I should never rise.

It is impossible for the mind to form any just conception of my feelings at this time. I have often attempted to call to mind how I felt, but in vain; it appears like a dream, and often, when reflecting on the event, I almost doubt its reality.

To remain stationary was certain death—so there was but one alternative left—move I must. There was an old dry log about fifty yards from me, and my life depended on my being able to reach it and strike a fire. Letting go the tree I ventured on this hazardous experiment, and moving my feet but a few inches at first, I succeeded, after much exertion of nearly an hour, in gaining the log. Having cut some dry pieces of cotton from my shirt, and loaded one of my pistols with them, I discharged it against a dry part of the log. My agonising fears and suspense were soon relieved by the success of this effort to start a fire, and soon my frozen clothing began to yield to the influence of the heat, and it was not long before my sense of pain returned.

The pain I had suffered from cold, during the last twelve hours, was, I thought, as great as the human system could endure; but it was comparatively nothing to that I felt in getting warm. Had my hands and feet been held in the fire until consumed, the pain certainly could not have been greater. When entirely restored to a proper warmth, my hands and feet stung and smarted as if they had been burned, and the skin peeled off them.

Three days had now elapsed since I had tasted food, and it required the exercise of all the fortitude and courage I was master of to keep me from sinking down with fatigue and hunger. The hope of soon seeing my lost child, added a new vigour to my body, and summoning all my remaining strength I pursued my journey.

I had not proceeded far, before night came on, and having made a good fire, I sunk down upon the cold, damp ground, to rest. My fatigue acted as an opiate, and I soon yielded myself to the arms of Morpheus, with but little hopes of ever again awaking in this world. I slept soundly all night; and although my fire had gone out, and my clothes were frozen to the ground, my hair a mat of ice, and my limbs benumbed, God, in His merciful preservation, enabled me to rise and rekindle the fire. After my clothes were thawed and partially dried, my limbs again became controllable, and I pursued my journey. I could not tell whether I had passed Mr. Pace's or not; but to attempt to return to the settlement I had left, would be vain; so, exercising my best judgment, I directed my course, with scarcely a hope of surviving until night.

I suppose I travelled that day about fifteen miles. The sun was now setting, and I almost hoped I would not live to see it rise. Darkness came on apace; and oh, how horrible was the thought of having to spend another night in the wild wilderness, eight hundred miles from home, with the frozen ground for a bed, and the blue dome of heaven my only shelter. As these thoughts were revolving in my mind, I heard a calf bleat—and the songs of angels could not have been sweeter to my ear, or more charming to my soul, than was the bleat of that calf. With an energy that astonished me, I pushed on in the direction from whence the sound came; and just at dark a grateful heart to God for his wonderful mercies, I found myself seated in Pace's house, by a comfortable fire; while his kind wife was preparing me a cup of coffee.

My joy at the escape I had made from a miserable death in the wilderness, was, however, soon turned to mortification and sorrow, for I learned that the woman that had been brought in was not my daughter, but a Mrs. Yorkins. She had gone on to Samuel B. Marshall's, and I did not get to see her.

At Pace's however, I met with some of Coffee's traders, who gave me direct intelligence of my daughter. They informed me that she was in charge of a band of Indians, who, they said, were then encamped about 60 miles from Mr. Pace's. They also informed me that the Indians had killed my daughter's child. The intelligence kindled anew the flame that was raging in my breast; and I immediately determined to go to the camp of the Indians, and at the risk of my life, recover my daughter.

I remained at Pace's two nights and one day, during which time, I received all the attention and kindness he and his family could bestow, for which I shall ever feel grateful.

On the morning of my departure from Mr. Pace's, his kind lady prepared me some bread and venison to take with me, though it was not more than enough to last one day. In very little better condition than when I arrived at Mr. Pace's, I directed my course to the Indian camp, which I did not reach until the fourth day in the afternoon. The Indians, I found, had left there just after the heavy rain before spoken of. As I could now follow them by their trail, I started on, and on the 6th day, I arrived at Red River. The Indians had crossed the river, and as I knew that in my enfeebled condition I could not swim it, and there being no timber near with which I could make a raft, I was compelled to retrace my steps.

On turning homeward and contemplating my situation, I felt as certain as that I was then alive, that I should never again see home. Faint with hunger and fatigue, and all hopes of ever again seeing my unfortunate daughter, being, as I thought, cut off, I resigned myself to my fate. I looked down the river and saw some timber, and feeling that I would rather die among the trees than in an open prairie, thither I directed my steps; and just as the sun was setting, I reached the spot which I never expected to leave. I pray God that when the final hour does come, and He shall call me hence, that I may feel as willing to obey as I did then.

I had been seated on a log in these woods but a few minutes, when I heard a rustling in the leaves; and on looking round, I saw a skunk near me; and at the same moment I saw it, I felt that the kind protecting care of Providence was yet around, and I was firmly convinced in my mind that I should again see my family, as I had been a few moments before persuaded that I should not.

Inscrutable, indeed, are the ways of Providence! Often, when we have the least occasion to fear death, we are stricken down without a moment's warning; whilst, on the other hand, when we have no reason to hope for life, and sincerely pray for death, the hand of the all-wise and merciful God is stretched forth, and we are plucked from the cold embrace of the "King of Terrors," as a "brand from the burning!"

I speedily despatched the skunk, and soon had a part of it broiling on the fire; and though I ate but a small portion that night, it strengthened and revived me so much, that the next morning I set about making a raft. This was the first food I had tasted in the last six days.

The reader doubtless thinks it strange that I had not a gun with me on such a tour. I neglected to mention, that when I arrived at Mr. Tinnie's, soon after I had started on this journey, he proposed to go and engage some Shawnee Indians to go in search of the prisoners, and required the loan of my gun. I let him have it, and he did not return before I left, so I went on without it.

Having burned some logs that lay near the river, into several pieces, I soon tied them together with bark and grape vines. Upon this raft I descended Red River, to Mr. Fitzgerald's, where I arrived on the 22nd, after an absence of twenty days. Mr. Fitzgerald had not written to my family, as I directed, not having met with an opportunity of sending the letter.

Considering all efforts to regain my daughter, fruitless, my duty to my family required my immediate return home, which I reached on the 17th day of November.

Congress being now in session, at Columbia, I determined to go there and petition that body for some assistance. But a treaty was urged as the best and only means of effecting the release of the prisoners, and I was doomed again to return home in sorrowful hopelessness.

Having firmly determined never to cease my efforts to facilitate the release of the prisoners, I concluded to visit Gen. T. J. Rusk and Maj. J. W. Burton, and try to enlist them in my cause. I found them both willing to render me all the assistance in their power; but they could do nothing. I again went to see Col. R. Sparks, but to no effect.

I now determined to return to Red River, and see what could be done; and taking leave of my family on the 25th day of February, 1837, I started on this, my second tour, among the Indians. I arrived at Natchitoches on the 7th of March, where I received many kindnesses from Mr. Joseph S. March, Mr. Clark, near Spanish Town, and others. Here I offered a reward of $300 for every prisoner then among the Indians that might be brought in; and to Mr. D. P. Despelier, I am under obligations for the gratuitous insertion of the advertisement in his paper.

On the 10th, I left Natchitoches for Monroe, to endeavour to collect some money due me, in order to pay the offered rewards, if needed. The waters being very high, and having many streams to cross, my progress was very slow and disagreeable, which was greatly increased by an unceasing toothache, with which I suffered nearly the whole way. On the 19th. I lost my pocket-book, and had to return a distance of twenty miles before I found it. I arrived at Monroe on the 20th, where I succeeded in collecting a small sum of money, and where I remained until the 29th, when I left for Red River. I cannot but mention the kindness extended to me by Mr. A. Ludwig and his kind lady, at whose house I stayed four nights.

On the 2nd of April, I arrived at Capt. Finn's on the lost prairie on Red River. From here I went to Marshall's trading house, on Blue River. I succeeded in securing Mr. Marshall's efforts in my behalf, and I purchased his stock of goods, as also the goods of Messrs. Colwell & Wallace, amounting in all to about $1000, with which they agreed to go on to try and purchase the prisoners.

Leaving Mr. Marshall's, I returned to Smith's trading house, and succeeded in securing his goods, subject to my order, provided I should need them in purchasing the prisoners' freedom. Here I met with a Shawnee Indian, from whom I learned that a white woman had been purchased by Mr. Sprawling, one of Mr. Marshall's traders. I immediately returned to Marshall's, who, having heard the same news, had started out the day before my arrival, and had left for me the following note:

My Friend, James W. Parker,

Sir:—Having received good news, I start after the prisoner tomorrow morning. Mr. Sprawling has purchased a woman; I hope it is your daughter. Keep yourself here. The Comanches are now at Coffee's. You must stay here until I come back, and if God spares my life I will have the prisoners. I have got three Indians engage at two dollars per day. For God Almighty's sake stay here until I come back, and see what can be done.

In haste, your friend,

Samuel B. Mashall.

April, 1837.

It will be discovered by Marshall's note, that he was extremely anxious that I should remain at his trading house until his return. This grew out of his fears that I would venture among the Indians, in which event he knew I would be killed. Under these circumstances, who of my readers that ever felt in his breast the pure and holy vibrations of paternal love, could have commanded himself in obedience to the more cautious and calm requirements of one, who though he might feel all the interest benevolence and philanthropy could prompt, yet felt comparatively nothing. Can it be supposed then that I obeyed his directions? I did not; for I immediately started for the traders' camp, where I supposed my daughter was. When I arrived at the camp, I was chagrined to learn that the woman was not my daughter. I remained with the traders several days, exerting every means to regain my child, but to no effect.

It was now the 21st of April, and having lost all hope of regaining my daughter by the plan I had laid, I determined to go among the Indians and reconnoitre their camps, with the hopes of seeing her, and by stealth effecting her release. With this view, I prepared myself with a good rifle, four pistols and a bowie knife, a sufficient quantity of ammunition, and pen, ink and paper. I would remark, that, knowing it was the custom of the Indians to make their prisoners carry all the water, and knowing that they never encamped but on the bank of a river or creek, my plan was, after discovering their encampment, to keep myself concealed until dark, and then while they were dancing, as is their custom every night after dark, to creep to the point from whence they procured their water, and having written notes directing any American into whose hands they might fall, where to come to me, to place them in positions where they would be likely to be found, and after doing this, to return to my hiding place. In this way, I hoped to get a note in to the hands of my daughter, and thus effect her release.

I accordingly started in company with one of the men belonging to a trading house, and we directed our course for the camps of the Comanches. On the 24th, having stopped for the night and hobbled our horses, we lay down, but we very soon found that we were among the Indians, and that they were trying to steal our horses. I immediately sprang to my feet, and I discovered an Indian not more than ten feet from me. I shot him with my rifle and fired at another with my pistol. He immediately ran off, and we, mounting our horses, followed his example.

We rode all night. The next' day at ten o'clock, we came upon a company of Indian's in ambush. We did not know that they were near us until the crack of their rifles and the stinging of my left ear and cheek from the graze of a ball, announced our perilous situation. As quick as thought, I had my trusty rifle to my shoulder, and seeing a very large Indian a few yards to my left, with his empty rifle yet to his face, I fired. He made no effort to rise, and my attention being directed to another spot, I saw another Indian preparing to fire a second time. I drew one of my pistols and fired it. He appeared to come to the conclusion not to fire a second time, for he immediately laid down as if to take some rest. My companion during this time had induced the third Indian to forego a second fire; and having no further business to transact at that particular spot, and hearing a short distance off a yell as if all the demons of hell were around us, we left, without taking time

31

to wish our three friends in ambush a comfortable rest and pleasant dreams. Nor did we wait to select our course; but, urging our faithful horses to do their duty, we soon left our pursuers far behind.

On the 26th, my companion left me and started for the trading house. I swam the Ouachita, or Cash Fork of Red River, and left my horse, finding that I could proceed on foot with less danger than on horseback. I then swam Red River and found the Indians.

I reconnoitred them until the second of June, practising all the plans I had arranged without being able to make any discoveries. Being now almost exhausted, having reconnoitred the Indians more than a month, during which time I had gone without food as long as six days at one time, and often four or five days, I determined to return home. It is probably necessary to remark, that when I did eat anything, I had to go a sufficient distance from the Indians to prevent them from hearing the report of my gun whenever I shot a buffalo. Sometimes, when the Indians moved, I would wait until they had proceeded some eight or ten miles, and then kill my game and satisfy my hunger.

The limits to which I have prescribed this narrative prevent me from relating many interesting incidents that occurred in this and the other tours I made in search of my daughter; but I must relate one here, and leave the reader to picture to himself many similar ones.

One evening after the Indians had moved, but not to a sufficient distance to be out of hearing of my gun, and being very hungry, I shot a buffalo, and proceeded to the bank of a stream not far off, where I kindled a fire for the purpose of broiling a piece of meat. On returning to the buffalo, I found my right to it disputed—not by an Indian, but by a very large white wolf, peculiar only to this section of country. I tried to scare him away, but he was bold and determined, and often cautioned me not to trust too much to his good humour, by showing me the length and condition of his long tusks. I was afraid to shoot a second time, as the Indians doubtless heard the first report, and were perhaps, listening to catch the sound of another.

Finding, however, that his wolfship was not to be moved by menaces, and my hunger increasing as the opportunity of satisfying it was before me, I determined after a long time to risk another fire, and accordingly gave my ungenerous companion of the wilderness a leaden pill to work off the hearty supper he had made on my buffalo. Luckily the Indians did not hear the report of my gun, and after having sated my craving appetite, I lay down and had a good night's rest.

On many other occasions when I was afraid to shoot game, I have carried water in my hat a considerable distance to drown out the prairie dogs from their burrows, and in this way procured the food that kept me from starving.

Having returned to the Cash Forks of Red River, and procured my horse, I returned home, after an absence of five months. On the 19th of June, I arrived at the city of Houston, and on the same day Gen Houston gave me the commission of the Commander-in-Chief of a military company, to be denominated the "Independent Volunteers of Texas," without limit as to numbers.

It now being evident that the Indians would not enter into a treaty, President Houston had at last agreed to order an expedition against them; and I, as above stated, having been honoured with the command of the expedition, immediately set about raising a company of volunteers for that purpose.

I Raise a Company

My brother, Nathaniel Parker, of Charleston, Ill., then and now, (1926), a member of the Senate of that State, had arrived in Texas; and assisted by him and my brother Joseph, I soon succeeded in raising a company of as brave men as that young republic could boast. My arrangements were fast being matured for an effective expedition against the Indians, when to my great surprise and mortification, I received orders from Gen. Houston to abandon the expedition and to disband the company I had partly raised! It appears that he was induced to do this by the misrepresentations of some evil disposed persons. He had been made to believe that I premeditated an attack upon some friendly and well-disposed Indian tribes near the frontier of Texas; which was entirely destitute of truth, as the testimony of Col. Jos. Williams, Daniel Montague, N. Parker, Majors William Lloyd and W. T. Henderson, and many others, all worthy men, will clearly prove.

My brother Nathaniel finding he could render me no assistance, returned home to Illinois. Brother Joseph and myself disbanded the men, but went ourselves into the Indian territory, determined to try what we could do.

We had travelled about 500 miles, when from the excessive heat and the want of proper food and water, we were both taken sick and compelled to return home, where we arrived on the 31st of August.

On the 7th of September, having partially recovered from my indisposition, I started again on another tour, with as firm a determination never to cease my efforts until the prisoners were released, as I had formed when I first started in pursuit of them.

This tour was a long and painful one to me, owing to the bad state of my health; though nothing of interest to the reader occurred. Finding my indisposition increasing, I was again compelled to return to my family.

After remaining at home four or five days, and my health becoming better, I again left home on the 27th of October, and went to see if the Indian traders whom I had engaged, had done or learned any thing. Finding they had done nothing, nor learned any tidings of my daughter, I pursued my course among the Indian tribes, then on the frontier of the United States. On arriving at an Indian town, I would stop and make inquiries for my daughter.

At one of these towns I met with an Indian who had on one of my vests. I told one of my companions that if it was my vest, the button moulds were made of the rind of a gourd; and to decide whether it was in truth my vest, I cut off one of the buttons, and soon recognised it as having been made by my own hands at Fort Parker. I interrogated the Indian as to where he procured the vest, and he being unable to give me a definite account of it—the treacherous capture of Fort Parker—the inhuman butchery of my aged father and my affectionate brothers—the galling captivity and slavish bondage of my dear child and innocent and helpless grand-children and nieces—all, rushed upon my mind at the same moment, and the firm belief that this was one of the authors of all my woe, kindled in my breast feelings that I leave the reader to imagine, for my pen cannot describe them. Every nerve of my system involuntarily trembled, and I felt it was necessary that I should leave the town; so directing my companions to start on, assuring them that I would soon follow *with all possible speed,* I mounted my horse, and taking a "last, fond look" at my vest—*with one eye through the sight of my trusty rifle*—I "turned and left the spot," with the assurance that my vest had *got a new button hole!*

The Indians of the town, as I passed them, appeared desirous that I should make a longer stay, which was manifested by their frequent attempts to catch my bridle and in other ways to arrest my progress; but some well aimed blows with my sword soon cleared the track, and my spirited steed quickly bore me beyond their reach. On coming up with my companions, we pursued our journey without further molestation.

We soon reached Sabine River, and having crossed it, entered an Indian town. The Indians at this town were drinking whiskey very freely when we arrived, and many were intoxicated. We soon found that our safety required as short a stay here as possible, and therefore did not alight from our horses. Just as we were about to start, an Indian, evidently much intoxicated, seized my bridle and drew a knife. I soon found it necessary for my own safety, to knock him down with my rifle, in doing which it was broken and rendered useless. Now, it was necessary that we should, not only leave immediately, but flee for our lives, as the Indians had become enraged and were rushing to attack us. We soon left them far behind, and we pursued the remainder of our journey homeward without molestation.

I arrived at home, from this tour, on the 28th of October. Finding that my health was much impaired from travelling, I started my son-in-law, (Mr. Nixon,) to see what my traders had done. On the 30th of November at a late hour of the night, a Mr. G. S. Parks arrived at my house, and informed me that he had met Mr. Nixon, and that he had directed him to go on to Independence, Missouri, where Mrs. Plummer was, she having been brought into that place by some Santa Fe traders.

Reader, I leave you to your own conceptions of what were my feelings on hearing this joyful news. My wife rushed eagerly to my side to hear the glad tidings, and so overjoyed was she to hear that her child was yet alive, that she fell, senseless, in my arms, whilst my little children gathered around me, all anxiously inquiring: "Father, does sister Rachel still live?"

How chequered are the ways of Providence. Though my sorrows and sufferings, for the past two years, had been greater than it would be thought human nature could bear, the joy I felt that night overbalanced them all, whilst I poured forth to Almighty God, the humble thanks of a grateful heart for the merciful deliverance of my child from a cruel bondage. How truly does the inspired writer say, that He chasteneth when it seemeth fit, and maketh the sorrowful heart to rejoice in due season.

On the 19th of February, Mr. Nixon and Mrs. Plummer arrived at my house, and great indeed was the joy on her return to the bosom of her friends. She presented a most pitiable appearance; her emaciated body was covered with scars, the evidences of the savage barbarity to which she had been subject during her captivity.

She was in very bad health, and although everything was done to restore her, she lived but a short time to enjoy the company of her kind husband and affectionate relatives. In about one year from the time she returned to her paternal home, she calmly breathed out her spirit to Him who gave it, and her friends committed her body to the silent grave.

During her protracted illness, she was seldom heard to murmur at her own sufferings, past or present, which she knew would soon end; but her whole soul appeared continually engaged in prayer to God for the preservation and deliverance of her dear and only child, James Pratt, from the inhuman bondage he was suffering. She often said that this life had no charms for her, and that her only wish was, that she might live to see her son restored to his friends. Although she was denied this happiness, I rejoice to feel that her prayers were heard and answered, in the deliverance of her child, as the following chapter discloses.

For a full account of her sufferings, during her captivity, the reader is referred to her own narrative which is appended to and closes this volume.

NARROW ESCAPE FROM THE INDIANS

Having recovered my daughter, and not feeling certain that my grandson and my brother's children were yet alive, I partially ceased my exertions to regain them. I, however, let no opportunity escape, where I thought there was the least prospect of hearing of them. I also made a tour once a year through the Indian country in search of them, but could hear nothing certain about them until the first of September, 1841, when I heard that two children had been brought into the Chickasaw Depot, about 800 miles from my house. At this time I was very sick with a fever; but in hopes that I might be able to reach the Depot, and thinking that travelling might perhaps help me, I started. I was scarcely able to mount my mule, when I started, yet it is no less strange than true that I travelled fifty miles the first day.

When I got among the Indians, I found that I was in great danger, owing to some difficulties that had taken place between the frontier Texans and the Chickasaw and Choctaw tribes of Indians. It was necessary, therefore, that I should pass myself as a citizen of Arkansas, in order to pass unmolested. I succeeded in reaching the depot on the 22nd of September. There were many Indians at the depot when I arrived, and to my horror I found that many of them were of the same tribe to which the Indian belonged that had on my vest, the particulars of which are previously related.

Maj. Jones, the chief proprietor of the depot, I found to be a gentleman and a friend, and to him I communicated the object of my visit. He informed me that the children that had been brought in were not those I was looking for, but said that his traders knew of some children among the Comanches that no doubt were those I was in search of. His traders were just about starting when I arrived, and he called in two of the head men and directed them to purchase these children at any price, becoming himself responsible for the amount they might cost.

One of these traders, an old Delaware, with whom I was well acquainted, took me aside and told me that I was in danger, and pointed out an Indian in the crowd who had said I had killed his brother. This Indian was probably a brother of the one that had on my vest. After the traders had started, Maj. Jones gave me the same caution that old Frank, the Delaware, had given me, and added, that he would invite me to stay at the depot that night, but he knew if I stayed the Indians would steal my mule.

Soon after Maj. Jones had left me, the Indian pointed out to me by the old trader, stepped up to me and asked, with apparent unconcern, if I was going to leave that evening? I replied I was. He asked me which road I was going? I told him the Fort Towson road. He then left me, and I saw him conversing with his companions.

Well acquainted, as I was, with the Indian character, it cannot be supposed that I was not perfectly aware of the danger I was in. In this case, as in all my other difficulties with the Indians, I was not the least alarmed. I mean, I was perfectly in possession of my presence of mind, and could control my feelings and actions so entirely, that I was enabled to act for the best. To remain at the depot I knew would be inexpedient, as the Indians would steal my mule, and then all hopes of escape would be cut off. So there was but one alternative left, and that was to start home.

Soon after the Indian above spoken of, had interrogated me, I saw him and forty or fifty others mount their mules and start down the road I was compelled to travel. I studied a few moments on the best course to pursue, and after they had been gone about one hour, I started. I had observed as I came up the Fort Towson road, a very heavy ambush about two miles from the depot, where I was sure these Indians intended to kill me. The road forked about half way between the depot and this ambush, the right hand fork leading to Blue River. This road I determined to take, and thus avoid the ambush. I was entirely unarmed, and I knew that my only means of escape was in flight.

Just as I came to the forks of the road I met two of these Indians, who had no doubt returned to watch me, and if I had taken the Blue River road I am confident they would have shot me; so I was compelled to go the Fort Towson road.

Soon after I met them I observed that they turned round and followed me. I was about two hundred yards ahead of them and was nearly in sight of the ambush, when a short turn in the road concealed me from their view. I now turned short to the right, and urging my mule with whip and spur, I was soon out of sight of the road, and crossing the Blue River road, took a straight direction through a boggy prairie. I did not slacken my pace until I had gone seven or eight miles, but kept looking behind to ascertain if I was pursued. I was now near a high piece of land, that bordered on the prairie, and in order to let my mule rest, and to ascertain whether I was pursued, I went to the most elevated point near me, and reconnoitred the prairie as far as I could see. I soon discovered the whole body of Indians, about two miles behind, running directly towards me. Remounting my mule, and applying whip and spur, I urged him, at full speed, for nearly two hours.

Having arrived at the foot of a mountain, and there being no point in sight but what appeared insurmountable, I almost despaired of escaping. As there was no time for delay, I started to climb the mountain, which I succeeded in doing, after much labour and great danger to myself and mule. When I reached the top, the sun was just setting, and my mule being very tired, I permitted him to rest, while I climbed a tree, to see if the Indians were still pursuing me; I could see nothing of them, and concluded they had given up the chase.

Descending the tree, I was soon on my way, and directing my course so as to intersect the Blue River road, which I gained about twelve o'clock that night, and about two in the morning crossed Blue River, where I found a good hiding place and lay down and slept until daybreak, when I pursued my journey and was soon out of all danger from the Indians.

I have not narrated here all my plans and difficulties in making my escape; but enough has been said to induce my readers to agree with me in ascribing the preservation of my life to the protecting care of a kind Providence.

Nothing further of interest transpired in this tour. I arrived at home on the 8th of October. My family and friends were as much grieved as myself, at my disappointment in not finding the children.

Having learned from the public papers, and otherwise, that two children had been brought in to Fort Gibson, I started for that place on the 22nd of December, 1842. Nothing of note occurred on this journey. I arrived at Fort Gibson on the 15th of January, 1843, where I was rejoiced to find my grandson, James Pratt Plummer, and my nephew, John Parker.

I found Capt. Brown, the commandant of the Fort, a perfect gentleman. He treated me very kindly, and rendered me all the aid necessary. I soon convinced him that the children were those I was in search of.

When the children were brought to me, although seven years had elapsed since I had seen them, and they had altered very much by growth, and from the ill usage of the Indians, I recognized in the features of my grandson, those of his mother, Mrs. Plummer; and my joy at rescuing him from Indian barbarity was not a little abated by the reminiscences brought to mind by his striking resemblance of his mother. The sympathising officers of the garrison appeared to partake of the mingled feelings of joy and grief, it was beyond my power to restrain on the occasion.

My grandson, learning that I had come after him, ran off, and went to the Dragoon encampment, about one mile from the Garrison. Poor child, how my heart bled, when he thus avoided me. Torn, as he had been, in his infancy, from the tender care of a mother and father; unused, as he had been, (until he arrived at this place) to enjoying kind treatment from anybody; ignorant, as he was, of any of those tender feelings of love and kind attentions which are the offspring of paternal affection, it is not to be thought strange that he was incapable of appreciating my kind intentions toward him.

Being much fatigued, I retired to rest, but my sufferings and trials for the last seven years, passing in retrospect across my mind, sleep was driven from my eyes, and I arose in the morning but little refreshed.

Early the next morning Capt. Brown sent a sergeant after my grandson. When he arrived, the captain and some of the other officers joined with me in persuading him to go with me. After more than two hours conversation, we succeeded in making him understand how I was related to him, at which he appeared much astonished, and asked me if he had a mother. I told him he had not, as she had died. He then asked if he had a father. I told him he had, and if he would go with me he should see him. He then consented to accompany me.

It will be recalled that the children were very young when taken

39

by the Indians, and consequently could now talk very little English. As I could not well understand them, nor they me, I was relieved from the pain of listening to their recital of the sufferings they had endured whilst among the Indians. The evidences, however, of the free exercise of savage barbarity, were visible upon the backs of these unfortunate children; for there was scarcely a place wherever the finger could be laid, without its covering a scar made by the lash.

After these children became able to make themselves understood, their own recital of their sufferings would make any heart bleed.

Capt. Brown made out the necessary documents to the Executive of Texas, and we were soon on our way home. The two boys rode my horse, and I walked, until we reached Fort Smith. Finding that I could walk no farther, I here purchased a pony.

We now pursued our journey, and a severe time we had of it. The children, as well as myself, were very thinly clad; and there having been a heavy fall of rain, we found the road in many places almost impassable. Added to this, the weather was very cold; and we all suffered very much. Soon after we crossed Red River, one of our horses was bogged, and it was sometime in the night before we succeeded in getting him out.

We arrived at home on the 27th of February, much fatigued. My wife and many of my neighbours met me at Cincinnati, on the Trinity River, twelve miles from my house, and joyous indeed was our meeting. I had now completed another tour of suffering; and grateful were my feelings to God on finding myself again with my family, and all in good health.

The boys soon became attached to me and my family. They soon learned to speak English, and are now doing well.

I cannot close this chapter without an acknowledgment of the kind treatment I received from many persons in going to and returning from Fort Gibson; among whom I would name Capt. Rogers and Capt. Bliss, of Fort Smith; Col. Lumas, of Fort Towson; Parson Potts, missionary among the Choctaws; and Mr. Donoho, of Clarksville.

A BRIEF SYNOPSIS OF THE FOREGOING CHAPTERS

In writing out the foregoing chapters, which cover the most interesting part of my narrative, it has been necessary to abridge as much as possible. In doing this, many interesting events and amusing anecdotes have unavoidably been omitted for want of space. To enter minutely into all the particulars, and to rehearse all that transpired in my journeyings in search of the prisoners, would occupy, at least, three hundred pages; the expense of printing which I am not able to bear. Another reason for omitting a detail of many of my sufferings and miraculous escapes, is, that I am confident few, of any, would believe them.

The reader no doubt thinks that what I have already related of my sufferings is miraculous enough; but, could I retrace my life, and endure again my past sufferings, and make him an eyewitness to them, then he would agree with me, that what I have narrated is nothing, when compared with the awful reality.

From the capture of the fort, up to the time my daughter was recovered, at least three-fourths of my time was spent in the wilderness. Sometimes I would not see a human being, except Indians, and they at a distance off, for two months. My only food was wild meat, without salt or bread, and that often uncooked. My only resting place, the cold ground; and my only covering, the arched dome of Heaven. Often I was without a mouthful of food for five or six days at a time; and frequently hope fled my bosom, and despair, horrible despair seized upon me. More than twenty times have I calmly and sincerely wished that death would end my sufferings; and on one or two occasions, I was on the eve of aiding the fell monster in the work with my own hands.

My feet being very tender, from freezing, I could often have been traced by the blood that marked my every step over the frozen ground. Sometimes, in the heat of summer, whilst reconnoitring the Indians in the large prairies, the vertical rays of the mid-day sun would so blister and parch my face and hands, that the skin would peel from them; and often my thirst was so great, that I would have given a mountain of pure gold, had I possessed it, for one draught of water.

Most of the country over which I travelled, was infested by beasts of prey and venomous reptiles; and not unfrequently have I narrowly escaped being destroyed by the ravenous jaws of the former, or the venomous fangs of the latter.

My readers may feel some surprise that I always went on these tours alone. A moment's reflection will convince them of the propriety of my doing so. I was not permitted to take a sufficient number of men with me to fight the Indians, and my only hope was to steal the prisoners from the enemy. The fewer in company then, less was the danger of my being discovered by the savages and killed. But, to return to a continuation of my narrative.

In February, 1844, information was received in Texas that a girl had been purchased from the Comanches and brought to Jasper county, Missouri, who, from the description given of her, I thought was my niece, now the only prisoner that was taken at Fort Parker, that had not been recovered.

I procured my passport from the Executive of Texas, and set about arranging my affairs for a journey to Missouri to see this girl. I first tried to raise some money, but although I offered to sell property for one-tenth of its real value, for that purpose, I failed. I tried to borrow money from Gen. Houston, and others, but there was scarcely any money in the country, and consequently all my endeavours to raise funds availed me nothing. Having prepared to start, I determined to wait no longer for money; and on the 21st day of June took leave of my family, assuring them that this should be the last journey I would go in pursuit of the prisoner.

When I reached Clarksville, in Texas, I stopped a few days for the purpose of getting some money due me there. I collected five dollars. When that was expended, I solicited work that I might get some more, but could find no one who had money to pay for the kind of work I could do.

I now pursued my journey to Missouri; and although I had but a few dollars, it is no less strange than true, that it was as much as I needed. On my whole route, the people whom I met treated me with a kindness and liberality I little looked for from entire strangers. It is true that to many of them I was personally a stranger; yet, they knew me well by character.

With the exception of the extreme warm weather, and much annoyance from the horse flies in the western part of Arkansas and Missouri, I had a pleasant journey. I reached Jasper County, Missouri, on the 5th of August, and found that the girl I went to see was not my niece, but, as I believed, the daughter of a Mrs. Williams of Texas. I proposed to take her with me to Texas, on my return, which created some unpleasant feelings between one of the citizens of that county and myself. However, I resolved that she should accompany me to Texas on my return.

Having learned that there was a white girl among the Kickapoo Indians, I determined to go to see her, and accordingly set out for that purpose. I arrived at Maj. Robert Cummins' (Indian Agent,) near Westport, Missouri, on the 15th of August. Maj. C, as soon as I presented him my authority from my government, set out with me to the Kickapoo nation. We went by the way of Fort Leavenworth, and the stationed officers there promptly rendered all the necessary aid. We soon found the girl, who proved to be of the same nation of Indians, but having some white blood in her. They wished to pass her off as a white girl for the purpose of gain.

To Maj. Cummins I am under lasting obligations for his prompt attention to my call, as well as many signal favours rendered me.

On the 20th of August, I put an advertisement in the *Western Expositor*, published at Independence, Missouri, offering a reward of $300 for any prisoner that might be brought in, and $500 for my niece. Having enlisted the good feelings of several of the leading men of Independence in my favour, and secured the assistance of Col. Alvaier, the U. S. Minister to Santa Fe, Dr. Waldo, and Maj. Rickman, in forwarding my object, I determined to go to brother Nathaniel Parker's, in Charleston, Illinois.

On this route, as well as the one from Texas to Independence, I had many interesting meetings. I attended the Mount Gilead Association, 35 miles from Quincy, Ill., where I had the pleasure of cultivating an acquaintance with many of the brethren, among whom were Elders Harper, Hogan, Roberts, Williams, Dr. James M. Clarkson, and many others. I reached my brother's, in Charleston, on the 20th of September. I remained sometime in that county; and it was here my friends again urged upon me to have my journal published.

Here I met with Elder B. B. Piper, who urged me to accompany him to Louisville, and proffered me all the aid in his power in getting the work through the press. We arrived in Louisville on the 18th day of October. I have found in Louisville a magnanimous people, among whom I have found *friends indeed*. Among those from whom I have received particular kindnesses, and to whom I shall ever feel under obligations, I cannot forego naming Mr. and Mrs. Kennedy, Mrs. Breckenridge, Mr. A. L. Shotwell and lady, Mr. W. N. Haldeman, Mr. R. B. J. Twyman and lady, and Mr. J. M. Stephens and lady.

In Sellersburg, Indiana, I have also met with many kind friends, whose favours I shall remember with the most lively gratitude, among whom I could name Elder M. W. Sellers, Mr. Wm. Jackson, Mr. Sparks and Mr. Wm. Parker.

Since I have been in Louisville, I have tried, under much affliction, to preach. I have also visited several of the neighbouring churches—at New Albany, Sellersburg, Elk Creek, Buckrun, &c. I hope, through the mercy of Providence, soon to be on my home, where I shall endeav-

PICTURE OF CYNTHIA ANN PARKER, WITH HER BABE NURSING, PRAIRIE FLOWER, TAKEN A FEW DAYS AFTER HER CAPTURE BY SULL ROSS, MOTHER OF QUANAH PARKER, COMANCHE INDIAN CHIEF.

our to spend the remainder of my days in the faithful discharge of my duty to my God, my country and my family.

James W. Parker.

MRS. RACHEL LOFTON, GREAT-GRANDDAUGHTER OF
JAMES W. PARKER, OWNER OF THE TRUSTY RIFLE, SPOKEN
OF IN THE LITTLE BOOK, WITH THE RIFLE IN HAND.

Narrative of the Capture and Subsequent Sufferings of Mrs. Rachel Plummer

Written By Herself.

PREFACE

In my preface to the first edition of this narrative, I promised a second edition, should the first meet with public patronage. The patronage extended to it has far exceeded my most sanguine expectations, for which I embrace the present opportunity to return my most sincere thanks to my friends and the public in general. In redemption of my promise, I present this second edition, revised and corrected, confidently anticipating the favourable consideration and renewed patronage of a generous public.

I hope it is unnecessary to ask my readers to throw over my awkward phraseology, ungrammatical sentences, and uncouth style, the veil of charity, as they cannot but recognise, at once, my want of education and practical experience in writing. Should this humble narrative be read with a critic's eye, and feeling injustice will be done me, and the object I have in view, in again appearing before the public will fail of being attained, *viz*: 1st. To make the reader acquainted with the manners and customs of the largest nation of Indians upon the American continent. 2nd. To warn all who are, or may be placed in a situation where they may be liable to fall a prey to savage barbarity, of what I have suffered, and thus induce them to avoid my fate; whilst at the same time I hope to excite a sympathy for those who are now, or hereafter may be prisoners among the Indians, and thus induce greater efforts for their release. 3rd. To briefly describe a country, yet known to but few of my readers, and which is destined, at no distant day, to excite much interest among the inhabitants of the United States and Texas.

With these remarks, I submit the following pages to the perusal of a generous public, feeling assured that before they are published, the hand that penned them will be cold in death.

Rachel Plummer.

City of Houston, Texas, Dec. 3, 1839.

NARRATIVE

On the 19th of May, 1836, I was living in Fort Parker, on the headwaters of the river Navasott. My father, (James W. Parker,) and my husband and brother-in-law were cultivating my father's farm, which was about a mile from the fort. In the morning, say 9 o'clock, my father, husband, brother-in-law, and brother, went to the farm to work. I do not think they had left the fort more than an hour before some one of the fort cried out, "Indians!" The inmates of the fort had retired to their farms in the neighbourhood, and there were only six men in it, *viz*: my grandfather, Elder John Parker, my two uncles, Benjamin and Silas Parker, Samuel Frost and his son Robert, and Frost's son-in-law, G. E. Dwight. All appeared in a state of confusion, for the Indians (numbering something not far from eight hundred) had raised a white flag.

On the first sight of the Indians, my sister (Mrs. Nixon,) started to alarm my father and his company at the farm, whilst the Indians were yet more than a quarter of a mile from the fort, and I saw her no more. I was in the act of starting to the farm, but I knew I was not able to take my little son, (James Pratt Plummer.) The women were all soon gone from the fort, whither I did not know; but I expected towards the farm. My old grandfather and grandmother, and several others, started through the farm, which was immediately adjoining the fort. Dwight started with his family and Mrs. Frost and her little children. As he started, uncle Silas said, "Good Lord, Dwight, you are not going to run? He said, "No, I am only going to try to hide the women and children in the woods." Uncle said, "Stand and fight like a man, and if we have to die we will sell our lives as dearly as we can.

The Indians halted; and two Indians came up to the fort to inform the inmates that they were friendly, and had come for the purpose of making a treaty with the Americans. This instantly threw the people off their guard, and uncle Benjamin went to the Indians, who had now got within a few hundred yards of the fort. In a few minutes he returned, and told Frost and his son and uncle Silas that he believed the Indians intended to fight, and told them to put everything in the best order for defence. He said he would go back to the Indians and see if the fight could be avoided.

Uncle Silas told him not to go, but to try to defend the place as well as they could; but he started off again to the Indians, and appeared to pay but little attention to what Silas said. Uncle Silas said, "I know they will kill Benjamin;" and said to me, "do you stand here and watch the Indians' motions until I run into my house"—I think he said for his shot pouch. I suppose he had got a wrong shot-pouch as he had four or five rifles. When Uncle Benjamin reached the body of Indians they turned to the right and left and surrounded him. I was now satisfied they intended killing him. I took up my little James Pratt, and thought I would try to make my escape. As I ran across the fort, I met Silas returning to the place where he left me. He asked me if they had killed Benjamin. I told him, "No; but they have surrounded him."

He said, "I know they will kill him, but I will be good for one of them at least." These were the last words I heard him utter.

I ran out of the fort, and passing the corner I saw the Indians drive their spears into Benjamin. The work of death had already commenced. I shall not attempt to describe their terrific yells, their united voices that seemed to reach the very skies, whilst they were dealing death to the inmates of the fort. It can scarcely be comprehended in the wide field of imagination. I know it is utterly impossible for me to give every particular in detail, for I was much alarmed.

I tried to make my escape, but alas, alas, it was too late, as a party of the Indians had got ahead of me. Oh! how vain were my feeble efforts to try to run to save myself and little James Pratt. A large sulky looking Indian picked up a hoe and knocked me down. I well recollect of their taking my child out of my arms, but whether they hit me any more I do not know, for I swooned away. The first I recollect, they were dragging me along by the hair. I made several unsuccessful attempts to raise to my feet before I could do it. As they took me past the fort, I heard an awful screaming near the place where they had first seized me. (I think Uncle Silas was trying to release me, and in doing this he lost his life; but not until he had killed four Indians). I heard some shots. I then heard Uncle Silas shout a triumphant huzza! I did, for one moment, hope the men had gathered from the neighbouring farms, and might release me.

I was soon dragged to the main body of the Indians, where they had killed Uncle Benjamin. His face was much mutilated, and many arrows were sticking in his body. As the savages passed by, they thrust their spears through him. I was covered with blood, for my wound was bleeding freely. I looked for my child but could not see him, and was convinced they had killed him, and every moment expected to share the same fate myself. At length I saw him. An Indian had him on his horse; he was calling, mother, oh, mother! He was just able to lisp the name of mother, being only about 18 months old. There were two Comanche women with them, (their battles are always brought on by a woman), one of whom came to me and struck me several times with a whip. I suppose it was to make me quit crying.

I now expected my father and husband, and all the rest of the men were killed. I soon saw a party of the Indians bringing my aunt Elizabeth Kellogg and Uncle Silas' two oldest children, Cynthia Ann, and John; also some bloody scalps; among them I could distinguish that of my grandfather by the grey hairs, but could not discriminate the balance.

Most of the Indians were engaged in plundering the fort. They cut open our bed ticks and threw the feathers in the air, which was literally thick with them. They brought out a great number of my father's books and medicines. Some of the books were torn up, and most of the bottles of medicine were broken; though they took on some for several days.

★★★★★★

Among them was a bottle of pulverised arsenic, which the Indians mistook for a kind of white paint, with which they painted their faces and bodies all over, after dissolving it in their saliva. The bottle was brought to me to tell them what it was. I did not do it, though I knew it, for the bottle was labelled. Four of the Indians painted themselves with it as above described, and it did not fail to kill them.

★★★★★★

I had few minutes to reflect, for they soon started back the same way they came up. As I was leaving, I looked back at the place where I was one hour before, happy and free, and now in the hands of a ruthless, savage enemy.

They killed a great many of our cattle as they went along. They soon convinced me that I had no time to reflect upon the past, for they commenced whipping and beating me with clubs, &c, so that my flesh was never well from bruises and wounds during my captivity. To undertake to narrate their barbarous treatment would only add to my present distress, for it is with feelings of the deepest mortification that' I think of it, much less to speak or write of it; for while I record this painful part of my narrative; I can almost feel the same heart-rending pains of body and mind that I then endured, my very soul becomes sick at the dreadful thought.

About midnight they stopped. They now tied a plaited thong around my arms, and drew my hands behind me. They tied them so tight that the scars can be easily seen to this day. They then tied a similar thong around my ankles, and drew my feet and hands together. They now turned me on my face and I was unable to tun over, when they commenced beating me over the head with their bows, and it was with great difficulty I could keep from smothering in my blood; for the wound they gave me with the hoe, and many others, were bleeding freely.

I suppose it was to add to my misery that they brought my little James Pratt so near me that I could hear him cry. He would call for mother; and often was his voice weakened by the blows they would give him. I could hear the blows. I could hear his cries; but oh, alas, could offer him no relief. The rest of the prisoners were brought near me, but we were not allowed to speak one word together. My aunt called me once, and I answered her; but, indeed, I thought she would never call or I answer again, for they jumped with their feet upon us, which nearly took our lives. Often did the children cry, but were soon hushed by such blows that I had no idea they could survive. They commenced screaming and dancing around the scalps; kicking and stamping the prisoners.

I now ask you, my Christian reader, to pause. You who are living secure from danger—you who have read the sacred scriptures of truth—who have been raised in a land boasting of Christian philanthropy—I say, I now ask you to form some idea of what my feelings were. Such dreadful, savage yelling! enough to terrify the bravest hearts. Bleeding and weltering in my blood; and far worse, to think of my little darling Pratt! Will this scene ever be effaced from my memory? Not until my spirit is called to leave this tenement of clay; and may God grant me a heart to pray for them, for *"they know not what they do."*

Next morning, they started in a northern direction. They tied me every night, as before stated, for five nights. During the first five days, I never ate one mouthful of food, and had but a very scanty allowance of water. Notwithstanding my sufferings, I could not but admire the

51

country—being prairie and timber, and very rich. I saw many fine springs. It was some 70 or 80 miles from the fort to the Cross Timbers. This is a range of timber-land from the waters of Arkansas, bearing a southwest direction, crossing the False Ouachita, Red River, the heads of Sabine, Angelina, Natchitoches, Trinity, Brazos, Colorado, &c, going on southwest, quite to the Rio Grande.

The range of timber is of an irregular width, say from 5 to 35 miles wide, and is a very diversified country; abounding with small prairies, skirted with timber of various kinds—oak, of every description, ash, elm, hickory, walnut and mulberry. There is more post oak on the up-lands than any other kind; and a great deal of this range of timber land is very rough, bushy, abounds with briers, and some of it poor. West, or S. W. of the Brazos, it is very mountainous. As this range of timber reaches the waters of the Rio Grande, (Big River,) it appears to widen out, and is directly adjoining the timber covering the table lands be-tween Austin and Santa Fe. This country, particularly southwest of the Brazos, is a well watered country, and part of it will be densely inhab-ited. The purest atmosphere I ever breathed was that of these regions.

After we reached the Grand Prairie, we turned more to the east; that is, the party I belonged to. Aunt Elizabeth fell to the Kitchawas, and my nephew and niece to another portion of the Comanches.

I must again call my reader to bear with me in rehearsing the continued barbarous treatment of the Indians. My child kept crying, and almost continually calling for "Mother," though I was not allowed even to speak to it. At the time they took off my fetters, they brought my child to me, supposing that I gave suck. As soon as it saw me, it, trembling with weakness, hastened to my embraces. Oh, with what feelings of love and sorrow did I embrace the mutilated body of my darling little James Pratt. I now felt that my case was much bettered, as I thought they would let me have my child; but oh, mistaken, in-deed, was I; for as soon as they found that I had weaned him, they, in spite of all my efforts, tore him from my embrace. He reached out his hands towards me, which were covered with blood, and cried, "Mother, Mother, oh, Mother!" I looked after him as he was borne from me, and I sobbed aloud. This was the last I ever heard of my little Pratt. Where he is, I know not.

Progressing farther and farther from my home, we crossed Big Red River, the head of Arkansas, and then turned more to the northwest. We now lost sight of timber entirely.

For several hundred miles after we had left the Cross Timber country, and on the Red River, Arkansas, &c, there is a fine country. The timber is scarce and scrubby. Some streams as salt as brine; and others, fine water. The land, in part, is very rich, and game plenty.

We would travel for weeks and not see a riding switch. Buffalo dung is all the fuel. This is gathered into a round pile; and when set on fire, it does very well to cook by, and will keep fire for several days.

In July, and in part of August, we were on the Snow Mountains. There it is perpetual snow; and I suffered more from cold than I ever suffered in my life before. It was very seldom I had anything to put on my feet, but very little covering for my body. I had to mind the horses every night, and had a certain number of buffalo skins to dress every moon. This kept me employed all the time in daylight; and often would I have to take my buffalo skin with me, to finish it whilst I was minding the horses. My feet would be often frozen, even while I would be dressing skins, and I dared not complain; for my situation still grew more and more difficult.

In October, I gave birth to my second son. As to the months, &c, it was guess work with me, for I had no means of keeping the time. It was an interesting and beautiful babe. I had, as you may suppose, but a very poor chance to comfort myself with any thing suitable to my situation, or that of my little infant. The Indians were not as hostile now. as I had feared they would be. I was still fearful they would kill my child; and having now been with them some six months, I had learned their language. I would often expostulate with my mistress to advise me what to do to save my child; but all in vain. (Having fallen into the hands of an old man that had only his wife and one daughter, who composed his family, I was compelled to reverence the both women as mistresses). My child was some six or seven weeks old, when I suppose my master thought it too much trouble, as I was not able to go through as much labour as before.

One cold morning, five or six large Indians came where I was suckling my infant. As soon as they came in I felt my heart sick; my fears agitated my whole frame to a complete state of convulsion; my body shook with fear indeed. Nor were my fears vain or ill-grounded. One of them caught hold of the child by the throat; and with his whole strength, and like an enraged lion actuated by its devouring nature, held on like the hungry vulture, until my child was to all appearance entirely dead. I exerted my whole feeble strength to relieve it; but the other Indians held me. They, by force, took it from me, and threw it up in the air, and let it fall on the frozen ground, until it was

53

apparently dead.

They gave it back to me. The fountain of tears that had hitherto given vent to my grief, was now dried up. While I gazed upon the bruised cheeks of my darling infant, I discovered some symptoms of returning life. Oh, how vain was my hope that they would let me have it if I could revive it. I washed the blood from its face; and after some time, it began to breathe again; but a more heart-rending scene ensued. As soon as they found it had recovered a little, they again tore it from my embrace and knocked me down. They tied a platted rope round the child's neck, and drew its naked body into the large hedges of prickly pears, which were from eight to twelve feet high. They would then pull it down through the pears. This they repeated several times. One of them then got on a horse, and tying the rope to his saddle, rode round a circuit of a few hundred yards, until my little innocent one was not only dead, but literally torn to pieces.

I stood horror struck. One of them then took it up by the leg, brought it to me, and threw it into my lap. But in praise to the Indians, I must say, that they gave me time to dig a hole in the earth and bury it. After having performed this last service to the lifeless remains of my dear babe, I sat down and gazed with joy on the resting place of my now happy infant; and I could, with old David, say, "*You cannot come to me, but I must go to you;*" and then, and even now, whilst I record the awful tragedy, I rejoice that it has passed from the sufferings and sorrows of this world. I shall hear its deathly cries no more; and fully and confidently believing, and solely relying on the imputed righteousness of God in Christ Jesus, I feel that my happy babe is now with its kindred spirits in that eternal world of joys. Oh! will my dear Saviour, by his grace, keep me through life's short journey, and bring me to dwell with my happy children in the sweet realms of endless bliss, where I shall meet the whole family of Heaven—those whose names are recorded in the *Lamb's Book of Life*.

I would have been glad to have had the pleasure of laying my little James Pratt with this my happy infant. I do really believe I could have buried him without shedding a tear; for, indeed, they had ceased to flow in relief of my grief. My heaving bosom could do no more than breathe deep sighs. Parents, you little know what you can bear. Surely, surely, my poor heart must break.

We left this place and as usual, were again on a prairie, We soon discovered a large lake of water. I was very thirsty; and although we travelled directly towards it, we could never get any nearer to it. It did not appear to be more than forty or fifty steps off, and always kept the same distance. This astonished me beyond measure. Is there any thing like magic in this, said I. I never saw a lake, pond, or river, plainer in my life. My thirst was excessive, and I was panting for a drop of water; but I could get no nearer to it. I found it to be a kind of gas, as I supposed, and I leave the reader to put his own construction upon it. It is, by some, called water gas. It looks just like water, and appears even to show the waves. I have often seen large herds of buffalo feeding in it. They appeared as if they were wading in the water; and their wakes looked as distinct as in real water. (This was the mirage, common to large deserts and prairies. Those travellers in the East, who have passed over the deserts of Asia and Africa, make frequent mention of these phenomena).

In those places, the prairies are as level as the surface of a lake, and can better be described by at once imagining yourself looking at a large lake. I have but a faint idea of the cause; but from the number of sea shells, (oysters', &c.,) I have no doubt that this great prairie was once a sea.

I was often on the salt plains. There the salt some little resembles dirty snow on a very cold day, being very light. The wind will blow it for miles. I have seen it in many places half leg deep; whilst other parts of the ground would be naked, owing to the strong winds drifting it.

I was at some of the salt lakes, which are very interesting to the view. Thousands of bushels of salt—yea, millions—resembling ice; a little on the muddy or milky order. It appears that there would not be consumption for this immense amount of salt in all the world; for it forms anew when it is removed, so that it is inexhaustible.

These prairies abound with such a number and variety of beasts, that pages could not describe them.

1st. The little prairie dog is as large as a gray squirrel. Some of them are as spotted as a leopard; but they are mostly of a dark colour, and live in herds. They burrow in the ground. As a stranger approaches them, they set up a loud barking; but will soon sink down into their holes. They are very fat, and fine to eat.

2nd. The prairie fox is a curious animal: It is as tall as a small dog— its body not larger than a grey squirrel, but three times as long. Their legs are remarkably small; being but little larger than a large straw. They can run very fast. Seldom fat.

3rd. The rabbit rivals the snow in whiteness, and is as large as a small dog. They are very active, and are delicious to eat. They can run very fast. I have thought they were the most beautiful animal I ever saw.

4th. The mountain sheep are smaller than the common sheep, and have long hair. They will feed on the brink of the steepest precipice, and are very active. They are very plentiful about the mountains.

5th. Buffalo, the next largest animal known, except the elephant. Their number no one can tell. They are found in the prairies and seldom in the timber even when there is any. Their flesh is the most delicious of all the beef kind I have seen. I have often seen the ground covered with them as far as the eye could reach.

The Indians shoot them with their arrows from their horses. They kill them very fast, and will even shoot an arrow entirely through one of these large animals.

6th. The elk, the largest of the deer species, with very large horns, and often more than six feet long. There are but few of them found in the same country with the buffalo; but they range along the Missouri River in parts of the Rocky Mountains. Their flesh is like venison.

7th. The antelope. This is, I believe, the fleetest animal in the world. They go in large flocks or herds. They will see the stranger a great way off, will run towards him till they get within twenty or thirty steps, and then the whole herd (perhaps some thousands) will wheel at the same moment, and are soon two or three miles off. They will again approach you, but not quite so near as at first, and then wheel again. They generally make about three or four of these visits, still wheeling from you at a greater distance. They will then leave you. They are much like the goat, and are by some called the wild goat.

8th. There are a great variety of wolves on the prairies; the large grey wolf, the large black wolf, the prairie wolf, and, I believe, the proper jackal. There is a large white wolf which will weigh 300 pounds, has very long hair of silvery white, and is very ferocious. They will kill a buffalo, and will not go out of the way of man or beast.

9th. There are four kinds of bears in the mountains; the white, grisley, red, and black bears. The grisley bear is the largest and most powerful. They will weigh 1200 or 1400 pounds. They cannot climb, but live in the valleys about the mountains. They are very delicious food. The white bear is very ferocious, and will attack either man or beast.

They are hard to conquer. The Indians are very fearful of them, and will not attack them; and even if attacked by them, will try to make their escape. They are of a silvery white, and are found along the brows of the Rocky Mountains. They are very fat and delicious food. The common black bear is scarce, as is also the red bear. The last species of bear is alone heard of in the western part of the Rocky Mountains. They are the most beautiful beast I ever saw, being red as vermillion.

10th. The common deer is in many places very plenty. In the mountains they grow much larger than they do in Texas.

11th. Turkeys, on the heads of Columbia River, are very numerous. They do not range on the prairies nor about the Snow mountains.

12th. Wild horses (Mustangs) are very plenty on the prairies. Thousands of the very finest horses, mules, jacks, &c, may be seen in one day. They are very wild. The Indians often take them by running them on their horses and throwing the lasso over their heads. They are easily domesticated.

13th. Man-Tiger. The Indians say that they have found several of them in the mountains. They describe them as being of the feature and make of a man. They are said to walk erect, and are eight or nine feet high. Instead of hands, they have huge paws and long claws, with which they can easily tear a buffalo to pieces. The Indians are very shy of them, and whilst in the mountains, will never separate. They also assert that there is a species of human beings that live in the caves in the mountains. They describe them to be not more than three feet high. They say that these little people are alone found in the country where the man-tiger frequents, and that the former takes cognizance of them, and will destroy any thing that attempts to harm them.

14th. The beaver is found in great numbers in the ponds, which are very numerous on the heads of the Columbia, Missouri, Arkansas, Rio Grande, Platte, and all the country between; though it is very mountainous, and sometimes the ponds are on the highest ground.

These strange animals, in many instances, appear to possess the wisdom of human beings. They appear to have their family connections, and each family lives separate, sometimes numbering more than a hundred in a family. A stranger is not allowed to dwell with them. They burrow in the ground when they cannot get timber to build huts. In case they can get timber, they will cut down quite large trees with their teeth, then cut them off in lengths to suit their purposes;

sometimes five or six feet long, and will then unite in hauling them to a chosen spot, and build up their houses in the edge of the water. The first storey of some three feet high—one door under the water. The next storey is not so high, has three doors, one next the water, one next the land, and one down through the floor into the first storey. There is continually a sentinel at the door next the land, and on the approach of any thing that alarms them, they are soon in the water.

They will move from one pond to another, and it is strange to see what a large road they make in removing. Their fur and size need no description. They are generally very fat, but the tail only is fit to eat. The bait with which the traps are baited, is collected from this animal, and is difficult to prepare, as there has to be a precise amount of certain parts of the animal. If there is too much of any one ingredient they will become alarmed, and even leave the pond. In preparing the bait, no part of your flesh must touch it, or they will not come near it. The bait has to be changed every few days by adding something; a small piece of spignard or annis root may be dropped into it. It is kept close in bladders, or skin bags, and nothing that goes into it must be touched with the hands.

15th. Muskrats in those ponds are beyond number. They also build houses in the ponds. They are built of any kind of trash they can find.

The most abrupt range of the Rocky Mountains embraces a large tract of country, and so incredibly high, and perpendicular are they in many places, that it is impossible to ascend them. At some places the tall sharp peaks of mountains resemble much the steeple on a church. Probably you can see twenty of these high peaks at one sight; and in other places the steep rock bluff, perhaps 200 feet high, will extend ten miles perfectly strait and uniform. In some places you will find a small tract of level country on the tops of the mountains. These levels are generally very rich. This range of mountains crosses the heads of the Missouri, and bears in a southwesterly direction to, and beyond the Rio Grande, even as far as I have ever been; also, bearing north, down the Columbia River as far as I went, and the head waters of the Platte, (perhaps I may be mistaken in the names of some of the rivers.)

They can better be described by saying they are a dreadful rough range of mountains, I suppose as high as any others in the world. The bottoms are very rich. It will be winter on the top of the mountains, and spring or summer in the valleys. There is a kind of wild flax that grows in these bottoms which yields a lint, out of which the Indians make ropes. It is very strong. As far as I was down on the tributaries of the Columbia, the bottoms were seldom more than one half mile wide; in some places a mile. The timber is indifferent in the bottoms, and more indifferent on the high land.

The buffalo sometimes finds it very difficult to ascend or descend these mountains, I have sometimes amused myself by getting on the top of one of these high pinnacles and looking over the country. You can see one mountain beyond another until they are lost in the misty air. Where you can see the valleys, you will often see them literally covered with the buffalo, sometimes the elk, wild horse, &c.

Northwest of the head of the Rio Grande, which is some 150 miles N.W. of Santa Fe, the country becomes more level. Part of this country is inhabited by a nation of Indians, called Apaches, and another tribe called Ferbelows. In this section of country there are some farms where fine wheat is raised.

This region of country is but very little known by the American people, being infested with such numerous tribes of Indians that Americans are very unsafe to be there. If the timber was not so indifferent, this country would be densely inhabited. The soil would fully justify the idea. In point of health it certainly is not surpassed in the world; and although very far to the north, is not excessively cold. I do not think it is colder than the state of Tennessee. The present inhabitants say there is nothing like fevers known in that country.

There are a great many caves in this high mountainous country. I must give my readers an account of one of my adventures in one of these caves. I am compelled to ask my reader to indulge me in the following adventure, as I am certain that this, as well as others of my adventures, will appear very remarkable; and reader, you will be compelled to fancy yourself in a condition where life has lost its sweetness, before you will be able to credit it. And here let me remark, that I have withheld stating many things, that are facts, because I well know that you will doubt whether any person could survive what I have undergone. I further assure you, my reader, that I have not written one word but what is fact. But to my story.

At one time, whilst on the Rocky Mountains, I had discovered a cave near the foot of the mountain. Having noticed some singular rocks, etc. at its mouth, that excited in me curiosity to explore this singular looking place, and the time drawing nigh, that we were to leave this encampment, I was much afraid I would not have an an opportunity of satisfying this curiosity. I had repeatedly asked my mistress to permit me to go into the cave, but she refused. A few days before we were to leave, however, she yielded a reluctant consent to my singular desire, and also permitted my young mistress to accompany me.

I immediately set about making my arrangements for this adventure. I procured some buffalo tallow, and made of a part of it some large candles, (if I may so call them) and took with me some tallow to make more, should I need them. I took with me the necessary instruments for striking fire, procured some light fuel, and thus prepared, we started into the cave. We had not proceeded more than 30 or 40 rods, when my companion became alarmed. I told her there was nothing alarming yet, and tried to persuade her to go on with me, but she refused to go any farther herself, or to let me go. I was, however, determined to proceed, and she appeared determined that I should return. A combat now ensued, and she struck at me with a piece of the wood we had with us. I dodged the blow, and knocked her down with another piece.

This made her yell most hideously; but being both out of sight and out of hearing of any person, I cared not for her cries, but firmly told her that if she attempted again to force me to return until I was ready, I would kill her. In the scuffle, being both down, the candle had fallen from my hand, and fortunately was not put out. I picked it up, and here a sight was presented to my view that surpasses all description. Innumerable stars, from the most diminutive size up to that of the full moon, studded the impenetrable gloom above and around us. I had not, until now, noticed the sublime and awful appearance of the cave. It was this sight that had alarmed my companion, and finding it impossible to induce her to proceed on the adventure with me, I agreed, on the condition that she would help me to mind the horses, to return with her to the mouth of the cave, which I did, and then returned to prosecute my adventure in the cave.

On reaching the battleground, I felt a great anxiety to find out the cause of this strange scene, which upon a close examination was more splendid than the mind can conceive. Reader, you may fancy yourself viewing, at once, an entirely new planetary system, a thousand times more sublime and more beautiful than our own, and you fall far short of the reality I here witnessed. I soon discovered that these lights proceeded from the reflections of the light of the candle by the almost innumerable crystallised formations in the rocks above, and on either side. The room I was in was large, say 100 feet wide, and its length was beyond my sight. The ceiling was about twelve feet high, and the floor was nearly smooth, and in many places was as transparent as the clearest glass. The sides and ceiling were thickly set with the same material, from which projected thousands of knobs or lumps, varying from 1 to 30 inches in length. The reflections of the light of the candle, from these transparent lumps, exactly resembling the clearest ice, proved to be the stars that had caused so much alarm in my young mistress, and wonder in me. Having satisfied my curiosity by a full examination of this singular apartment, I pursued my journey in the bowels of the earth.

For a distance of three or four miles, the cave differed in appearance and width, but nothing worthy of notice was observed. I now came to another place that excited my admiration. The cave forked, the ceiling or roof of the right hand fork being about 10 feet high and 6 feet wide. This avenue was obstructed by the intervention of bars of these transparent formations, reaching from the ceiling to the floor. They were to close together to permit my body to pass between them, and the room, into which I could look, surpassing, in splendour, any thing I had yet seen, I was anxious to explore it. After much labour, I succeeded in breaking one of these bars, and now entered one of the most spacious and splendid rooms my eyes ever beheld.

It was about 100 feet in diameter, and 10 feet high. It was nearly circular, and the walls, ceiling and floor being entirely transparent, presented a scene of which the mind can form no just conception, much less the pen describe. I know my readers would not credit if I were to attempt to describe it. I therefore leave my readers to their own conjectures of how a room would look, prepared as a house of public worship, with a pulpit and three rows of seats around it, all of the same material, as has been described, on one side, and on the other a beautiful clear stream of water.

The water of this river, or creek, was so clear that I could have seen a pin on the bottom. It was about 50 yards wide, and varied from one to two feet deep. I crossed it, and after going down it a mile or more, I heard most terrific roaring. I continued my course in the direction from whence it came until I reached a place where this stream fell down a precipice, the depth of which I could form no conjecture, but from deafening roar that it made, it must have been immense.

Being much fatigued, and having come to the end of my journey, I sat down to rest. I had not been seated here long before I fell asleep, as I suppose, and in the confused roar of the waters I fancied I could hear the dying screams of my infant. I thought of home and my friends far away, that I must never see again. My wounded body appeared to bleed afresh, as my mind reverted back to the cruelties inflicted upon me by my barbarian captivators, when there appeared to me the form of a human being. He held in his hand a bottle containing a liquid, with which he bathed my wounds, which ceased paining, and strange to say never hurt me afterwards. (This I know is not fancy, and sometimes, in reflecting upon this adventure, I am lost in doubt as to whether this whole scene was reality or only a dream.) He consoled me with kind words, that I well remember, but shall not here relate. Oh, could it have been possible that He who comforts the afflicted and gives strength to the weak, that God, in His bountiful mercy could have extended His hand to a poor wretch like me. whilst thus buried in the earth. How inscrutable are thy ways, Oh, God; and thy mercy and wisdom, how unsearchable. Were I to go give vent to my feelings, and possessed the mental capacity equal to the task, it would swell this humble narrative far beyond the limits I have prescribed to it.

Having renewed my light, I retraced my steps. I found the distance much greater, on returning, (or it appeared so,) than I thought. On reaching the place where my young mistress turned back, I found that the Indians had been in the cave looking for me. I reached the camp just as the sun was setting, and was astonished to learn that I had spent two days and one night in the cave. I never, in my life, had a more interesting adventure, and although I am now in the city of Houston, surrounded by friends and all the comforts of life, to sit alone, and in memory, retrace my steps in this cave, gives me more pleasurable feelings than all the gaudy show and pleasing gaiety with which I am surrounded. The impressions made upon my mind in this cave, have since served as a healing balm to my wounded soul.

There are some interesting incidents connected with this adventure, which I do not think proper to give the public at this time; they may, perhaps, be published hereafter. I have given but a very partial description of one of the most interesting scenes that occurred.

About the middle of March, all the Indian bands—that is, the Comanches, and all the hostile tribes, assembled and held a general war council. They met on the head waters of the Arkansas, and it was the largest assemblage I ever saw. The council was held upon a high eminence, descending every way. The encampments were as close as they could stand, and how far they extended I know not; for I could not see the outer edge of them with my naked eye.

I had now been with them so long that I had learned their language, and as the council was held in the Comanche language, I determined, (for I yet entertained a faint hope that I would be released,) to know the result of their proceedings. It being contrary to their laws to permit their squaws to be present in their councils, I was several times repulsed with blows, but I cheerfully submitted to abuse and persevered in listening to their proceedings.

A number of traditionary ceremonies were performed, such as would be of but little interest to the reader. This ceremony occupied about three days, after which they came to a determination to invade and take possession of Texas. It was agreed that those tribes of Indians who were in the habit of raising corn, should cultivate the farms of the people of Texas; the prairie Indians were to have entire control of the prairies, each party to defend each other. After having taken Texas, killed and driven out the inhabitants, and the corn growing Indians had raised a good supply, they were to attack Mexico. There they expected to be joined by a large number of Mexicans who are disaffected with the government, as also a number that would or could be coerced into measures of subordination, they would soon possess themselves of Mexico. They would then attack the United States.

They said that the white men had now driven the Indian bands from the East to the West, and now they would work this plan to drive the whites out of the country; they said that the white people had got almost around them, and in a short time they would drive them again. I do believe that almost every band or nation of Indians was represented in that Council, and there was but one thing that was left unsettled, that was the time of attack— some said, the spring of 1838, and others said the spring of 1839; though this matter was to be left measurably to the Northern Indians, and to be communicated to the chiefs of the Comanches. The Council continued in session seven days, and at the end of that period, they broke up. One Indian came to me on the prairie, and stated that he was a Beadie, that he lived on the San Jacinto River, and that they were determined to make servants of the white people, and cursed me in the English language, which were the only English words I had heard during my captivity.

On one occasion, my young mistress and myself were out a short distance from town. She ordered me to go back to the town and get a kind of instrument with which they dig roots. Having lived as long, and indeed longer than life was desirable, I determined to aggravate them to kill me.

I told her I would not go back. She, in an enraged tone, bade me

63

go. I told her I would not. She then with savage screams ran at me. I knocked, or, rather, pushed her down. She, fighting and screaming like a desperado, tried to get up; but I kept her down; and in the fight I got hold of a large buffalo bone. I beat her over the head with it, although expecting at every moment to feel a spear reach my heart from one of the Indians; but I lost no time. I was determined if they killed me, to make a cripple of her. Such yells as the Indians made around us—being nearly all collected—a Christian mind cannot conceive. No one touched me. I had her past hurting me, and indeed, nearly past breathing, when she cried out for mercy. I let go my hold of her, and could but be amazed that not one of them attempted to arrest or kill me, or do the least thing for her. She was bleeding freely; for I had cut her head in several places to the skull. I raised her up and carried her to the camp.

A new adventure this. I was yet undetermined what would grow out of it. All the Indians seemed as unconcerned as if nothing had taken place. I washed her face and gave her water. She appeared remarkably friendly. One of the big chiefs came to me, and appeared to watch my movements with a great deal of attention. At length he observed—

> You are brave to fight—good to a fallen enemy—you are directed by the Great Spirit. Indians do not have pity on a fallen enemy. By our law you are clear. It is contrary to our law to show foul play. She began with you, and you had a right to kill her. Your noble spirit forbid you. When Indians fight, the conqueror gives or takes the life of his antagonist—and they seldom spare them.

This was like balm to my soul. But my old mistress was very mad. She ordered me to go and get a large bundle of straw. I soon learned it was to burn me to death. I did not fear that death; for I had prepared me a knife, with which I intended to defeat her object in putting me to death by burning, having determined to take my own life. She ordered me to cross my hands. I told her I would not do it. She asked me if I was willing for her to burn me to death without being tied. I told her that she should not tie me. She caught up a small bundle of the straw, and setting it on fire, threw it on me. I soon found I could not stand fire. I told her that I should fight if she burnt me any more, (she had already burnt me to blisters in many places.) An enraged tiger could not have screamed with more terrific violence than she did. She set another bundle on fire, and threw it on me. I was as good as my word. I pushed her into the fire, and as she raised, I knocked her down into the fire again, and kept her there until she was as badly burned as I was. She got hold of a club and hit me a time or two. I took it from her, and knocked her down with it.

So we had a regular fight. I handled her with more ease than I did the young woman. During the fight, we had broken down one side of the house, and had got fully out into the street. After I had fully overcome her, I discovered the same diffidence on the part of the Indians as in the other fight. The whole of them were around us, screaming as before, and no one touched us. I, as in the former case, immediately administered to her. All was silent again, except now and then, a grunt from the old woman. The young woman refused to help me into the house with her. I got her in, and then fixed up the side of the house that we had broken.

Next morning, twelve of the chiefs assembled at the Council House. We were called for, and we attended; and with all the solemnity of a church service, went into the trial. The old lady told the whole story without the least embellishment.

I was asked if these things were so. I answered, "Yes."

The young woman was asked, "Are these things true?"

She said they were. We were asked if we had anything to say.

Both of the others said "No."

I said I had. I told the court that they had mistreated me—they had not taken me honourably; that they had used the white flag to deceive us, by which they had killed my friends—that I had been faithful, and had served them from fear of death, and that I would now rather die than be treated as I had been. I said that the Great Spirit would reward them for their treachery and their abuse to me. The sentence was, that I should get a new pole for the one that we had broken in the fight. I agreed to it, provided the young woman helped me. This was made a part of the decree, and all was peace again.

This answered me a valuable purpose afterwards, in some other instances. I took my own part, and fared much the better by it.

I shall next speak of the manners and customs of the Indians, and in this I shall be brief—as their habits are so ridiculous that this would be of but little interest to any.

They never stay more than three or four days in one place, unless it is in very cold weather; in that case, they stay until the weather changes. Their houses are made of skins, stretched on poles, which they always carry with them. Their poles are tied together, and put on each side of a mule, whilst one end drags on the ground. The women do all the work, except killing the meat. They herd the horses, saddle and pack them, build the houses, dress the skins, meat, etc. The men dance every night, during which, the women wait on them with water.

No woman is admitted into any of their Councils; nor is she allowed to enquire what their councils have been. When they move, the women do not know where they are going. They are no more than servants, and are looked upon and treated as such.

I knew one young man have his mother hung for refusing to get him feathers for his arrows, and appeared rejoiced at her death.

They are traditionary in their manner of cooking. It is considered a great sin, and sure defeat, to suffer meat to be broiled and boiled on the same fire at the same time. Every kind of provision has to be cooked and eaten by itself. When meat is broiling, or boiling, no person is allowed to pass so near as to suffer their shadow to pass over the meat, or it is not fit to eat. They often eat their meat entirely raw. When they kill meat, they suffer nothing to be lost. They have rigid laws, and rigorously enforce them when violated. They know no such thing as mercy. They have no language to express gratitude, only to say I am glad.

Dancing is a part of their worship. Torturing their prisoners is another. They pay their homage to a large lump of platina, (which lays in the Cross Timbers, on the waters of the Brazos. Every year, the chiefs collect sacrifices, and offer them to this their God.

★★★★★★

Platina is a scarce and valuable metal, heavier and more durable than gold. The Indians make arrow spikes of it sometimes. It is very malleable. This lump will weigh some thousands of pounds.

★★★★★★

These offerings consist of beads, muscle shells, periwinkles, &c. There are several bushels of beads that have been left there as sacrifices. They worship different things while on the prairie. Some worship a pet crow—some a deer skin, with the sun and moon pictured on it. The band that I was with, worshipped an eagle's wing. Those things are kept as sacredly by them, as the Holy Scriptures are by us. They drink water every morning until they vomit—particularly when they are going to war. They believe in a Supreme Being—the resurrection of the body, and in future rewards and punishments. I am informed, however, that some tribes do not believe in these things. These Indians are not countenanced by the others.

Their manner of doctoring by faith is amusing. When any of the men are sick, the principal civil chiefs order two of the wigwams to be joined together, though open between. A hole is dug in each of these camps, about two feet deep. In one of them a fire is built; on the side of the other, is a lump of mud as large as a man's head. All around the hole, as well as this lump of mud, the ground is stuck full of willow sprouts. At sunrise, the sick man and musicians enter the camps, and the music is kept up all day. No one must pass near enough to allow his shadow to fall on the camp, or the patient is sure to die; but if every thing is done right, he is sure to get well. If he dies, it is attributed to a failure in some of the ceremonies.

Having said as much on this subject as is necessary, I shall now return to my narrative.

On the head of Columbia River, I could sometimes get some dry brush to make me a light to work by. We were now in a very deep valley. One evening, I was going in search of some dry brush, and discovered some shining particles on the ground.

I picked up one of them. It was about three-fourths of an inch in circumference, of an oblong shape. I found it gave light, which superseded, ever afterward, the necessity of using dry brush. It was perfectly transparent. I leave my reader to judge what it was. I thought it was a diamond. There were unnumbered thousands of pieces. In some places, I could see the little ravine on which they were, at the distance of a mile, by the light which emanated from them. I lost this stone a few days before I was purchased. I have good reason to believe that one of the richest gold mines ever discovered may be found in that valley; and it would be a pity for so much wealth to remain undiscovered. The Indians often found pieces large enough to make arrow spikes, which is the only use they have for it. They would at any time exchange one of these arrow spikes for an iron one—the latter being harder and lighter. I may hereafter say more on this subject.

In the province or country called Senoro, I found many curiosities. (I, perhaps, may be mistaken as to the country; as all I know of it, I learned from the Indians and Mexican prisoners). This country, I think, was a northwest course from Santa Fe, about 700 miles. Here I found a great curiosity in a kind of thorn, which is as complete a fish-hook as ever I saw, having several strong beards on each hook; and what is still more strange, there are various sizes on the same shrub.

These hooks are quite as strong as any that are made of steel, and more elastic. I have two of them now that I have caught many a fish with. I took them off the bush myself, and have kept them ever since I have been released. I have often been offered five dollars for one of them, but I have never been induced to part with them. They often bring to my recollection the distant country where I obtained them.

In this region of country, nearly every shrub and tree bears a thorn or briar. The timber, what little there is, is very low and scrubby. I wish I had language to give a fair description of this part of the country, with its present inhabitants. There are some Mexicans residing here. I tried to get one of them to buy me. I told him that even if my father and husband were dead, I knew I had land enough in Texas to fully in-demnify him; but he did not try to buy me, although he agreed to do it. Some of the inhabitants are Indians. I am not certain of what tribe they are; but they cultivate the land, and raise some corn and potatoes. I was allowed to be among them but very little; neither. do I believe them to be friendly with the Comanches—though I saw no quarrel between them; but the Comanches stole their horses and killed some of them as we were about leaving.

I learned from the women that it was very seldom the Coman-ches went into that country. I saw here some springs that were truly a curiosity. The water, or kind of liquid, was about the consistency of tar, which would burn like oil, and was as yellow as gold. The earth, in many places, is also yellow. There are very few places in all this country, but what looks to be very poor. From the time that we left the coun-try of the Rocky Mountains, and during the whole time we were in this region, I do not think I saw one tree more than fifteen feet high; and those, as before stated, covered with thorns. The healthiest looking Indians I ever saw, lived here. Notwithstanding it is a healthy country, I do not think it ever will be settled by white men, as I saw nothing to induce white men to settle there. I have neglected to mention that the Indians have very rigid laws in the collection of debts. If one man owes another, it stands perpetually as a debt until paid.

When a creditor brings a suit for a debt, it is done by informing the civil chiefs. They immediately find out the amount due, which is recovered in buffalo skins, furs, mules, horses, bows, arrows, &c, ac-cording to the amount. The debtor is immediately informed of the amount that stands against him, and if he does not at once discharge the debt, it is in the power of the creditor, at any time, to enforce this judgment—which amounts to disfranchisement—that is, the debtor can hold no office, not even that of musician. He is not allowed to dance with his tribe, nor to hunt with them. If the debt is still unpaid when the debtor dies, his children are held under the same restrictions as those incurred by the father; nor are their wives allowed to associate with other women.

There are among them delinquent debtors, who are doubtless now bound for debts contracted by their forefathers five hundred years ago. Some use great exertions to pay the debt; but the last cent must be paid.

They have their different grades of officers, both civil and military. In many cases, these offices are hereditary. They enforce their laws most rigorously, even among themselves. They are strangers to any thing like mercy or sympathy, unless it is in war. They appear to be much enraged at the death of one of their men—particularly if their dead are scalped. If their dead are not scalped, they do not mind it so much.. When they have a battle, every exertion to prevent their dead from falling into the hands of the enemy is made, even to the extent of risking their own lives, which they often lose in trying to save, or carry off their dead from the field of battle. If they cannot get the body, they take off the scalp or head of their slain—such is their aversion to the enemy becoming possessed of the scalp The scalps of their enemies are kept as securities of good luck. This good luck is transferable from the father to the son.

On one occasion, they had a very severe battle with the Osage Indians, in which the Comanches lost several men. Part of them fell into the hands of the Osages. They secured the heads of some, and from others they took their scalps; yet the Osages got some of them. They grieved much more for those who had been scalped, than for those that were not.

In this battle, the Comanches got hold of several of the Osages that were killed, and brought their bodies to the town. They cut them up, broiled and boiled and ate them. My young mistress got a foot, roasted it, and offered me part of it. They appear to be very fond of human flesh. The hand or foot, they say, is the most delicious.

These inhuman cannibals will eat the flesh of a human being and talk of their bravery or abuse their cowardice with as much unconcern as if they were mere beasts.

One evening as I was at my work, (being north of the Rocky Mountains,) I discovered some Mexican traders.

★★★★★★

I had dreamed, the night before, that I saw an angel, the same I saw in the cave. He had four wings. He gave them to me, and immediately I was on the wing, and was soon with my father. But, when I awoke, behold! it was all a dream.

★★★★★★

Hope instantly mounted the throne from whence it had long been banished. My tottering frame received fresh life and courage, as I saw them approaching the habitation of sorrow and grief where I dwelt. They asked for my master, and we were directly with him. They asked if he would sell me. No music, no sounds that ever reached my anxious ear, was half so sweet as *"ce senure"* (yes, sir.) The trader made an offer for me. My owner refused. He offered more, but my owner still refused. Utter confusion hovers around my mind while I record this part of my history; and I can only ask my reader, if he can, to fancy himself in my situation; for language will fail to describe the anxious thoughts that revolved in my throbbing breast when I heard the trader say he could give no more. Oh! had I the treasures of the universe, how freely I would have given it; yea, and then consented to have been a servant to my countrymen. Would that my father could speak to him; but my father is no more. Or one of my dear uncles; yes, they would say "stop not for price."

Oh! my good Lord, intercede for me. My eyes, despite my efforts, are swimming in tears at the very thought. I only have to appeal to the treasure of your hearts, my readers, to conceive the state of my desponding mind at this crisis. At length, however, the trader made another offer for me, which my owner agreed to take. My whole feeble frame was now convulsed in an ecstasy of joy, as he delivered the first article as an earnest of the trade. *Memorable Day!*

Col. Nathaniel Parker, of Charleston, Illinois, burst into my mind; and although I knew he was about that time in the Illinois Senate, I knew he would soon reach his suffering niece, if he could only hear of her. Yes, I knew he would hasten to my relief, even at the sacrifice of a seat in that honourable body, if necessary.

Thousands of thoughts revolved through my mind as the trader was paying for me. My joy was full. Oh! shall I ever forget the time when my new master told me to go with him to his tent? As I turned from my prison, in my very soul I tried to return thanks to my God who always hears the cries of his saints:

My God was with me in distress,

My God was always there;
Oh! may I to my God address
Thankful and devoted prayer.

I was soon informed by my new master that he was going to take me to Santa Fe. That night, sleep departed from my eyes. In my fancy I surveyed the steps of my childhood, in company with my dear relations. It would, I suppose, be needless for me to say that I watched with eagerness the day to spring, and that the night was long filled with gratitude to the Divine Conservator of the divine law of heaven and earth.

In the morning quite early, all things being ready, we started. We travelled very hard for seventeen days, when we reached Santa Fe. Then, my reader, I beheld some of my countrymen, and I leave you to conjecture the contrast in my feelings when I found myself surrounded by sympathising Americans, clad in decent attire. I was soon conducted to Col. William Donoho's residence. I found that it was him who had heard of the situation of myself and others, and being an American indeed, his manly and magnanimous bosom, heaved with sympathy characteristic of a Christian, had devised the plan for our release. (Mrs. Harris had also been purchased by his arrangements, her narrative can be found in *Captives* also published by Leonaur).

Here I was at home. I hope that every American that reads this narrative may duly appreciate this amiable man, to whom, under the providence of God, I owe my release. I have no language to express my gratitude to Mrs. Donoho. I found in her a mother, to direct me in that strange land, a sister to condole with me in my misfortune, and offer new scenes of amusement to me to revive my mind. A friend? yes, the best of friends; one who had been blessed with plenty, and was anxious to make me comfortable; and one who was continually pouring the sweet oil of consolation into my wounded and trembling soul, and was always comforting and admonishing me not to despond, and assured me that every thing should be done to facilitate my return to my relatives; and though I am now separated far from her, I still owe to her a debt of gratitude I shall never be able to repay but with my earnest prayers for the blessing of God to attend her through life.

The people of Santa Fe, by subscription, made up $150 to assist me to my friends. This was put into the hands of Rev. C———, (at the request of my father I forbear publishing his name), who kept it and never let me have it; and but for the kindness of Mr. and Mrs.

71

Donoho, I could not have got along. Soon after I arrived in Santa Fe, a disturbance took place among the Mexicans. They killed several of their leading men. Mr. Donoho considered it unsafe for his family, and started with them to Missouri, and made me welcome as one of his family. The road led through a vast region of prairie, which is nearly one thousand miles across. This, to many, would have been a considerable undertaking, as it was all the way through an Indian country. But we arrived safely at Independence, in Missouri, where I received many signal favours from many of the inhabitants, for which I shall ever feel grateful. I stayed at Mr. Donoho's but I was impatient to learn something of my relatives.

My anxiety grew so great that I was often tempted to start on foot. I tried to pray, mingling my tears and prayers to Almighty God to intercede for me, and in his providence to devise some means by which I might get home to my friends. Despite of all the kind entreaties of that benevolent woman, Mrs. Donoho, I refused to be comforted; and who, I ask, under these circumstances, could have been reconciled?

One evening I had been in my room trying to pray, and on stepping to the door, I saw my brother-in-law, Mr. Nixon. I tried to run to him, but was not able. I was so much overjoyed I scarcely knew what to say or how to act. I asked, "are my father and husband alive?" He answered affirmatively. "Are mother and the children alive?" He said they were. Every moment seemed an hour. It was very cold weather, being now in dead of winter.

Mr. Donoho furnished me a horse, and in a few days we started, Mr. Donoho accompanying us. We had a long and cold journey of more than one thousand miles, the way we were compelled to travel, and that principally through' a frontier country. But having been accustomed to hardships, together with my great anxiety, I thought I could stand any thing, and the nearer I approached my people, the greater my anxiety grew. Finally on the evening of the 19th day of February, 1838, I arrived at my father's house in Montgomery county, Texas. Here united tears of joy flowed from the eyes of father, mother, brothers and sisters; while many strangers, unknown to me, (neighbours to my father) cordially united in this joyful interview.

I am now not only freed from my Indian captivity, enjoying the exquisite pleasure that my soul has long panted for.

Oh! God of Love, with pitying eye
Look on a wretch like me;

That I may on thy name rely,
Oh, Lord! be pleased to see.

How oft have sighs unuttered flowed
From my poor wounded heart,
Yet thou my wishes did reward,
And sooth'd the painful smart.

The following lines were written by Mrs. Plummer just before her death. Although they will not bear a critic's eye, yet we have thought we would append them to her narrative.

Ye careless ones, who wildly stroll
On life's uneven tide—
List to the sorrows of my soul,
My heaving bosom hide.

Oh, parents will you lend an ear,
And listen to my grief;
Will you let fall for me one tear,
Or could this give relief?

But, oh, my soul! my darling babe,
Was from my bosom torn,
It lies now in deaths gloomy shade,
And I am left to mourn.

Good LORD, I cried can I endure,
Such sorrow and deep grief,
His holy spirit kind and pure,
Give my poor soul relief.

It is very much to be regretted, that this little history of the capture of the Parker Fort by the Indians, and the trials and suffering the survivors had to endure, was not kept intact, we feel it our duty to republish all that is left intelligible of this little book, every effort to obtain a full copy having failed.

The Cynthia Ann Parker Account

PREFACE

In the month of June, 1884, there appeared in the columns of the Forth Worth *Gazette* an advertisement signed by the Comanche chief, Quanah Parker, and dated from the reservation near Fort Sill, in the Indian Territory, enquiring for a photograph of his late mother, Cynthia Ann Parker, which served to revive interest in a tragedy which has always been enveloped in a greater degree of mournful romance and pathos than any of the soul-stirring episodes of our pioneer life, so fruitful of incidents of an adventurous nature.

From the valued narratives kindly furnished us by Victor M. Ross, Major John Henry Brown and Gen. L. S. Ross, supplemented by the Jas. W. Parker book and copious notes from Hon. Ben. F. Parker, together with most of the numerous partial accounts of the fall of Parker's Fort and subsequent relative events, published during the past fifty years; and after a careful investigation and study of the whole, we have laboriously and with much painstaking, sifted out and evolved the foregoing narrative of plain, unvarnished facts, which form a part of the romantic history of Texas.

In the preparation of our little volume the thanks of the youthful author are due to Gen. L. S. Ross, of Waco; Major John Henry Brown of Dallas; Gen. Walter P. Lane of Marshall; Col. John S. Ford of San Antonio; Rev. Homer S. Thrall—the eminent historian of Texas; Mr. A. F. Corning of Waco; Capt. Lee Hall, Indian Agent, I. T., and Mrs. C. A. Westbrook of Lorena, for valuable assistance rendered.

To Victor M. Ross of Laredo, Texas, the author has been placed under many and lasting obligations for valuable data so generously placed at his disposal, and that too at considerable sacrifice to the donor.

From this source we have obtained much of the matter for our

CYNTHIA ANN PARKER,
AFTER HER RETURN TO THE PARKER FAMILY

narrative.

In submitting our little work—the first efforts of the youthful author—we assure the reader that while there are, doubtless, many defects and imperfections, he is not reading fiction, but facts which form only a part of the tragic and romantic history of the Lone Star State.

James T. Deshields,

Belton, Texas, May 19, 1886.

CHAPTER 1
THE PARKER PORT MASSACRE, ETC.

Contemporary with, and among the earliest of the daring and hardy pioneers that penetrated the eastern portion of the Mexican province of Texas, were the "Parker family," who immigrated from Cole county, Illinois, in the fall of the year 1833, settling on the west side of the Navasota creek, near the site of the present town of Groesbeck, in Limestone county, one or two of the family coming a little earlier and some a little later.

The elder John Parker was a native of Virginia, resided for a time in Elbert county, Georgia, but chiefly reared his family in Bedford county, Tennessee, whence in 1818 he removed to Illinois.

The family, with perhaps one or two exceptions, belonged to one branch of the primitive Baptist church, commonly designated as "two seed," or "hard shell" Baptists.

In the spring of 1834 the colonist erected Parker's Fort, a kind of wooden barricade, or wall around their cabins, which served as a means of better protecting themselves against the numerous predatory bands of Indians into that, then, sparsely settled section.

★★★★★★

The reader will understand by this term, not only a place of defence, but the residence of a small number of families belonging to the same neighbourhood. As the Indian mode of warfare was an indiscriminate slaughter of all ages, and both sexes, it was as requisite to provide for the safety of the women and children as for that of the men. Dodridge's faithful pen picture of early pioneer forts, will perhaps give the reader a glimpse of old Fort Parker in the dark and bloody period of its existence. He says: "The fort consisted of cabins, blockhouses, and stockades. A range of cabins commonly formed on one side at least of the fort. Divisions, or portions of logs, separated the cabins from each other. The walls on the outside were ten or twelve feet

77

high, the slope of the roof being turned wholly inward. A very few of these cabins had puncheon floors, the greater part were earthen. The blockhouses were built at the angles of the fort. They projected about two feet beyond the outer walls of the cabins and stockades. Their upper storeys were about eighteen inches every way larger in dimension than the under one, leaving an opening at the commencement of the second to prevent the enemy from making a lodgement under their walls. In some forts, instead of blockhouses the angles of the fort were furnished with bastions. A large folding gate, made of thick slabs, nearest the spring, closed the fort. The stockades, bastions, cabins, and blockhouse walls, were furnished with port-holes at proper heights and distances. The whole of the outside was completely bullet-proof.

It may be truly said that "necessity is the mother of invention"; for the whole of this work was made without the aid of a single nail or spike of iron; and for this reason such things were not to be had. In some places, less exposed, a single blockhouse, with a cabin or two, constituted the whole fort. Such places of refuge may appear very trifling to those who have been in the habit of seeing the formidable military garrisons of Europe and America, but they answered the purpose, as the Indians had no artillery. They seldom attacked, and scarcely ever took one of them.

★★★★★★

As early as 1829 the "Prairie Indians" had declared war against the settlers, and were now actively hostile, constantly committing depredations in different localities.

Parker's colony at this time consisted of only some eight or nine families, *viz*: Elder John Parker, patriarch of the family, and his wife; his son James W. Parker, wife, four single children and his daughter, Mrs. Rachel Plummer, her husband, L. M. T. Plummer, and infant son, fifteen months old; Mrs. Sarah Nixon, another daughter, and her husband L. D. Nixon; Silas M. Parker (another son of Elder John), his wife and four children Benjamin F. Parker, an unmarried son of the Elder; Mrs. Nixon, sr., mother of Mrs. James W. Parker; Mrs. Elizabeth Kellogg, daughter of Mrs. Nixon; Mrs. —— Duty; Samuel M. Frost, wife and two children; G. E. Dwight, wife and two children in all thirty-four persons.

★★★★★★

Elder Daniel Parker, a man of strong mental powers, a son of Elder John, does not figure in these events. He signed the Declaration of Independence in 1836, and preached to his people till his death in Anderson county in 1845. Ex-Representative Ben. F. Parker, is his son and successor in preaching at the same place. Isaac Parker, above mentioned, another son, long represented Houston and Anderson counties in Senate and House, and in 1855 represented Tarrant county. He died in Parker county, not long since, not far from 88 years of age. Isaac D. Parker of Tarrant is his son.

★★★★★★

Besides those mentioned, old man ——— Lunn, David Faulkenberry and his son Evan, Silas Bates, and Abram Anglin, a boy, had erected cabins a mile or two distant from the fort, where they resided.

These families were truly the advance guard of civilization of that part of our frontier. Fort Houston, in Anderson county, being the nearest protection, except their own trusty rifles.

Here the struggling colonist remained, engaged in the avocations of a rural life, tilling the soil, hunting buffalo, bear, deer, turkeys and smaller game, which served abundantly to supply their larder at all times with fresh meat, in the enjoyment of a life of Arcadian simplicity, virtue and contentment, until the latter part of the year 1835, when the Indians and Mexicans forced the little band of compatriots to abandon their homes, and flee with many others before the invading army from Mexico.

On arriving at the Trinity River they were compelled to halt in consequence of an overflow. Before they could cross the swollen stream the sudden and unexpected news reached them that Santa Anna and his vandal hordes had been confronted and defeated at San Jacinto, that sanguinary engagement which gave birth to the new sovereignty of Texas, and that *Texas was free from Mexican tyranny.*

On receipt of this news the fleeing settlers were overjoyed, and at once returned to their abandoned homes.

The Parker colony now retraced their steps, first going to Fort Houston, where they remained a few days in order to procure supplies, after which they made their way back to Fort Parker to look after their stock and to prepare for a crop.

These hardy sons of toil spent their nights in the fort, repairing to their farms early each morning.

On the night of May 18, 1836, all slept at the fort, James W. Parker,

Nixon and Plummer repairing to their field a mile distant on the Navasota, early next morning, little thinking of the great calamity that was soon to befall them.

About 9 o'clock a.m. the fort was visited by several hundred Comanche and Kiowa Indians. On approaching to within about three hundred yards of the fort the Indians halted in the prairie, presenting a white flag; at the same time making signs of friendship.

★★★★★★

Different accounts have variously estimated the number of Indians at from 300 to 700. One account says 300, another 500, and still another 700. There were perhaps about 500 warriors.

★★★★★★

At this time there were only six men in the fort, three having gone out to work in the field as above stated. Of the six men remaining, only five were able to bear arms, *viz*: Elder John Parker, Benjamin and Silas Parker, Samuel and Robert Frost. There were ten women and fifteen children.

The Indians, artfully feigning the treacherous semblance of friendship, pretended that they were looking for a suitable camping place, and enquired as to the exact locality of a water-hole in the vicinity, at the same time asking for a beef to appease their hungry a want always felt by an Indian, when the promise of fresh meat loomed up in the distant perspective; and he would make such pleas with all the servile sicophancy of a slave, like the Italian who embraces his victim ere plunging the poniard into his heart.

Not daring to resent so formidable a body of savages, or refuse to comply with their requests, Mr. Benjamin F. Parker went out to them, had a talk and returned, expressing the opinion that the Indians were hostile and intended to fight, but added that he would go back and try to avert it. His brother Silas remonstrated, but he persisted in going, and was immediately surrounded and killed, whereupon the whole force their savage instincts aroused by the sight of blood—charged upon the works, uttering the most terrific and unearthly yells that ever greeted the ears of mortals. Cries and confusion reigned. The sickening and bloody tragedy was soon enacted.

Brave Silas M. Parker fell on the outside of the fort, while he was gallantly fighting to save Mrs. Plummer. Mrs. Plummer made a most manful resistance, but was soon overpowered, knocked down with a hoe and made captive. Samuel M. Frost and his son Robert met their fate while heroically defending the women and children inside the stockade. Old Granny Parker was outraged, stabbed and left for dead. Elder John Parker, wife and Mrs. Kellogg attempted to make their escape, and in the effort had gone about three-fourths of a mile, when they were overtaken and driven back near to the fort where the old gentleman was stripped, murdered, scalped and horribly mutilated. Mrs. Parker was stripped, speared and left for dead, but by feigning death escaped, as will be seen further on. Mrs. Kellogg was spared as a captive.

The result summed up, was as follows:

Killed—Elder John Parker, aged seventy-nine; Silas M. and Benjamin F. Parker; Samuel M. and his son Robert Frost.

Wounded dangerously—Mrs. John Parker; Old Granny Parker and Mrs. —— Duty.

Captured—Mrs. Rachel Plummer, (daughter of James W. Parker), and her son James Pratt Plummer, two years of age; Mrs. Elizabeth Kellogg; Cynthia Ann Parker, nine years old, and her little brother John Parker, aged six years, children of Silas M. Parker. The remainder of the inmates making their escape, as we shall narrate.

When the attack on the fort first commenced, Mrs. Sarah Nixon made her escape and hastened to the field to advise her father, husband and Plummer. On her arrival, Plummer hurried on horseback to inform the Faulkenberrys, Limn, Bates and Anglin. Parker and Nixon started to the fort, but the former met his family on the way, and carried them some five miles down the Navasota, secreting them in the bottom. Nixon, though unarmed, continued on towards the fort, and met Mrs. Lucy, wife of the dead Silas Parker, with her four children, just as they were intercepted by a small party of mounted and foot Indians. They compelled the mother to lift behind two mounted warriors her daughter Cynthia Ann, and her little son John. The foot Indians now took Mrs. Parker, her two youngest children and Nixon back to the fort.

Just as the Indians were about to kill Nixon, David Faulkenberry appeared with his rifle, and caused them to fall back. Nixon, after his narrow escape from death, seemed very much excited, and immediately left in search of his wife, soon falling in with Dwight, with his own and Frost's family. Dwight and party soon overtook J. W. Parker and went with him to the hiding place in the bottom.

Faulkenberry, thus left with Mrs. Parker and her two children, bade her to follow him. With the infant in her arms and leading the other child she obeyed. Seeing them leave the fort, the Indians made several feints, but were held in check by the brave man's rifle. Several mounted warriors, armed with bows and arrows strung and drawn, and with terrific yells would charge them, but as Faulkenberry would present his gun they would halt, throw up their shields, right about, wheel and retire to a safe distance. This continued for some distance, until they had passed through a prairie of some forty or fifty acres.

Just as they were entering the woods, the Indians made a desperate charge, when one warrior, more daring than the others, dashed up so near that Mrs. Parker's faithful dog seized his horse by the nose, whereupon both horse and rider somersaulted, alighting on their backs in a ravine. Just at this moment Silas Bates, Abram Anglin and Evan Faulkenberry, armed, and Plummer unarmed, came up, causing the Indians to retire, after which the party made their way unmolested.

As they were passing through the field where the three men had been at work in the morning, Plummer, as if aroused from a dream, demanded to know what had become of his wife and child. Armed only with a butcher knife, he left the party, in search of his loved ones, and was seen no more for six days.

The Faulkenberrys, Lunn, with Mrs. Parker and children, secreted themselves in a small creek bottom, some distance from the first party, each unconscious of the other's whereabouts.

At twilight Abraham Anglin and Evan Faulkenberry started back to the fort to succour the wounded and those who might have escaped. On their way, and just as they were passing Faulkenberry's cabin, Anglin saw his first and only ghost. He says:

It was dressed in white with long, white hair streaming down its back. I admit that I was worse scared at this moment than when the Indians were yelling and charging us. Seeing me hesitate, my ghost now beckoned me to come on. Approaching the object it proved to be old Granny Parker, whom the Indians had wounded and stripped, with the exception of her underwear. She had made her way to the house from the fort by crawling the entire distance. I took some bed clothing, and carrying her some distance from the house, made her a bed, covered her up and left her until we should return from the fort.

On arriving at the fort we could not see a single individual alive or hear a human sound. But the dogs were barking, the cattle lowing, the horses neighing and the hogs squealing, making a hideous and strange medley of sounds. Mrs. Parker had told me where she had left some silver, $106.50. This I found under a hickory bush by moonlight. Finding no one at the fort we returned to where I had hid Granny Parker. On taking her up behind me, we made our way back to our hiding place in the bottom, where we found Nixon, whom we had not seen since his cowardly flight at the time he was rescued by Faulkenberry from the Indians. (In the book published by James W. Parker, he states that Nixon liberated Mrs. Parker from the Indians and rescued old Granny Parker. Mr. Anglin, in his account contradicts, or rather corrects this statement. He says: "I positively assert that this is a mistake and I am willing to be qualified to the statement I here make and can prove the same by Silas H. Bates, now living near Graesbeck.")

On the next morning, Bates, Anglin and E. Faulkenberry went back to the fort to get provisions and horses and to look after the dead. On reaching the fort they found five or six horses, a few saddles and some meal, bacon and honey. Fearing an attack from the red devils who might still be lurking around, they left without burying the dead. Returning to their comrades in the bottom, they all concealed themselves until the next night, when they started through the woods to Fort Houston, which place they reached without material suffering.

Fort Houston, an asylum on this as on many other occasions, stood on what has been for many years the farm of a wise statesman, a chivalrous soldier and a true patriot—John H. Reagan—two miles west of Palestine.

After wandering around and travelling for six days and nights, during which time they suffered much from hunger and thirst, with their clothing torn into shreds, their bodies lacerated with briars and thorns, the women and children with unshod and bleeding feet, the party of James W. Parker ———— men, and ———— women and children reached Tinnin's, at the old San Antonio and Nacogdoches crossing of the Navasota. (We are unable to ascertain the exact number. Different accounts variously estimate the number from 10 to 20). Being informed of their approach, Messrs. Carter and Courtney, with five horses, met them some miles away, and thus enabled the women and children to ride. The few people around, though but returned to their deserted homes after the victory of San Jacinto, shared all they had of food and clothing with them.

Plummer, after six days of wanderings alone in the wilderness, arrived at the fort the same day.

In due time the members of the party located temporarily as best suited the respective families, most of them returning to Fort Parker soon afterwards.

A burial party of twelve men from Fort Houston went up and buried the dead. Their remains now repose near the site of old Fort Parker. Peace to their memories. Unadorned are their graves; not even a slab of marble or a memento of any kind has been erected to tell the traveller where rests the remains of this brave little band of pioneer heroes who wrestled with the savage for the mastery of this proud domain.

After the massacre the savages retired with their booty to their own wild haunts amid the hills and valleys of the beautiful Canadian and Pease Rivers.

CHAPTER 2

THE CAPTIVES CYNTHIA ANN AND JOHN PARKER

Of the captives we will briefly trace their subsequent checkered career.

After leaving the fort the two tribes, the Comanches and Kiowas, remained and travelled together until midnight. They then halted on an open prairie, staked out their horses, placed their pickets, and pitched their camp. Bringing all their prisoners together for the first time, they tied their hands behind them with rawhide thongs so tightly as to cut the flesh, tied their feet close together, and threw them upon their faces. Then the braves, gathering around with their yet bloody, dripping scalps, commenced their usual war dance. They danced, screamed, yelled, stamping upon their prisoners, beating them with bows until their own blood came near strangling them. The remainder of the night these frail women suffered and had to listen to the cries and groans of their tender little children.

Mrs. Elizabeth Kellogg, soon fell into the hands of the Keechis, from whom, six months after her capture, she was purchased by a party of Delawares, who carried her into Nacogdoches and delivered her to Gen. Houston, who paid them $150.00, the amount they had paid and all they asked.

On the way thence to Fort Houston, escorted by James W. Parker and others, a hostile Indian was slightly wounded and temporarily disabled by a Mr. Smith. Mrs. Kellogg instantly recognised him as the savage who had scalped the patriarch, Elder John Parker, whereupon, without judge, jury or court-martial, or even dallying with "Judge Lynch," he was involuntarily hastened to the "happy hunting grounds" of his fathers.

Mrs. Rachel Plummer remained a captive about eighteen months. Soon after her capture she was delivered of a child. The crying of her infant annoyed her captors, and the mother was forced to yield up her offspring to the merciless fiends,—in whose veins the milk of human sympathy had never flowed, to be murdered before her eyes with all the demoniacal demonstrations of brutality intact in those savages. The innocent little babe but six weeks old was torn madly from the mother's bosom by six giant Indians, one of them clutched the little prattling innocent by the throat, and like a hungry beast with defenceless prey, he held it out in his iron grasp until all evidence of life seemed extinct. Mrs. Plummer's feeble efforts to save her child were utterly fruitless. They tossed it high in the air and repeatedly let it fall on rocks and frozen earth.

Supposing the child dead they returned it to its mother, but discovering traces of lingering life, they again, by force, tore it angrily from her, tied plaited ropes around its neck and threw its unprotected body into hedges of prickly pear. They would repeatedly pull it through these lacerating rushes with demonic yells. Finally, they tied the rope attached to its neck to the pommel of a saddle and rode triumphantly around a circuit until it was not only dead but literally torn to shreds. All that remained of that once beautiful babe was then tossed into the lap of its poor, distracted mother. With an old knife the weeping mother was allowed to dig a grave and bury her babe.

After this she was given as a servant to a very cruel old squaw, who treated her in a most brutal manner. Her son had been carried off by another party to the far West and she supposed her husband and father had been killed at the massacre. Her infant was dead, and death to her would have been a sweet relief. Life was a burden, and driven almost to desperation, she resolved no longer to submit to the intolerant old squaw. One day when the two were some distance from, although still in sight of the camp, her mistress attempted to beat her with a club. Determined not to submit to this, she wrenched the club from the hands of the squaw and knocked her down.

The Indians, who had witnessed the whole proceedings from their camp, now came running up, shouting at the top of their voices. She fully expected to be killed, but they patted her on the shoulder, crying, "*Bueno! bueno!!*' (Good! good!!) or well done! She now fared much better and soon became a great favourite and was known as the "Fighting Squaw." She was eventually ransomed through the agency of some Mexican Santa Fe traders, by a noble-hearted, American merchant of that place, Mr. William Donahue. She was purchased in the Rocky Mountains so far north of Santa Fe that seventeen days were consumed in reaching that place. She was at once made a member of her benefactor's family, where she received the kindest of care and attention. Ere long she accompanied Mr. and Mrs. Donahue on a visit to Independence, Missouri, where she had the pleasure of meeting and embracing her brother-in-law, L. D. Nixon, and by him was escorted back to her people in Texas.

★★★★★★

During her stay with the Indians, Mrs. Plummer had many thrilling adventures, which she often related after her reclamation. In narrating her reminiscences, (the previous story in this book), she said that in one of her rambles, after she had been with the Indians some time, she discovered a cave in the mountains, and in company with the old squaw that guarded her, she explored it and found a large diamond, but her mistress immediately demanded it, and she was forced to give it up. She said also here in these mountains she saw a bush which had thorns on it resembling fish-hooks which the Indians used to catch fish with, and she herself has often caught trout with them in the little mountain streams.

★★★★★★

On the 19th of February, 1838, she reached her father's house, exactly twenty-one months from her capture. She had never seen her little son, James Pratt, since soon after their capture, and knew nothing of his fate. She wrote, or dictated a thrilling and graphic history of her capture and the horrors of her captivity of the tortures and hardships she endured, and all the incidents of her life with her captors, with observations among the savages. In this book she tells the last she saw of Cynthia Ann and John Parker. She died on the 19th of February, 1839, just one year after reaching home. As a remarkable coincidence it may be stated that she was born on the 19th, married on the 19th, captured on the 19th, released on the 19th, reached Independence on the 19th, arrived at home on the 19th, and died on the 19th of the month.

Her son, James Pratt Plummer, after six long and weary years of captivity and suffering, during which time he had lived among many different tribes and travelled several thousand miles, was ransomed and taken to Fort Gibson late in 1842, and reached home in February, 1843, in charge of his grandfather. He became a respected citizen of Anderson county. Both he and his father are now dead.

This still left in captivity Cynthia and John Parker, who, as subsequently learned, were held by separate bands. The brother and sister thus separated, gradually forgot the language, manners and customs of their own people, and became thorough Comanches as the long years stole slowly away. How long the camera of their young brains retained impressions of the old home within the fort, and the loved faces of their pale-faced kindred, no one knows; though it would appear that the fearful massacre should have stamped an impress indelible while life continued. But the young mind, as the twig, is inclined by present circumstances, and often forced in a way wholly foreign to its native and original bent.

John grew up with the little semi-nude Comanche boys of his own age, and played at "hunter" and "warrior" with pop-guns made of the elder stem, or bows and arrows, and often flushed the *chaparral* for hare and grouse, or entrapped the finny denizens of the mountain brooks with the many peculiar and ingenious devices of the wild man for securing for his repast the toothsome trout which abounds so plentifully in that elevated and delightful region, so long inhabited by the lordly Comanches.

When just arrived at manhood, John accompanied a raiding party down the Rio Grande and into Mexico. Among the captives taken was a young Mexican girl of great beauty, to whom the young warrior felt his heart go out. The affection was reciprocated on the part of the fair Dona Juanita, and the two were soon engaged to be married, so soon as they should arrive at the Comanche village. Each day as the cavalcade moved leisurely, but steadily along, the lovers could be seen riding together, and discussing the anticipated pleasures of connubial life, when suddenly John was prostrated by a violent attack of smallpox. The cavalcade could not tarry, and so it was decided that the poor fellow should be left all alone in the vast *Llano Esticado* to die or recover as fate decreed. But the little Aztec beauty refused to leave her lover, insisting on her captors allowing her to remain and take care of him. To this the Indians reluctantly consented.

With Juanita to nurse and cheer him up, John lingered, lived, and ultimately recovered, when, with as little ceremony, perhaps, as consummated the nuptials of the first pair in Eden, they assumed the matrimonial relation; and Dona Juanita's predilections for the customs and comforts of civilization were sufficiently strong to induce her lord to abandon the wild and nomadic life of a savage for the comforts to be found in a straw-thatched *Jackal*.

"They settled," says Mr. Thrall, the historian of Texas, "on a stock ranch in the far West."

When the civil war broke out John Parker joined a Mexican company in the Confederate service, and was noted for his gallantry and daring. He, however, refused to leave the soil of Texas, and would, under no circumstances, cross the Sabine into Louisiana. He was still living on his ranch across the Rio Grande a few years ago, (as at 1886), but up to that time had never visited any of his relatives in Texas.

Of Cynthia Ann Parker (we will anticipate the thread of the narrative). Four long years have elapsed since she was cruelly torn from a mother's embrace and carried into captivity. During this time no tidings have been received of her. Many efforts have been made to ascertain her whereabouts, or fate, but without success; when in 1840, Col. Len. Williams, an old and honoured Texian, Mr. —— Stoat, a trader, and a Delaware Indian guide, named "Jack Harry," packed mules with goods and engaged in an expedition of private traffic with the Indians.

On the Canadian River they fell in with Pa-ha-u-ka's band of Comanches, with whom they were peaceably conversant. And with this tribe was Cynthia Ann Parker, who from the day of her capture had never seen a white person. She was then about fourteen years of age and had been with the Indians nearly five years.

Col. Williams found the Indian into whose family she had been adopted, and proposed to redeem her, but the Comanche told him all the goods he had would not ransom her, and at the same time "the fierceness of his countenance," says Col. Williams, "warned me of the danger of further mention of the subject." But old Pa-ha-u-ka prevailed upon him to let them see her. She came and sat down by the root of a tree, and while their presence was doubtless a happy event to the poor stricken captive, who in her doleful captivity had endured everything but death, she refused to speak a word.

As she sat there, musing, perhaps, of distant relatives and friends, and the bereavements at the beginning and progress of her distress, they employed every persuasive art to evoke some expression. They told her of her playmates and relatives, and asked what message she would send them, but she had doubtless been commanded to silence, and with no hope or prospect of return was afraid to appear sad or dejected, and by a stoical effort in order to prevent future bad treatment, put the best face possible on the matter. But the anxiety of her mind was betrayed by the perceptible quiver of her lips, showing that she was not insensible to the common feelings of humanity.

As the years rolled by Cynthia Ann speedily developed the charms of womanhood, as with the dusky maidens of her companionship she performed the menial offices of drudgery to which savage custom consigns women,—or practiced those little arts of coquetry maternal to the female heart, whether she be a *belle* of Madison Square, attired in the most elaborate toilet from the *élite* bazaars of Paris, or the half naked savage with matted locks and claw-like nails.

Doubtless the heart of more than one warrior was pierced by the Ulyssean darts from her laughing eyes, or charmed by the silvery ripple of her joyous laughter, and laid at her feet the game taken after a long and arduous chase among the Antelope Hills.

Among the number whom her budding charms brought to her shrine was Peta Nocona. a Comanche war chief, in prowess and renown the peer of the famous and redoubtable "Big Foot," who fell in a desperately contested hand-to-hand encounter with the veteran ranger and Indian fighter, Captain S. P. Ross, now living at Waco, and whose wonderful exploits and deeds of daring furnished themes for song and story at the war dance, the council, and the camp-fire.

Cynthia Ann,—stranger now to every word of her mother tongue save her own name became the bride of Pata Nocona, performing for her imperious lord all the slavish offices which savageism and Indian custom assigns as the duty of a wife. She bore him children, and we are assured *loved* him with a species of fierce passion, and wifely devotion; "for some fifteen years after her capture," says Victor M. Rose, "a party of white hunters, including some friends of her family, visited the Comanche encampment on the upper Canadian, and recognizing Cynthia Ann—probably through the medium of her name alone, sounded her in a secret manner as to the disagreeableness of a return to her people and the haunts of civilization.

She shook her head in a sorrowful negative, and pointed to her little, naked barbarians sporting at her feet, and to the great greasy, lazy buck sleeping in the shade near at hand, the locks of a score of scalps dangling at his belt, and whose first utterance upon arousing would be a stern command to his meek, pale-faced wife. Though in truth, exposure to sun and air had browned the complexion of Cynthia Ann almost as intensely as were those of the native daughters of the plains and forest.

She retained but the vaguest remembrance of her people—as dim and flitting as the phantoms of a dream; she was accustomed now to the wild life she led, and found in its repulsive features charms which "upper tendom" would have proven totally deficient in:—"I am happily wedded," she said to these visitors. "I love my husband, who is good and kind, and my little ones, who, too, are his, and I cannot forsake them!"

What were the incidents in the savage life of these children which in after times became the land marks in the train of memory, and which with civilized creatures serves as incentives to reminiscence?

Mr. Rose says:—

Doubtless, Cynthia Ann arrayed herself in the calico borne from the sacking of Linville, and fled with the discomfited Comanches up the Gaudaloupe and Colorado, at the ruthless march of John H. Moore, Ben McCulloch and their hardy rangers. They must have been present at the battle of Antelope Hills, on the Canadian, when Col. John S. Ford, "Old Rip" and Captain S. P. Ross encountered the whole force of the Comanches, in 1858; perhaps John Parker was an actor in that celebrated battle; and again at the Wichita."

Theirs must have been a hard and unsatisfactory life the Comanches are veritable Ishmaelites, their hands being raised against all men, and every man's hand against them. Literally, *eternal vigilance was the price of liberty* with them, and of life itself. Every night the dreaded surprise was sought to be guarded against; and every copse was scanned for the anticipated ambuscade while upon the march. Did they flout the blood-drabbled scalps of helpless whites in fiendish glee, and assist at the cruel torture of the unfortunate prisoners that fell into their hands? Alas! forgetful of their race and tongue, they were thorough savages, and acted in all particulars just as their Indian comrades did. Memory was stored but with the hard ships and the cruelties of the life about them; arid the stolid indifference of mere animal existence furnishes no finely wrought springs for the rebound of reminiscence.

★ ★ ★ ★ ★ ★ ★ ★

The year 1846, one decade from the fall of Parker's Fort, witnessed the end of the Texian Republic, in whose councils Isaac Parker served as a senator, and the blending of the *Lone Star* with the galaxy of the great constellation of the American Union—during which time many efforts were made to ascertain definitely the whereabouts of the captives, as an indispensable requisite to their reclamation sometimes by solitary scouts and spies, sometimes through the medium of negotiation and sometimes by waging direct war against their captors,—but all to no avail.

★ ★ ★ ★ ★ ★ ★ ★

Another decade passes away, and the year 1856 arrives. The hardy pioneers have pushed the frontier of civilization far to the north and west, driving the Indian and the buffalo before them. The scene of Parker's Fort is now in the heart of a dense population; farms, towns, churches, and school houses lie along the path by which the Indians marched from their camp at the "water-hole" in that bloody May of 1836, Isaac Parker is now a Representative in the Legislature of the State of Texas. It is now twenty years since the battle of San Jacinto twenty years since John and Cynthia Ann were borne into a captivity worse than death the last gun of the Mexican war rung out its last report over the conquered capital of Mexico ten long years ago; but John and Cynthia Ann Parker have sent no tokens to their so long anxious friends that they even live: Alas! time even blunts the edge of anxiety, and sets bounds alike to the anguish of man, as well as to his hopes.

The punishment of Prometheas is not of this world!

CHAPTER 3

THE BATTLE OF ANTELOPE HILLS

Brave Colonel Ford the commander and ranger bold,
On the South Canadian did the Comanches behold,
On the 12th of May, at rising of sun,
The armies did meet and the battle begun.

The Battle of the South Canadian or "Antelope Hills," fought in 1858, was probably one of the most splendid scenic exhibitions of Indian warfare ever enacted upon Texas soil. This was the immemorial home of the Comanches here they sought refuge from their marauding expeditions into Texas and Mexico; and here, in their veritable "city of refuge," should the adventurous and daring rangers seek them, it was certain that they would be encountered in full force—Pohebits Quasho—"Iron Jacket," so called from the fact that he wore a coat of scale mail, a curious piece of ancient armour, which doubtless had been stripped from the body of some unfortunate Spanish Knight slain, perhaps, a century before—some *chevalier* who followed Coronado, De Leon, La Salle—was the war chief. He was a "Big Medicine" man, or Prophet, and claimed to be invulnerable to balls and arrows aimed at his person, as by a necromantic puff of his breath the missives were diverted from their course, or charmed, and made to fall harmless at his feet.

Peta Nocono, the young and daring husband of Cynthia Ann Parker, was second in command.

About the 1st of May, in the year above named, Col. John S. Ford, ("Old Rip,") at the head of 100 Texian Rangers—comprising such leaders as Capts. S. P. Ross, (the father of Gen. L. S. Ross); W. A. Pitts, Preston, Tankersley, and a contingent of 111 Toncahua Indians, the latter commanded by their celebrated chief, Placido—so long the faithful and implicitly trusted friend of the whites—marched on a campaign against the marauding Comanches, determined to follow them up to their stronghold amid the hills of the Canadian river, and if possible surprise them and inflict a severe and lasting chastisement.

After a toilsome march of several days the Toncahua scouts reported that they were in the immediate vicinity of the Comanche encampment. The Comanches, though proverbial for their sleepless vigilance, were unsuspicious of danger and so unsuspected was the approach of the rangers, that on the day preceding the battle, Col. Ford and Capt. Ross stood in the old road from Fort Smith to Santa Fe, just north of the Rio Negro or "False Wichita," and watched through their glasses the Comanches running buffalo in the valleys still more to the north. That night the Toncahua spies completed the hazardous mission of locating definitely the position of the enemy's encampment. The next morning (May 12) the rangers and "reserve" or friendly Indians, marched before sunrise to the attack.

Placido claimed for his "red warriors" the privilege of wreaking vengeance upon their hereditary enemies. His request was granted, □and the Toncahuas effected a complete surprise. The struggle was short, sharp and sanguinary. The women and children were made prisoners, but not a Comanche brave surrendered. Their savage pride preferred death to the restraints and humiliations of captivity. Not a single warrior escaped to bear the sorrowful tidings of this destructive engagement to their people.

A short time after the sun had lighted the tops of the hills, the rangers came in full view of the hostile camp, pitched in one of the picturesque valleys of the Canadian, and on the opposite side of the stream, in the immediate vicinity of the famous "Antelope Hills."

The panorama thus presented to the view of the rangers was beautiful in the extreme, and their pent-up enthusiasm found vent in a shout of exultation, which was speedily suppressed by Col. Ford. Just at this moment a solitary Comanche was descried riding southward, evidently heading for the village which Placido had so recently destroyed. He was wholly unconcious of the proximity of an enemy. Instant pursuit was now made; he turned, and fled at full speed toward the main camp across the Canadian, closely followed by the rangers.

He dashed across the stream, and thus revealed to his pursuers the locality of a safe ford across the miry and almost impassable river. He rushed into the village beyond, sounding the notes of alarm; and soon the Comanche warriors presented a bold front of battle-line between their women and children and the advancing rangers. After a few minutes occupied in forming line of battle, both sides were arrayed in full force and effect. The friendly Indians were placed on the right, and thrown a little forward. Col. Ford's object was to deceive the Comanches as to the character of the attacking force, and as to the quality of arms they possessed.

Pohebits Quasho, arrayed in all the trappings of his "war toggery"□coat of mail, shield, bow and lance, completed by a head-dress decorated with feathers and long red flannel streamers; and besmeared in "war paint,"—gaily dashed about on his "war-horse" mid way of the opposing lines, delivering taunts and challenges to the whites. As the old chief dashed to and fro a number of rifles were discharged at him in point blank range without any effect whatever; which seeming immunity to death encouraged his warriors greatly; and induced even some of the more superstitious among the rangers to enquire within themselves if it were possible that "Old Iron Jacket" really bore a charmed life?

Followed by a few of his braves, he now bore down upon the rangers, described a few "charmed circles," gave a few necromantic puffs with his breath and let fly several arrows at Col. Ford, Capt. Ross and chief Placido; receiving their fire without harm. But as he approached the line of the Toncahuas, a rifle directed by the steady nerve and unerring eye of one of their number, Jim Pockmark, brought the "Big Medicine" to the dust. The shot was a mortal one. The fallen chieftain was instantly surrounded by his braves, but the spirit of the conjuring brave had taken its flight to the "happy hunting grounds."

These incidents occupied but a brief space of time, when the order to charge was given; and then ensued one of the grandest assaults ever made against the Comanches. The enthusiastic shouts of the rangers and the triumphant yell of their red allies greeted the welcome order. It was responded to by the defiant "war-hoop" of the Comanches, and in those virgin hills, remote from civilization, the saturnalia of battle was inaugurated. The shouts of enraged combatants, the wail of women, the piteous cries of terrified children, the howling of frightened dogs, the deadly reports of rifle and revolver, constituted a discordant confusion of sounds, blent together in an unearthly mass of infernal noise.

The conflict was sharp and quick—a charge; a momentary exchange of rifle and arrow shots, and the heart-rending wail of discomfiture and dismay, and the beaten Comanches abandoned their lodges and camp to the victors, and began a disorderly retreat. But sufficient method was observed to take advantage of each grove of timber, each hill and ravine, to make a stand against their pursuers; and thus enable the women and children to make their escape. The noise of battle now diverged from a common centre like the spokes of a wheel, and continued to greet the ear for several hours, gradually growing fainter as the pursuit disappeared in the distance.

But another division, under the vigilant Peta Nocona, was soon marching through the hills north of the Canadian, to the rescue. Though ten miles distant, his quick ear had caught the first sounds of the battle; and soon he was riding, with Cynthia Ann by his side, at the head of (500) five hundred warriors.

About 1 o'clock of the afternoon the last of the rangers returned from the pursuit of Pohebits Quasho's discomfited braves, just in time to anticipate this threatened attack.

As Capt. Ross (who was one of the last to return) rode up, he enquired "What hour of the morning is it, Colonel?"

"Morning!" exclaimed Col. Ford, "it is one o'clock of the afternoon;" so unconscious is one of the flight of time during an engagement, that the work of hours seems comprised within the space of a few moments.

"Hello! what are you in line of battle for?" asked Ross. "Look at the hills there, and you will see," calmly replied Col. Ford, pointing to the hills some half a mile distant, behind which the forces of Peta Nocona were visible; an imposing line of 500 warriors drawn up in battle array.

Col. Ford had with 221 men fought and routed over 400 Comanches, and now he was confronted by a stronger force, fresh from their village still higher up on the Canadian. They had come to drive the "pale faces" and their hated copper-coloured allies from the captured camp, to retake prisoners, to retake over four hundred head of horses and an immense quantity of plunder. They did not fancy the defiant state of preparations awaiting them in the valley, however, and were waiting to avail themselves of some incautious movement on the part of the rangers, when the wily Peta Nocona with his forces would spring like a lion from his lair, and with one combined and desperate effort swoop down and annihilate the enemy. But his antagonist was a soldier of too much sagacity to allow any advantage to a vigilant foe.

The two forces remained thus contemplating each other for over an hour; during which time a series of operations ensued between single combatants illustrative of the Indian mode of warfare, and the marked difference between the nomadic Comanche and his semi-civilized congeners, the Tonchua. The Tonchuas took advantage of ravines, trees and other natural shelter. Their arms were rifles and "six-shooters." The Comanches came to the attack with shield and bow and lance, mounted on gaily caparisoned and prancing steeds, and flaunting feathers and all the "gorgeous" display incident to savage "finery" and pomp. They are probably the most expert equestrians in the world. A Comanche warrior would gaily canter to a point half way between the opposing lines, yell a defiant "war hoop," and shake his shield. This was a challenge to single combat.

Several of the friendly Indians who accepted such challenges were placed *hors de combat* by their more expert adversaries, and in consequence Col. Ford ordered them to decline the savage banters; much to the dissatisfaction of Placido, who had conducted himself throughout the series of engagements with the bearing of a savage hero.

Says Col. Ford: "In these combats the mind of the spectator was vividly carried back to the days of chivalry; the jousts and tournaments of knights and to the concomitants of those scenic exhibitions of gallantry. The feats of horsemanship were splendid, the lances and shields were used with great dexterity, and the whole performance was a novel show to civilized man."

Col. Ford now ordered Placido, with a part of his warriors, to advance in the direction of the enemy, and if possible draw them in the valley, so as to afford the rangers an opportunity to charge them. This had the desired effect, and the rangers were ready to deliver a charge, when it was discovered that the friendly Indians had removed the white badges from their heads because they served as targets for the Comanches, consequently the rangers were unable to distinguish friend from foe. This necessitated the entire withdrawal of the Indians. The Comanches witnessed these preparations and now commenced to recoil. The rangers advanced; the trot, the gallop, the headlong charge, followed in rapid succession. Lieut. Nelson made a skilful movement and struck the enemy's left flank.

The Comanche line was broken. A running fight for three or four miles ensued. The enemy was driven back wherever he made a stand. The most determined resistance was made in a timbered ravine. Here one of Placido's warriors was killed, and one of the rangers, young George W. Pascal wounded. The Comanches left some dead upon the spot and had several more wounded. After routing them at this point the rangers continued to pursue them some distance, intent upon taking the women and children prisoners but Peta Nocona, by the exercise of those commanding qualities which had often before signalized his conduct on the field, succeeded in covering their retreat, and thus allowing them to escape. It was now about 4 p.m., both horses and men were almost entirely exhausted, and Col. Ford ordered a halt and returned to the village.

Brave old Placido and his warriors fought like so many demons. It was difficult to restrain them, so anxious were they to wreak vengeance on the Comanches.

In all of these engagements seventy-five Comanches "bit the dust."

The loss of the rangers was small,—two killed and five or six wounded.

The trophies of Pohebits Quasho, including his lance, bow, shield, head-dress and the celebrated coat of scale mail, was deposited by Col. Ford in the State archives at Austin, where, doubtless, they may yet be seen,—as curious relics of by-gone days.

The lamented old chief, Placido, fell a victim to the revengeful Comanches during the latter part of the great civil war, between the North and South; being assassinated by a party of his enemies on the reservation, near Fort Sill.

The venerable John Henry Brown, some years since, paid a merited tribute to his memory through the columns of the Dallas *Herald*.

Of Placido it has been said that he was the "soul of honour," and "never betrayed a trust." That he was brave to the utmost, we have only to refer to his numerous exploits during his long and gratuitous service on our frontiers. He was implicitly trusted by Burleson and other partisan leaders; and rendered in valuable services in behalf of the early Texian pioneers; in recognition of which he never received any reward of a material nature, beyond a few paltry pounds of gunpowder and salt. Imperial Texas should rear a monument commemorative of his memory. He was the more than Tammany of Texas! But I am digressing from the narrative proper.

"Doubtless," says Rose, "Cynthia Ann rode from this ill-starred field with her infant daughter pressed to her bosom, and her sons□ two youths of about ten and twelve years of age, at her side,—as fearful of capture at the hands of the hated whites, as years ago immediately after the massacre of Parker's Fort—she had been anxious for the same."

CHAPTER 4
GENL. L. S. ROSS.—BATTLE OF THE WICHITA

It is not our purpose in this connection, to assume the role of biographer to so distinguished a personage as is the chevalier Bayard of Texas—General Lawrence Sullivan Ross. That task should be left to an abler pen; and besides, it would be impossible to do anything like justice to the romantic, adventurous, and altogether splendid and brilliant career of the brave and daring young ranger who rescued Cynthia Ann Parker from captivity, at least in the circumscribed limits of a brief biographical sketch, such as we shall be compelled to confine ourselves to; yet, some brief mention of his services and exploits as a ranger captain, by way of an introduction to the reader beyond the limits of Texas, where his name and fame are as household words, is deemed necessary, hence we beg leave here to give a brief sketch of his life.

The author of *Ross' Texas Brigade* says:—

Texas, though her annals be brief, counts upon her 'roll of honour' the names of many heroes, living and dead. Their splendid services are the inestimable legacies of the past and present, to the future. Of the latter, it is the high prerogative of the State to embalm their names and memories as perpetual examples to excite the generous emulation of the Texian youth to the latest posterity. Of the former it is our pleasant province to accord them those honours which their services, in so eminent a degree, entitle them to receive. Few lands, since the days of the

'Scottish Chiefs,' have furnished material upon which to predicate a Douglas, a Wallace, or a Ravenswood; and the adventures of chivalric enterprise, arrant quest of danger, and the personal combat, were relegated, together with the knight's armorial trappings, to the rusty archives of 'Tower' and 'Pantheon,' until the Comanche Bedouins of the Texian plains tendered in bold defiance the savage gauntlet to the pioneer knights of progress and civilization. And though her heraldic roll glows with the names of a Houston, a Rusk, Lamar, McCulloch, Hayes, Chevellie, which illumine the pages of her history with an effulgence of glory, Texas never nurtured on her maternal bosom a son of more filial devotion, of more loyal patriotism, or indomitable will to do and dare, than L. S. Ross.

Lawrence Sullivan Ross was born in the village of Bentonsport, Ohio, in the year 1838. His father, Captain S. P. Ross, emigrated to Texas in 1839, casting his fortunes with the struggling pioneers who were blazing the pathway of civilization into the wilds of a *terra incognita*, as Texas then was.

Captain S. P. Ross was, for many years, pre-eminent as a leader against the implacable savages, who made frequent incursions into the settlements. The duty of repelling these forays usually devolved upon Captain Ross and his neighbours, and, for many years, his company constituted the only bulwark of safety between the feeble colonist and the scalping knife. The rapacity and treachery of his Comanche and Kiowa foes demanded of Captain Ross sleepless vigilance, acute sagacity, and a will that brooked no obstacle or danger. It was in the performance of this arduous duty that he slew, in single combat, 'Big Foot,' a Comanche chief of great prowess, and who was for many years the scourge of the early Texas frontier. The services of Captain S. P. Ross are still held in grateful remembrance by the descendants of his compatriots, and his memory will never be suffered to pass away while Texians feel a pride in the sterling worth of the pioneers who laid the foundation of Texas' greatness and glory.—*Vide Ross' Texas Brigade.*

The following incident, as illustrative of the character and spirit of the man and times, is given:

On one occasion, Captain Ross, who had been visiting a

neighbour, was returning home, afoot, accompanied by his little son, 'Sul,' as the general was familiarly called. When within half a mile of his house, he was surrounded by fifteen or twenty mounted Comanche warriors, who commenced an immediate attack. The captain, athletic and swift of foot, threw his son on his back, and outran their ponies to the house, escaping unhurt amid a perfect shower of arrows.

Such were among the daily experiences of the child, and with such impressions stamped upon the infantile mind, it was but natural that the enthusiastic spirit of the ardent youth should lead him to such adventures upon the "war-path," similar to those that had signalized his honoured father's prowess upon so many occasions.

Hence, we find "Sul" Ross, during vacation from his studies at Florence Weslean University, Alabama, though a beardless boy, scarcely twenty years of age, in command of a contingent of 135 friendly Indians, co-operating with the United States cavalry under the dashing Major Earl Van Dorn, in a campaign against the Comanches.

★ ★ ★ ★ ★ ★ ★ ★

Notwithstanding the severe chastisement that had been inflicted on the Comanches at "Antelope Hills," they soon renewed their hostilities, committing many depredations and murders during the summer of 1858.

Early in September Major Van Dorn received orders from Gen. Twiggs, to equip four companies, including Ross' "red warriors," and go out on a scouting expedition against the hostile Indians. This he did, penetrating the heart of the Indian country where he proceeded to build a stockade, placing within it all the pack mules, extra horses and supplies, which was left in charge of the infantry.

Ross' faithful Indian scouts soon reported the discovery of a large Comanche village near the Wichita Mountains, about ninety miles away. The four companies, attended by the spies, immediately set out for the village, and after a fatiguing march of thirty-six hours, causing the men to be continuously in the saddle the latter sixteen hours of the ride, arrived in the immediate vicinity of the Indian camp just at daylight on the morning of October 1st.

A reconnoissance showed that the wily Comanches were not apprehensive of an attack, and were sleeping in fancied security. The horses of the tribe, which consisted of a *caballado* of about 500 head, were grazing near the outskirts of the village. Major Van Dorn directed Captain Ross, at the head of his Indians, to "round up" the horses, and drive them from the camp, which was effected speedily, and thus the Comanches were forced to fight on foot—a proceeding extremely harrowing to the proud warriors' feelings.

Victor M. Rose, whose graphic narrative we again quote, says:—

Just as the sun was peeping above the eastern horizon, Van Dorn charged the upper end of the village, while Ross' command, in conjunction with a detachment of United States cavalry, charged the lower. The village was strung out along the banks of a branch for several hundred yards. The morning was very foggy, and after a few moments of firing the smoke and fog became so dense that objects at but a short distance could be distinguished only with great difficulty. The Comanches fought with absolute desperation, and contended for every advantage, as their women and children, and all their possessions, were in peril.

A few moments after the engagement became general, Ross discovered a number of Comanches running down to the branch, about one hundred and fifty yards from the village, and concluded that they were beating a retreat. Immediately, Ross, Lieutenant Van Camp of the United States Army, Alexander, a 'regular' soldier, and one Caddo Indian, of Ross' command, ran to the point with the intention of intercepting them. Arriving, it was discovered that the fugitives were the women and children. In a moment, another posse of women and children came running immediately past the squad of Ross, who, discovering a little white girl among the number, made his Caddo Indian grab her as she was passing. The little pale-face—apparently about twelve years of age—was badly frightened at finding herself a captive to a strange Indian and stranger white men, and was hard to manage at first.

Ross now discovered, through the fog and smoke of the battle, that a band of some twenty-five Comanche warriors had cut his small party off from communication with Van Dorn, and were bearing immediately down upon them. They shot Lieutenant Van Camp through the heart, killing him ere he could fire his double-barrelled shot-gun. Alexander, the United States Cavalryman, was likewise shot down before he could fire his

GENERAL L S ROSS.

gun (a rifle). Ross was armed with a Sharp's rifle, and attempted to fire upon the exultant red devils, but the cap snapped. 'Mohee,' a Comanche warrior, seized Alexander's rifle and shot Ross down.

The indomitable young ranger fell upon the side on which his pistol was borne, and though partially paralyzed by the shot, he turned himself, and was getting his pistol out when 'Mohee' drew his butcher-knife, and started towards his prostrate foe— some fifteen feet away—with the evident design of stabbing and scalping him. He made but a few steps, however, when one of his companions cried out something in the Comanche tongue, which was a signal to the band, and they broke away in confusion.

'Mohee' ran about twenty steps, when a wire-cartridge, containing nine buck-shot, fired from a gun in the hands of Lieutenant James Majors, (afterwards a Confederate General), struck him between the shoulders, and he fell forward on his face, dead. 'Mohee' was an old acquaintance of Ross, as the latter had seen him frequently at his father's post on the frontier, and recognized him as soon as their eyes met. The faithful Caddo held on to the little girl throughout this desperate *mêlée*, and, strange to relate, neither were harmed. The Caddo, doubtless, owed his escape to the fact that the Comanches were fearful of wounding or killing the little girl.

This whole scene transpired in a few moments, and Captain N. G. Evans' company of the Second United States Cavalry, had taken possession of the lower end of the Comanche village, and Major Van Dorn held the upper, and the Comanches were running into the hills and brush; not, however, before an infuriated Comanche shot the gallant Van Dorn with an arrow. Van Dorn fell, and it was supposed that he was mortally wounded. In consequence of their wounds, the two chieftains were compelled to remain on the battle ground five or six days.

After the expiration of this time, Ross' Indians made a 'litter,' after their fashion, borne between two gentle mules, and in it placed their heroic and beloved 'boy captain,' and set out for the settlements at Fort Belknap. When this mode of conveyance would become too painful, by reason of the rough, broken nature of the country, these brave Caddos—whose race and history are but synonyms of courage and fidelity—would vie with each other in bearing the burden upon their own shoulders. At Camp Radziminski, occupied by United States forces, an ambulance was obtained, and the remainder of the journey made with comparative comfort. Major Van Dorn was also conveyed to Radziminski. He speedily recovered of his wound, and soon made another brilliant campaign against the Comanches, as we shall see further on. Ross recovered sufficiently in a few weeks so as to be able to return to college at Florence, Alabama, where he completed his studies, and graduated in 1859.

This was the Battle of the Wichita Mountains, a hotly contested and most desperate hand to hand fight in which the two gallant and dashing young officers, Ross and Van Dorn, were severely wounded. The loss of the whites was five killed and several wounded.

The loss of the Comanches was, eighty or ninety warriors killed, many wounded, and several captured; besides losing all their horses, camp equipage, supplies, etc.

The return of this victorious little army was hailed with enthusiastic rejoicing and congratulation, and the Wichita fight and Van Dorn and Ross were the themes of song and story for many years along the borders and in the halls and banqueting-rooms of the cities, and the martial music of the "Wichita March" resounded through the plains of Texas wherever the Second Cavalry encamped or rode off on scouts in after years.

The little girl captive of whose parentage or history nothing could be ascertained, though strenuous efforts were made was christened "Lizzie Ross," in honour of Miss *Lizzie* Tinsley, daughter of Dr. D. R. Tinsley, of Waco, to whom Ross at that time was engaged; and afterwards married—May, 1861.

Of Lizzie Ross, it can be said that, in her career, is afforded a thorough verification of Lord Byron's saying: *Truth is stranger than fiction!* She was adopted by her brave and generous captor, properly reared and educated, and became a beautiful and accomplished woman. Here were sufficient romance and vicissitude, in the brief career of a little maiden, to have turned the "roundelay's" of "troubadour and *meunesauger.*" A solitary lily, blooming amidst the wildest grasses of the desert plains. A little Indian girl in all save the Caucasian's conscious stamp of superiority. Torn from home, perhaps, amid the heart rending scenes of rapine, torture and death. A stranger to race and lineage—stranger even to the tongue in which a mother's lullaby was breathed. Affiliating with these wild Ishmaelites of the prairie—a Comanche in all things save the intuitive premonition *that she was not of them*! Finally, redeemed from a captivity worse than death by a knight entitled to rank, for all time in the history of Texas, *"primus inter pores"*—*Vide Ross Texas Brigade.*

Lizzie Ross accompanied Gen. Ross' mother on a visit to the State of California, a few years since, and while there, became the wife of a wealthy merchant near Los Angeles, where she now resides.

Such is the romantic story of "Lizzie Ross"—a story that derives additional interest because of the fact of its absolute truth in all respects.

★ ★ ★ ★ ★ ★ ★ ★ ★

The following letter from Gen. L. S. Ross, touching upon the battle of the Wichita Mountains and the recapture of "Lizzie Ross," is here appropriately inserted:

Waco, Texas, July 12. 1884.

Mr. James T. Deshields. Dear Sir:—My father could give you reliable data enough to fill a volume. I send you photograph of Cynthia Ann Parker, with notes relating to her on back of photo. On the 28th of October, 1858, I had a battle with the Comanches at Wichita Mts., and there recaptured a little white girl about eight years old, whose parentage, nor indeed any trace of her kindred, was ever found. I adopted, reared, and educated her, giving her the name of Lizzie Ross; the former name being in honour of the young lady—Lizzie Tinsley—to whom I was then engaged and afterwards married—May, 1861. Lizzie Ross grew to womanhood, and married a wealthy merchant living near Los Angeles, California, where she now resides. See *History of 'Ross' Brigade* by Victor M. Rose, and published by *Courier-Journal*, for a full and graphic description of the battle and other notable incidents. I could give you many interesting as well as thrilling adventures of self and father's family with the Indians in the early settlement of the country.

He can give you more information than any living Texian, touching the Indian character, having been their agent and warm and trusted friend, in whom they had confidence.

My early life was one of constant danger from their forays, and I was twice in their hands and at their mercy, as well as the other members of my father's family.

But I am just now too busy with my farm matters to give you such data as would subserve your purpose.

Yours truly,   L. S. Ross.

CHAPTER 5
BATTLE OF PEASE RIVER—CYNTHIA ANN PARKER

For some time after Ross' victory at the Wichita Mountains the Comanches were less hostile, seldom penetrating far down into the settlements. But in 1859-'60 the condition of the frontier was again truly deplorable. The people were obliged to stand in a continued posture of defence, and were in continual alarm and hazard of their lives, never daring to stir abroad unarmed, for small bodies of savages, quick-sighted and accustomed to perpetual watchfulness, hovered on the outskirts, and springing from behind bush or rock, surprised his enemy before he was aware of danger, and sent tidings of his presence in the fatal blow, and after execution of the bloody work, by superior knowledge of the country and rapid movements, safely retired to their inaccessible deserts.

In the Autumn of 1860 the indomitable and fearless Peta Nocona led a raiding party of Comanches through Parker county, so named in honour of the family of his wife, Cynthia Ann, committing great depredations as they passed through. The venerable Isaac Parker was at the time a resident of the town of Weatherford, the county seat; and little did he imagine that the chief of the ruthless savages who spread desolation and death on every side as far as their arms could reach , was the husband of his long lost niece and that the comingled blood of the murdered Parkers and the atrocious Comanche now coursed in the veins of a second generation—bound equally by the ties of consanguinity to murderer and murdered; that the son of Peta No-cona and Cynthia Ann Parker would become the chief of the proud Comanches, whose boast it is that their constitutional settlement of government is the purest democracy ever originated and administered among men. It certainly conserved the object of its institution—the protection and happiness of the people—for a longer period, and much more satisfactorily than has that of any other Indian tribe.

The Comanches claimed a superiority over the other Texian tribes and they unquestionably were more intelligent and courageous. The "Reservation Policy,"—necessary though it be—brings them all to an object level,—the plane of lazy beggars and thieves. The Comanche is the most qualified by nature for receiving education and for adapting himself to the requirements of civilization, of all the southern tribes, not excepting even the Cherokees, with their churches, school-houses and farms. The Comanches after waging an unceasing war for nearly fifty years against the United States, Texas and Mexico, still number 16,000 souls; a far better showing than any other tribe can make, though not one but has enjoyed privileges to which the Comanche was a stranger. It is a shame to the civilization of the age that a people so susceptible of a high degree of development should be allowed to grovel in the depths of heathenism and savagery. But we are digressing.

The loud and clamorous cries of the settlers along the frontier for protection, induced the government to organise and send out a regiment under Col. M. T. Johnson to take the field for public defence. But these efforts proved of small service. The expedition, though at great expense to the state, failed to find an Indian until returning, the command was followed by the wily Comanches, their horses "stampeded" at night and most of the men compelled to reach the settlements on foot, under great suffering and exposure.

Captain "Sul" Ross, who had just graduated from Florence Wesleyan University, of Alabama, and returned to Texas, was commissioned a captain of rangers, by Governor Sam Houston, and directed to organize a company of sixty men, with orders to repair to Fort Belknap, receive from Col. Johnson all government property, as his regiment was disbanded, and take the field against the redoubtable Peta Nocona, and afford the frontier such protection as was possible to this small force. The necessity of vigorous measures soon became so pressing that Capt. Ross determined to attempt to curb the insolence of these implacable enemies of Texas by following them into their fastnesses and carry the war into their own homes. In his graphic narration of this campaign Gen. L. S. Ross says:

> As I could take but forty of my men from my post, I requested Capt. N. G. Evans, in command of the United States troops, at Camp Cooper, to send me a detachment of the Second Cavalry. We had been intimately connected on the Van Dorn campaign, during which I was the recipient of much kindness from Capt. Evans while I was suffering from a severe wound received from an Indian in the Battle of the 'Wichita.' He promptly sent me a sergeant and twenty well mounted men. My force was still further augmented by some seventy volunteer citizens under command of the brave old frontiersman, Capt. Jack Cureton, of

Bosque county. These self-sacrificing patriots, without the hope of pay or reward, left their defenceless homes and families to avenge the sufferings of the frontier people. With pack-mules laden down with necessary supplies the expedition marched for the Indian country.

On the 18th of December, 1860, while marching up Pease River, I had some suspicions that Indians were in the vicinity, by reason of the buffalo that came running in great numbers from the north towards us, and while my command moved in the low ground I visited all neighbouring high points to make discoveries. On one of these sand hills I found four fresh pony tracks, and being satisfied that Indian *videtts* had just gone, I galloped forward about a mile to a higher point, and riding to the top, to my inexpressible surprise, found myself within 200 yards of a Comanche village, located on a small stream winding around the base of the hill.

It was a most happy circumstance that a piercing north wind was blowing, bearing with it clouds of sand, and my presence was unobserved and the surprise complete. By signalling my men as I stood concealed, they reached me without being discovered by the Indians, who were busy packing up preparatory to a move. By this time the Indians mounted and moved off north across the level plain. My command, with the detachment of the Second Cavalry, had out-marched and become separated from the citizen command, which left me about sixty men. In making disposition for attack, the sergeant and his twenty men were sent at a gallop, behind a chain of sand hills, to encompass them in and cut off their retreat, while with forty men I charged.

The attack was so sudden that a considerable number were killed before they could prepare for defence. They fled precipitately right into the presence of the sergeant and his men. Here they met with a warm reception, and finding themselves completely encompassed, everyone fled his own way, and was hotly pursued and hard pressed.

The chief of the party, Peta Nocona, a noted warrior of great repute, with a young girl about fifteen years of age mounted on his horse behind him, and Cynthia Ann Parker, with a girl child about two years of age in her arms and mounted on a fleet pony, fled together, while Lieut. Tom. Kelliheir and I pursued them. After running about a mile Killiheir ran up by the side of Cynthia's horse, and I was in the act of shooting when she held up her child and stopped. I kept on after the chief and about a half a mile further, when in about twenty yards of him I fired my pistol, striking the girl (whom I supposed to be a man, as she rode like one, and only her head was visible above the buffalo robe with which she was wrapped) near the heart, killing her instantly, and the same ball would have killed both but for the shield of the chief, which hung down, covering his back.

When the girl fell from the horse she pulled him off also, but he caught on his feet, and before steadying himself, my horse, running at full speed, was very nearly upon top of him, when he was struck with an arrow, which caused him to fall to pitching or 'bucking,' and it was with great difficulty that I kept my saddle, and in the meantime, narrowly escaped several arrows coming in quick succession from the chief's bow. Being at such disadvantage he would have killed me in a few minutes but for a random shot from my pistol (while I was clinging with my left hand to the pommel of my saddle) which broke his right arm at the elbow, completely disabling him.

My horse then became quiet, and I shot the chief twice through the body, whereupon he deliberately walked to a small tree, the only one in sight, and leaning against it, began to sing a wild, weird song. At this time my Mexican servant, who had once been a captive with the Comanches and spoke their language as fluently as his mother tongue, came up, in company with two of my men. I then summoned the chief to surrender, but he promptly treated every overture with contempt, and signalized this declaration with a savage attempt to thrust me with the lance which he held in his left hand. I could only look upon him with pity and admiration. For, deplorable as was his situation, with no chance of escape, his party utterly destroyed, his wife and child captured in his sight, he was undaunted by the fate that awaited him, and as he seemed to prefer death to life, I directed the Mexican to end his misery by a charge of buck shot from the gun which he carried.

Taking up his accoutrements, which I subsequently sent Gov. Houston, to be deposited in the archives at Austin, we rode back to Cynthia Ann and Killiheir, and found him bitterly cursing himself for having run his pet horse so hard after an 'old

Lizzie Ross

squaw.' She was very dirty, both in her scanty garments and her person. But as soon as I looked on her face, I said, 'Why, Tom, this is a white woman, Indians do not have blue eyes.' On the way to the village, where my men were assembling with the spoils, and a large *caballado* of 'Indian ponies,' I discovered an Indian boy about nine years of age, secreted in the grass. Expecting to be killed, he began crying, but I made him mount behind me, and carried him along. And when in after years I frequently proposed to send him to his people, he steadfastly refused to go, and died in McLennan county last year.

After camping for the night Cynthia Ann kept crying, and thinking it was caused from fear of death at our hands, I had the Mexican tell her that we recognized her as one of our own people, and would not harm her. She said two of her boys were with her when the fight began, and she was distressed by the fear that they had been killed. It so happened, however, both escaped, and one of them, 'Quanah' is now a chief. The other died some years ago on the plains. I then asked her to give me the history of her life with the Indians, and the circumstances attending her capture by them, which she promptly did in a very sensible manner.

And as the facts detailed corresponded with the massacre at Parker's Fort, I was impressed with the belief that she was Cynthia Ann Parker. Returning to my post, I sent her and child to the ladies at Cooper, where she could receive the attention her situation demanded, and at the same time dispatched a messenger to Col. Parker, her uncle, near Weatherford, and as I was called to Waco to meet Gov. Houston, I left directions for the Mexican to accompany Col. Parker to Cooper in the capacity of interpreter. When he reached there, her identity was soon discovered to Col. Parker's entire satisfaction and great happiness.

And thus was fought the Battle of "Pease River" between a superior force of Comanches under the implacable chief, Peta Nocona on one side, and sixty rangers led by their youthful commander, Capt. L. S. Ross, on the other. Ross, sword in hand, led the furious rush of the rangers; and in the desperate encounter of "war to the knife" which ensued, nearly all the warriors bit the dust.

So signal a victory had never before been gained over the fierce and war-like Comanches and never since that fatal December clay in 1860 have they made any military demonstrations at all commensurate with the fame of their proud campaigns in the past. The great Comanche confederacy was forever broken. The incessant and sanguinary war which had been waged for more than thirty years was now virtually at an end.

The blow was a most decisive one; as sudden and irresistable as a thunder-bolt, and as remorseless and crushing as the hand of Fate.

It was a short but desperate conflict. Victory trembled in the balance. A determined charge, accompanied by a simultaneous fire from the solid phalanx of yelling rangers and the Comanches beat a hasty retreat, leaving many dead and wounded upon the field. Espying the chief and a chosen few riding at full speed, and in a different direction from the other fugitives, from the ill-starred field, Ross quickly pursued. Divining his purpose, the watchful Pete Nocona rode at full speed, but was soon overtaken, when the two chiefs engaged in a personal encounter, which must result in the death of one or the other. Peta Nocona fell, and his last sigh was taken up in mournful wailings on the wings of defeat. Most of the women and children with a few warriors escaped. Many of these perished on the cold and inhospitable plains, in an effort to reach their friends on the head-waters of the Arkansas River.

The immediate fruits of the victory was some four hundred and fifty horses, and their accumulated winter's supply of food. But the incidental fruits are not to be computed on the basis of dollars and cents. The proud spirit of the Comanche was here broken, and to this signal defeat is to be attributed the measurably pacific conduct of these heretofore implacable foes of the white race during the course of the late civil war in the Union, a boon of incalculable value to Texas.

In a letter recognising the great service rendered the state by Ross in dealing the Comanches this crushing blow, Governor Houston said:

> Your success in protecting the frontier gives me great satisfaction. I am satisfied that with the same opportunities, you would rival, if not excel, the greatest exploits of McCulloch and Hays. Continue to repel, pursue, and punish every body of Indians coming into the State, and the people will not withhold their praise.   Signed: Sam Houston.

CHAPTER 6

CYNTHIA ANN PARKER—QUANAH PARKER

From May 19th, 1836, to December 18th, 1860, was twenty-four years and seven months. Add to this nine years, her age when captured, and at the later date Cynthia Ann Parker was in her thirty-fourth year. During the last ten years of this quarter of a century, which she spent as a captive among the Comanches, no tidings had been received of her. She had long been given up as dead or irretrievably lost to civilization.

Notwithstanding the long lapse of time which had intervened since the Capture of Cynthia Ann Parker, Ross, as he interrogated his "blue eyed" but bronzed captive, more than suspected that she was the veritable "Cynthia Ann Parker," of which he had heard so much from his boyhood. She was dressed in female attire, of course, according to the custom of the Comanches, which being very similar to that of the males, doubtless, gave rise to the erroneous statement that she was dressed in male costume. So sure was Ross of her identity that, as before stated, he at once dispatched a messenger to her uncle, the venerable Isaac Parker; in the meantime placing Cynthia Ann in charge of Mrs. Evans, wife of Capt. N. G. Evans, the commandant at Fort Cooper, who at once, with commendable benevolence, administered to her necessities.

Upon the arrival of Col. Parker at Fort Cooper, interrogations were made her through the Mexican interpreter, for she remembered not one word of English, respecting her identity; but she had forgotten absolutely everything, apparently, at all connected with her family or past history.

In despair of being able to reach a conclusion, Col. Parker was about to leave, when he said, "The name of my niece was Cynthia Ann." The sound of the once familiar name, doubtless the last lingering memento of the old home at the fort, seemed to touch a responsive chord in her nature, when a sign of intelligence lighted up her countenance, as memory by some mystic inspiration resumed its cunning as she looked up, and patting her breast, said, "Cynthia Ann! Cynthia Ann!" At the awakening of this single spark of reminiscence, the sole gleam in the mental gloom of many years, her countenance brightened with a pleasant smile in place of the sullen expression which habitually characterizes the looks of an Indian restrained of freedom. There was now no longer any doubt as to her identity with the little girl lost and mourned so long. It was in reality Cynthia Ann Parker,—but, oh, so changed!

But as savage-like and dark of complexion as she was, Cynthia Ann was still dear to her overjoyed uncle, and was welcomed home by relatives with all the joyous transports with which the prodigal son was hailed upon his miserable return to the parental roof.

As thorough an Indian in manner and looks as if she had been so born, she sought every opportunity to escape, and had to be closely watched for some time. Her uncle carried herself and child to his home, then took them to Austin, where the secession convention was in session. Mrs. John Henry Brown and Mrs. N. C. Raymond interested themselves in her, dressed her neatly, and on one occasion took her into the gallery of the hall while the convention was in session. They soon realized that she was greatly alarmed by the belief that the assemblage was a council of chiefs, sitting in judgement on her life. Mrs. Brown beckoned to her husband, Hon. John Henry Brown, who was a member of the convention, who appeared and succeeded in reassuring her that she was among friends.

Gradually her mother tongue came back, and with it occasional incidents of her childhood, including a recognition of the venerable Mr. Anglin, and perhaps one or two others.

The civil war coming on soon after, which necessitated the resumption of such primitive arts, she learned to spin, weave and to perform the domestic duties. She proved quite an adept in such work, and became a very useful member of the household.

The ruling passion of her bosom seemed to be the maternal instinct, and she cherished the hope that when the war was concluded she would at last succeed in reclaiming her two children who were still with the Indians. But it was written otherwise, and Cynthia Ann and her little "barbarian" were called hence ere "the cruel war was over." She died at her brother's in Anderson county, Texas, in 1864, preceded a short time by her sprightly little daughter, "Prairie Flower."

Thus ended the sad story of a woman far famed along the border.

★ ★ ★ ★ ★ ★ ★ ★

How fared it with the two young orphans we may only imagine. The lot of these helpless ones is too often one of trials, heart-pangs, and want, even among our enlightened people; and it would require a painful recital to follow the children of Peta Nocona and Cynthia Ann Parker from the terrible fight on Pease River, across trackless prairies, and rugged mountain-ways, in the inhospitable month of December, tired, hungry, and carrying a load upon their hearts far heavier than the physical evils which so harshly beset them. Their father was slain, and their mother a captive. Doubtless they were as intent upon her future recovery, during the many years in which they shared the vicissitudes of their people, until the announcement of her death reached them, as her own family had been for her rescue during her quarter of a century of captivity. One of the little sons of Cynthia Ann died some years after her recapture. The other, now known as Capt. Quanah Parker, born as he says in 1854, is the chief of Comanches, on their reservation in the Indian Territory.

Finally, in 1874, the Comanches were forced upon a "reservation," near Fort Sill, to lead the beggarly life of "hooded harlots and blanketed thieves," and it was at this place that the "war-chief" Quanah, learned that it was possible he might secure a photograph of his mother.

An advertisement to that effect was inserted in the Fort Worth *Gazette*, when General Ross at once forwarded him a copy. To his untutored mind it seemed that a miracle had been wrought in response to his "paper prayer;" and his exclamations, as he gazed intently and long upon the faithful representation of "Preloch," or Cynthia Ann, were highly suggestive of Cowper's lines on his mother's picture; and we take the liberty of briefly presenting a portion of the same in verse:

My mother! and do my weeping eyes once more
Half doubting—scan thy cherished features o'er?
Yes, 'tis the pictured likeness of my dead mother,
How true to life! It seems to breathe and move;
Fire, love, and sweetness o'er each feature melt;
The face expresses all the spirit felt;
Here, while I gaze within those large, dark eyes,
I almost see the living spirit rise;
While lights and shadows, all harmonious, glow,
And heavenly radiance settles on that brow.
What is the "medicine" I must not know,
Which thus can give to death life's bloom and glow.
O, could the white man's magic art but give
As well the happy power, and bid her live!
My name, me thinks, would be the first to break
The seal of silence, on those lips, and wake
Once more the smile that charmed her gentle face,
As she was wont to fold me in her warm embrace.
Yes, it is she, "Preloch," Nocona's pale-faced bride,

Who rode, a matchless princess, at his side,
'Neath many a bloody moon afar,
O'er tortuous paths devoted alone to war.
Long since she's joined him on that blissful shore,—
Where parting and heart-breakings are no more,—
And since our star with him went down in gloom,
No more to shine above the blighting doom,
'Neath which my people's hopes, alas, are fled,
I, too, but long that silent path to tread,—
A child, to be with her and him again,
Healed every wound an orphan's heart can pain!

Quanah Parker is a Nocone, which means wanderer, but on the capture of his mother, Preloch, and death of his father, Quanah was adopted and cared for by the Cohoites, and when just arrived at manhood, was made chief by his benefactors on account of his bravery. His name before he became a chief was Cepe. He has lived among several tribes of the Comanches. He was at one time with the Cochetaker, or Buffalo Eaters, and was the most influential chief of the Penatakers. Quanah is at present one of the four chiefs of the Cohoites, who each have as many people as he has. The Cohoite Comanches were never on a reservation until 1874, but are today, (1886), further advanced in civilization than any Indians on the "Comanche reservation." Quanah speaks English, is considerably advanced in civilization, and owns a ranch with considerable live stock and a small farm; wears a citizen's suit, and con forms to the customs of civilization—withal a fine-looking and dignified son of the plains. In 1884, Quanah, in company with two other prominent Comanche chiefs, visited Mexico. In reporting their passage through that city, the San Antonio *Light* thus speaks of them:

They bear relationship to each other of chief and two subordinates. Quanah Parker is the chief, and as he speaks very good English, they will visit the City of Mexico before they return. They came from Kiowa, Comanche and Wichita Indian Agency, and Parker bears a paper from Indian Agent Hunt that he, Parker, is a son of Cynthia Ann Parker, and is one of the most prominent chiefs of the half-breed Comanche tribe. He is also a successful stock man and farmer. He wears a citizen's suit of black, neatly fitting, regular "toothpick" dude shoes, a watch and gold chain and black felt hat. The only peculiar item in his

115

appearance is his long hair, which he wears in two plaits down his back. His two braves also wear civilization's garb. But wear heavy boots, into which their trousers are thrust in true western fashion. They speak nothing but their native language.

In 1885 Quanah Parker visited the World's Fair at New Orleans. The following extract from the Fort Worth *Gazette*, is a recent incident in his career:

"HE BLEW OUT THE GAS"
AND ON THAT BREATH THE SOUL OF YELLOW BEAR
FLEW TO ITS HAPPY HUNTING GROUNDS.

Another instance in which the noble red man succumbs to the influence of civilization!

A sensation was created on the streets yesterday by the news of a tragedy from asphyxiation at the Pickwick hotel, of which two noted Indians, Quanah Parker and Yellow Bear, were the victims.

The circumstances of the unfortunate affair were very difficult to obtain because of the inability of the only two men who were possessed of definite information on the subject to reveal it—one on account of death, and the other from unconsciousness. The Indians arrived here yesterday from the Territory, on the Fort Worth & Denver incoming train. They registered at the Pickwick and were assigned an apartment together in the second story of the building. Very little is known of their subsequent movements, but from the best evidence that can be collected it appears that Yellow Bear retired alone about 10 o'clock, and that in his utter ignorance of modern appliances, he blew out the gas. Parker, it is believed, did not seek his room until 2 or 3 o'clock in the morning, when, not detecting from some cause the presence of gas in the atmosphere, or not locating its origin in the room, he shut the door and scrambled into bed, unmindful of the deadly forces which were even then operating so disastrously.

The failure of the two Indians to appear at breakfast or dinner caused the hotel clerk to send a man around to awake them. He found the door locked and was unable to get a response from the inmates. The room was then forcibly entered, and as the door swung back the rush of the deathly perfume through the aperture told the story. A ghastly spectacle met the eyes of

116

QUANAH PARKER.

the hotel *employés*. By the bedside in a crouched position, with his face pressed to the floor, was Yellow Bear, in the half-nude condition which Indian fashion in night clothes admits. In the opposite corner near the window, which was closed, Parker was stretched at full length upon his back. Yellow Bear was stone dead, while the quick gasps of his companion indicated that he was in but a stone's throw of eternity. The chief was removed to the bed, and through the untiring efforts of Drs. Beall and Moore his life has been saved.

Finding Quanah sufficiently able to converse, the reporter of the *Gazette* questioned him as to the cause of the unhappy occurrence, and elicited the following facts:

'I came,' said the chief, 'into the room about midnight, and found Yellow Bear in bed. I lit the gas myself. I smelt no gas when I came into the room. When I went to bed I turned the gas off. I did not blow it out. After a while I smelt the gas, but went to sleep. I woke up and shook Yellow Bear and told him 'I'm mighty sick and hurting all over.' Yellow Bear says, 'I'm mighty sick, too.' I got up, and fell down and all around the room, and that's all I know about it.'

'Why didn't you open the door?' asked the reporter.

'I was too crazy to know anything,' replied the chief.

It is indeed, a source of congratulation that the chief will recover, as otherwise his tribe could not be made to understand the occurrence, and results detrimental to those having interests in the Territory would inevitably follow.

The new town of Quanah, in Hardeman county, Texas, was named in honour of chief Quanah Parker.

We will now conclude our little work by appending the following letter, which gives a true pen portrait of the celebrated chief as he appears at his home on the "reservation:"

Anadarko, I. T., Feb. 4, 1886.

We visited Quanah in his *tepee*. He is a fine specimen of physical manhood, tall, muscular—as straight as an arrow; gray, look-you-straight-through-the-eyes, very dark skin, perfect teeth, and a heavy, raven-black hair—the envy of feminine hearts—he wears hanging in two rolls wrapped around with red cloth. His hair is parted in the middle the scalp-lock is a portion of hair the size of a dollar, plaited and tangled, signifying: 'If you want

118

fight you can have it.'

Quanah is how camped with a thousand of his subjects at the foot of some hills near Anadarko. Their white *tepees*, and the inmates dressed in their bright blankets and feathers, cattle grazing, children playing, lent a weird charm to the lonely, desolate hills, lately devastated by prairie fire.

He has three squaws, his favourite being the daughter of Yellow Bear, who met his death by asphyxiation at Fort Worth in December last. He said he gave seventeen horses for her. His daughter Cynthia, named for her grandmother, Cynthia Parker, is an inmate of the Indian Agent's house. Quanah was at tired in a full suit of buck-skin tunic, leggins and *moccasins* elaborately trimmed in beads—a red breech-cloth, with ornamental ends hanging down. A very handsome and expensive Mexican blanket was thrown around his body; in his ears were little stuffed birds. His hair done with the feathers of bright plumaged birds. He was handsomer by far than any Ingomar the writer has ever seen—but there was no squaw fair enough to personate his Parthenia. His general aspect, manners, bearing, education, natural intelligence, show plainly that white blood trickles through his veins. When travelling he assumes a complete civilian's outfit—dude collar, watch and chain—takes out his ear-rings—he of course cannot cut off his long hair, saying that he could no longer be 'big chief.' He has a handsome carriage; drives a pair of matched grays, always travelling with one of his squaws (to do the chores). Minna-a-ton-ccha is with him now. She knows no English, but while her lord is conversing, gazes, dumb with admiration, at 'my lord'—ready to obey his slightest wish or command.

Tragedies of Cañon Blanco

Robert Goldthwaite Carter

THE TEXAS PANHANDLE

In 1836 the principal war chief of the Qua-ha-das was Peta Na-cona (the "Wanderer"). It was then the wildest and most hostile band of the Comanche tribe, and the most inveterate raiders on the Texas border.

PARKER'S FORT—THE ROMANCE OF QUANAH

On May 19, 1836, a few days after the Battle of San Jacinto was fought, these Indians, under Nacona, raided Parkers Fort, situated at the headwaters of Navasota Creek—a tributary of the Brazos—near where the town of that name is now located, sixty miles from the nearest white settlement, and two miles from the present town of Groesbeck, Limestone County, Texas. The post was occupied by six men and several women and children. The Indians shrewdly presented a white flag, and sent some of their number to the post to say they were friendly.

One of the inmates, Benjamin Parker (who was the father of Cynthia Ann Parker and the grandfather of Chief Quanah Parker), let them enter the fort, believing that they were friendly Indians and wanted to make a treaty with the whites, but when he was within their power they treacherously attacked and killed him and immediately captured the fort.

It was a stockade fort, occupied by several families who had just returned from the flight before the Mexican Army, commanded by General Santa Ana. After effecting an entrance into Parkers Fort by pretending to be friendly, the Indians massacred all the men and some of the women and children, carrying away captive Mrs. Plummer and her son, two years old; Mrs. Kellogg; Cynthia Ann Parker, then

QUANAH PARKER
PRINCIPAL WAR CHIEF OF THE QUA-HA-DA COMANCHES

nine years old, and her brother, aged six. After leaving the fort the Comanches and Kiowas travelled together until midnight. They then camped, brought their prisoners together, tied their hands behind them so tightly as to cut the flesh, tied their feet together, and threw them on their faces; then gathered around with the bloody scalps they had taken at the fort and commenced their war dance. They danced, screamed, yelled, and stamped upon the prisoners, beating them with bows until the blood flowed from their bruises, and the rest of the night the women had to listen to the cries and groans of the little children. When the tribes parted each of the bands took a captive.

Cynthia Ann Parker was claimed by the Comanche tribe, and became their permanent captive. Nothing was heard from her for many years, but in the meantime her relatives and friends and the Texas authorities did everything in their power to ascertain her fate and secure her release, if she was living.

In the autumn of 1860 the Comanches, in force under their chief, Peta Nacona, the father of Quanah Parker and the Indian husband of Cynthia Ann, raided through Parker and adjoining counties and inflicted great distress upon the white settlements.

But in December he was followed and surprised in his own camp on Pease River by a force of forty Texas Rangers and twenty dragoons of the Regular Army, in all sixty soldiers, under Captain "Sul" Ross, of the Rangers. His camp was captured and many slain. The chief fled at full speed, with another Indian behind him on the same horse, and his wife, with an infant in her arms, on a fleet pony beside him. The captain of the Rangers, with one attendant, pursued. They soon overtook the chief's wife, who held up her child and stopped. Leaving her with his attendant, the captain pursued the two Indians on one horse, and, coming up with them, fired with his heavy revolving pistol, killing the hindmost. The same ball would have also killed the chief, but his shield hanging on his back prevented. The hindmost, in falling, dragged the chief from his horse, but he lit upon his feet and plied his pursuers with arrows, wounding his horse.

The wound set the animal to rearing and plunging so violently that the ranger could not aim his weapon. Victory in the single combat seemed on the point of declaring for the savage. His well-directed arrows were sent rapidly; but a random shot from the Ranger broke his right arm and disabled him, both hands being indispensable to the use of the bow. The captain's horse becoming quiet, he shot the chief twice through the body, who then walked deliberately to a tree near by and, leaning against it, began to sing a wild, weird song—the death song of his tribe, a custom in many tribes in the presence of certain death.

The captain's men coming up with an interpreter, the chief was summoned to surrender, but he answered by a savage thrust at the captain with his lance held in his left hand. It was plain that he would surrender only to death. The captain directed one of his attendants to "finish him," and the death song ended. The Indian who had been riding behind the chief proved to be a young female, but her sex was not distinguished in the flight, because she was covered with a buffalo robe with only the head visible. The woman taken with the child, the fallen chief's wife, was seen to be a white woman, and she had blue eyes. She wept incessantly and the captain directed the interpreter to tell her that they recognised her as one of their own nation and would not hurt her. She replied that she was not weeping for herself, but for her two boys, who were in the battle, and, she feared, were slain.

She was sent to the white settlement, where she was speedily identified as Cynthia Ann Parker, who was captured when nine years old by the Comanches at Parkers Fort massacre in 1836. She was not reconciled to civilization, and had to be watched to prevent her escape. Her little child, named Prairie Flower, died, and in less than two years she died also and was laid beside her little barbarian. Of her sons, one died on the plains, but the other lived and became the famous chief, Quanah Parker. This battle ground was but about twenty miles above the town of Vernon, on Pease River, at the mouth of Mule Creek and in Foard County, Texas.

There have been many wild newspaper stories and legends concerning the capture of Cynthia Ann Parker. One was that she was taken in 1790 on the banks of the Scioto River, near the present site of Chillicothe, Ohio, and that her parents were from Virginia, etc.

The story, as the writer relates it, is not only official but absolutely reliable, coming as it does from the gallant Ranger, Captain Ross, who afterwards became a brigadier-general in the Confederate Army, and subsequently governor of the State of Texas. He died some fifteen or eighteen years ago, universally beloved by all Texans. While serving as governor he gave to Hon. John H. Stephens, M. C, all the particulars regarding her capture.

Quanah himself knew but little about the early life of his mother, or when and where she was captured.

Quanah was born about 1845. He grew up with the Qua-ha-da

band, and on the death of his father, Nacona, rapidly rose to more or less commanding influence as principal war chief of that band, as well as in the Comanche tribe.

In 1871 the band was still out under Quanah, moving about from place to place, but generally near the headwaters of Pease River, their old stamping ground, the Palo Duro Canon, in Cañon Blanco, and near the mouth of McClellan's Creek, a small tributary of the north fork of the Red River, although he was associated in these raids, reports of which were constantly reaching us, with Mow-wi (the "Handshaker") and Para-a-coom ("He Bear"); both subchiefs of the Qua-ha-da band. The village of Mow-wi, on McClellan's Creek, was destroyed in September, 1872, by our command operating from Fort Richardson, Texas.

The Fourth Cavalry had been out in the field from May 1 until about September 13, 1870, much of the time north of Red River in the Indian Territory (now Oklahoma), by direction of General Sherman, and had succeeded in driving in the Kiowas under Ton-ne-un-co ("Kicking Bird"), who had fled from the Fort Sill reservation in May of that year when he (General Sherman) had ordered the arrest at Fort Sill of the principal chiefs of that tribe, including the notorious war chiefs, See-ti-toh (Sa-tan-ta, "White Bear") and Quirl-par-ko ("Lone Wolf"), for the massacre of seven teamsters a few weeks before on Salt Creek prairie, two miles from Rock Creek Station, near Fort Richardson, Texas. Had a strong guard not been stationed in General Grierson's quarters, concealed from view, when General Sherman ordered their arrest at a council which was being held, he would have been killed through the treachery of the Indians, who went to the conference with arms concealed under their blankets, but were foiled by General Sherman's precautions. It came very near, however, to being another General Canby murder. The writer has a copy of General Sherman's letter written at that period, graphically describing the scene.

After having accomplished this duty of stampeding Kicking Bird into Fort Sill, in which we were ably (?) assisted by General Grierson, who, either through jealousy or fear, sent his post interpreter, Horace P. Jones, into Kicking Bird's camp on the Sweetwater—near where old Fort Elliott was later located—to warn him that the "Great Chief from Texas, Mackenzie, was about to attack him outside of the reservation, and to get in as soon as possible," and hearing that the Comanches had been raiding down the country again, and had already secured many horses, cattle, and, as rumour had it, killed some people and captured women and children, among them a child five years of age, Mackenzie determined to pay his attention now to the Indians of the Texas Panhandle in their fastnesses, the breaks and small cañons of the Staked Plains.

CAMP COOPER—THE RENDEZVOUS

On September 19, therefore, we left Fort Richardson again for a new campaign. We concentrated and reorganized at old Camp Cooper on Tecumseh's Creek, a small tributary of the Clear Fork of the Brazos, about five miles from Fort Griffin, Texas. General Robert E. Lee built this post some years before the Civil War, and occupied it for some time. General John B. Hood, a general in the Confederate Army, saw his first service here. It was a former reservation for the southern Comanches, and, at this period, was in ruins. On August 12, Lawrie Tatum, the Quaker Indian agent at Fort Sill, wrote General Grierson as follows:

> I should be very glad indeed if thee and General Mackenzie could get that little captive, and induce Mow-way (Mow-wi) and his band to come into the reservation and behave .. . . . Mow-way does not appear likely to bring in that poor little captive child of his own volition . . . . I did not get a definite idea of where Mow-way is.

A copy of this letter was furnished to General Mackenzie, who then determined to definitely locate the Qua-ha-das, punish them, and, if possible, bring in the child.

On September 25, eight (8) companies (or troops) of the Fourth Cavalry (A, B, D, F, G, H, K, and L), and two (2) companies of the Eleventh Infantry (F and I), with about twenty Ton-ka-way scouts, were in camp near Fort Griffin. On that, night a big band of Indians came in to Murphy's ranch, about twenty miles from the post, and, it was reported, ran off a herd of one hundred and twenty cattle and thirteen horses, and two citizens, Stockton and James, part owners of this stock, joined us at our camp, ready to take up the trail of their animals, assist in punishing these depredators and murdering thieves, and to identify, if possibly, their brands, if secured. General Mackenzie had not then arrived, and the settlers showed signs of anger at Capt. Wirt Davis, commanding camp, because he would not order out the command at once and take up the trail. But he had positive orders from Mackenzie to remain at this camp resting the men and animals. Up to this period the writer had been field adjutant and a general "*Pooh Bah*" of the command—topographical engineer, etc.—but was now attached, first to "K" Troop (his own troop "E" having been left at Fort Richardson) and later to "B" Troop for duty, and to command it, as Captain Clarence Mauck of that troop now commanded the squadron, then composed of two troops.

On the morning of September 30 the writer was ordered to take eight men and five "Tonk" trailers or scouts, proceed up the Clear Fork, and select a good camp for the command and some kind of a practicable road for the wagon train. Upon his return, on October 3, we moved out. The writer rode at the head of the column, directing the scouts in advance, and guiding it over the trail he had made to the bend of the stream.

The March for the "Panhandle"—The "Double Mountain" Fork—A "Close Shave"

We left our bivouac on the beautiful bend of the Clear Fork the next morning, with about six hundred men and nearly one hundred pack mules, all in fine condition, although the horses were somewhat thin and worn by their long campaign since May. The Indian scouts, our faithful "Tonks," under Lieutenant P. M. Boehm, were far in advance, well fanned out, combing the country for trails, with a selected advance guard in close support if necessary, and to guard against surprise. All were cheerful, and our old song rang out, "Come home, John, don't stay long; Come home soon to your own Chick-a-biddy!" California and Paint Creeks, both quicksand streams, with rather steep banks and no regular fords, were crossed.

Plenty of buffalo and antelope were seen on the flanks, but no hunting was now permitted. Other and different game was our objective. Mackenzie sent the writer to the rear several times to assist Lawton, our newly joined regimental quartermaster, in crossing these creeks and numerous "sloughs" or "arroyos," saying: "You men of the Civil War have had more experience in that work, in 'speeding up' wagon trains, than my other and younger officers, and if you and Lawton can't make time I don't know who can."

Our next camp was but a few miles from the Double Mountains, which were in plain sight. Marching early the next morning we crossed the Double Mountain Fork of the Brazos, and at night camped near "Flat Top," or "Cottonwood Springs." Here we found the vilest water, but excellent grazing for the animals. We saw immense herds of buffalo all day, and at night we were literally in their midst, for they only moved off a mile or two for our accommodation, and to avoid the scent of our command coming down the wind. Only enough were killed to furnish fresh meat for the entire command, as was our custom. The writer was in charge of the guard that night. This included herd guards, "sleeping parties," all camp guards and picket outposts. Preparatory to midnight inspection of all the posts, he lay down in a buffalo robe near the sergeant in charge of the picket re-serve, to protect himself from a cold wind that had now increased to a stiff gale, making it difficult to hear any sounds outside the camp.

Suddenly, however, he heard above the din of the gale a tremen-dous tramping and an unmistakable snorting and bellowing. Placing his ear to the ground, he could hear it plainer, and this time there was a heavy jarring. Throwing off his robe, he could distinctly see com-ing through the darkness an immense, black, moving mass, which he knew at once were the herds of buffalo. They were making directly for the reserve and our horse herds which had inadvertently been staked or lariated directly across the paths or water trails leading to their usual drinking holes. There was no time to lose, even to alarm the sleeping camp. The writer did not dare to fire upon them to break the heads of the herds, as that might alarm and also stampede the horses, and besides orders had been given that no shots should be fired now that we were in the enemy's country. He jumped to his feet, shouted to the sergeant to rout out his guard, and to carry their blankets forward and, by meeting the mass, waving them, and yelling, to try and turn them aside.

The men acted promptly and effectively. The immense herds of brown monsters were caromed off and they stampeded to our left at breakneck speed, rushing and jostling, but flushing only the edge of one of our horse herds, and were soon crowding down the banks to the flats below, thundering off in the black gloom of night with a noise that aroused every sleeper in camp, who supposed for a mo-ment that our horses had broken away from their lariats and had gone. As we watched their grotesque shadows and brown masses troop off in the darkness in countless hundreds, with a noise like the mighty rumbling of thunder, making the ground fairly tremble with their tramping, one could hardly repress a shudder at what might have been the result of this nocturnal visit, for although the horses were strongly "lariated out," "staked" or "picketed," nothing could have saved them from the terror which this headlong charge would have inevitably created, had we not heard them just in time to turn the leading herds. It was a close shave, and might have proved a sad disaster.

The writer slept no more that night, but rolling himself in his buffalo robe tried to ward off the piercing wind.

Duck Creek—The Unsuccessful Scout

Moving early we reached Duck Creek—no water on the road, and our trail was mostly over a rolling prairie thinly covered with mesquite, but thickly covered with dog towns, populated by prairie-dogs, and immense herds of buffalo as far as the eye could reach. The water in the creek was clear, contained in large waterholes, all impregnated with gypsum, an improvement, however, over the last camp. We discovered this day the trading stations of the Mexicans with the Indians, consisting of curiously built caves in the high banks or bluffs, the earth being propped up or kept in place by a framework of poles, giving these subterranean abodes the appearance of grated prison doors or windows, reminding us of the cave dwellers of Arizona and New Mexico. These trading stations were now abandoned. At night, after much persuasion, the "Tonks" were sent out to find, if possible, any signs of the Comanche villages, it being Mackenzie's intention, as soon as they, the "Tonks" returned, to make a night march and surprise the enemy. Our Indian scouts were very timid when sent out in a new country without an escort or supporting column, for fear our own men might mistake them for hostiles, before they could be recognized, especially at night, and fire upon them.

Here we located our supply camp from which we could load the pack mules for mobility and quick movements in any direction; the two infantry companies to be left as a sufficient guard, and Lawton to control the supplies. Here the writer was directed to take a small detachment and scout to the head of the creek to reconnoitre for signs and, if possible, strike the trail of our "Tonks." It proved unsuccessful as our route was too far to the east.

Night March in the—"Bad Lands" for a Surprise—The Barrier

Upon our return the same day, Mackenzie announced his intention to strike out that night and make a quick march to surprise the hostiles. The wagons were therefore corralled or parked, the mules packed, and, without waiting for the return of the "Tonks," and under cover of darkness, leaving our cook fires to deceive the enemy, we started.

After many trials, tribulations, and much hard talk verging upon profanity, and many bruises, we all brought up at midnight in a small box canon or break, against the high and rocky face of an impassable wall, which, in the inky blackness of a starless and moonless night, we could not see our way clear to scale, and unable to find any way out, after many rather comical scenes, floundering among the ravines and arroyos forming this barrier, we bivouacked without fires until morning, the heels of the pack mules sharply defining our limits, and the companies hardly moving from column as they halted, for fear of inextricable confusion and injury by accident. Cold "snacks" were all we could obtain for "eats." At daybreak, or just before it was fairly light, we moved by a flank around the obstacle, which we found too steep to climb, and after a rapid and hard march over rough country of about five hours we reached the Freshwater Fork of the Brazos River, the objective we ought to have gained at daylight.

To our surprise the water was really fresh, and its name was not misleading. We unsaddled, built fires, and ate breakfast. Until now no signs of the missing Ton-ka-ways had been discovered; nothing was known thus far but what our march had been a success. Lieutenant Boehm recognised the spot as being near where Captain Carrol of the Ninth Cavalry and he had had a fight with this same band of Comanches the year before. A hasty reconnaissance revealed the brush huts or "wickey-ups," and remnants of lodges or "*tepees*" could be seen on high ground near the stream and to our left. In the early afternoon a squadron under Captain E. M. Heyl was sent out on a reconnaissance, while the balance of the command rested after their hard struggle of the previous night.

THE "TONKS" DISCOVER THE COMANCHES

The "Tonk" scouts soon espied our column and came in, but while hastening along some ravines, on high ground, ran rather unexpectedly upon four Comanches, also busily intent upon watching our reconnoitring squadron, and our "surprise" (?) column. The "Tonks" gave chase, which, for a time, proved quite exciting, but the hostiles being better mounted soon distanced their pursuers and vanished into the hills. The scouts all looked the worse for wear, being fagged out, dirty, and with scalp-locks looking tousled and tangled. Having been without sleep or food since leaving our camp on Duck Creek, they were nearly famished and as ravenous as wolves.

They reported their belief in having discovered the trail leading to the Qua-ha-da village. At three p. m. the writer was detailed as officer-of-the-day, and immediately after the short ceremony of guard mount, word was passed along—"boots and saddle" never being sounded in an Indian country—for the command to "pack up." The column was soon in motion, and with a strong guard I followed in rear with the entire pack train of nearly one hundred mules. The Fresh Fork was full of quick-sands, and in crossing the train a number of the animals "bogged," which, fortunately, we got out upon dry land very soon, but not without hard work, and were just congratulating ourselves when a shot was heard, and then another, either at the head of the column, or of the pack train, now strung out at some length.

The main column was alarmed. Mackenzie came galloping to the rear, and with some excitement inquired where the shots came from, fearing that Captain Mauck's squadron, which had been sent back to the camp we had left, as a "blind," had been attacked. Without waiting to learn the cause of the shots, he directed the writer to ride at a gallop to the head of the column and tell Captain Wirt Davis to counter-march the command, and move it rapidly to the rear. Mackenzie, upon meeting it, however, after having ascertained that a careless soldier of the rear guard had discharged his piece, caused it to move to the front again. Much valuable time had been thus lost. The country was rough, with some foothills and small arroyos. Frequent halts were made and it was nearly dark before the command was straightened out and ready to go into camp.

The absent squadron was sent for, and under the shadow of some abrupt hills, scarcely one hundred yards from the stream, we went into bivouac. It was a pocket valley. The horses were "staked out" with "cross side lines," picket pins securely driven, and the men allowed to make small fires, which, in the writer's judgment, was a grave error, as will be seen. The missing squadron came in after dark, and, not finding much room, crowded pretty close to the rear company, the horses being somewhat huddled upon their grazing ground—another unfortunate error.

We were in a narrow pocket, with a line of small bluffs or foothills close to us on one side, and a treacherous quicksand stream on the other, with a wily enemy always to be accounted for—an excellent camp in time of peace, or even an ideal theoretical camp in time of war—*provided no Indians were about.*

The pickets were posted, the necessary instructions were given, and, without taking my pistol off, loosening my belt, or removing my boots, but uncoiling my lariat and driving my picket pin close to my hand so that I could quickly seize it, my horse remaining saddled (the only one in the command), I lay down until time to inspect the posts. Nearby were Lieutenants P. M. Boehm and W. A. Thompson, and the two cattlemen, Stockton and James, already referred to, who were accompanying us to recover their stock.

It had been a most eventful day. Our thoughts were of the exciting incidents of the march at early dawn; reaching the Fresh Fork; the chase of the four Comanches by our scouts; the shot and rapid counter-march—but especially the poor camp we were now in. It was, in fact, a rapid review of this day's events, and we all made our comments.

It drew near midnight. All was still except the night noises of the horse herds grazing at the end of their lariats. Small fires had been allowed (another error of indulgence to the men), and a few slumbering embers of the one nearest to us flashed up, sparkled and died down, and all was dark, almost inky blackness, when suddenly a yell, followed by a shot, rang down the valley; then a succession of unearthly, blood-cuddling yells, a dozen shots in quick succession, one after the other, a rush, and, in an instant, our whole camp was aroused.

The camp was attacked! The rapid flashes of the carbines and pistols from the rear squadron, now in action, showed us, at intervals, that the ridge, or line of small foothills which skirted our entire camp, was alive with wild Indians, riding by at full speed, shaking dried buffalo robes, ringing bells, yelling like wild demons, and by every other possible device trying to stampede our animals. The answering whoops of our Ton-ka-ways and the loud bangs of carbines, with the shouts of the men, could now be heard, mingled with the hoarse commands of the officers, "Get to your horses!"

For a few moments all was uproar and confusion, but above all this din of arms, yells, whoops of Indians and shouts of soldiers came another sound, like the rumbling of heavy thunder, never to be mistaken when once heard by a cavalry command, which told us all too surely but sadly that all of our horses were stampeding. Upon them was staked almost our very existence in this far-off wilderness. Unless checked, their total loss seemed inevitable. Now came the loud commands: "Every man to his lariat!" "Stand by your horses!"—heard amidst all the tumult.

The scene beggars all description by tongue or pen. There was no "artist on the spot!" At every flash the horses and mules, nearly six hundred in number, could be seen rearing, jumping, plunging, running and snorting, with a strength that terror and brute frenzy alone can inspire. They trembled and groaned m their crazed fright, until they went down on their knees, straining all the time to free themselves from their lariats. As they plunged and became inextricably intermingled and more and more tangled up, the lariats could be heard snapping and crackling like the reports of pistols. Iron picket pins were hurtling, swishing, and whistling more dangerous than bullets. Men, crouching as they ran, vainly endeavoured to seize the pins as they whirled and tore through the air, only to be dragged and thrown among the heels of the horses with hands lacerated and burnt by the ropes running rapidly through their fingers. To one who has never seen or heard a night stampede of horses, mules, or of buffalo such a description would give no adequate conception of this midnight debacle.

The herds thundered off in the distance; the men secured all they could.

The hissing and spitting of the bullets sounded viciously and the yells of the retreating Indians from the distance came back on the midnight air with a peculiar, taunting ring, telling all too plainly that the Qua-ha-das, Quanah's wild band of Comanches, had been among us.

We had found them at last! Or, at least, *they had found us!* The tangled masses of horses, lariats, picket pins, and side lines were straightened out in the darkness as well as conditions would permit, and firing parties were thrown forward to the crest of the ridge. The busy hum of many tongues, all intent upon relating the adventures of this nocturnal visitation, sounded strangely upon the crisp midnight air.

Confusion gradually subsided; every endeavour was made to ascertain our losses in men, horses, etc. Companies were sent out, after being formed. The horses could only be saddled in the darkness by one man holding his struggling and thoroughly terror-stricken brute, while another man adjusted the saddle and bridled him (no easy task), and until the gray of morning a sharp watch was kept to guard against another stampede.

It was ascertained that about seventy of our best horses and mules were gone, this loss falling principally upon "G" and "K" troops, as the Indians struck their flank first. It is doubtful if either of these troops had any "sleeping parties" among their herds. General Mackenzie lost a fine gray pacer, which he prized very highly, and his adjutant, Lieutenant Lynch, also lost a very valuable horse.

******

General Frank Baldwin, U. S. A., retired, told the writer on February 6, 1914, that when he was Indian agent at Fort Sill, Indian Territory (now Oklahoma), about 1876, and in almost daily conference with Quanah, that the latter told Mackenzie in an interview which he (Quanah) sought, that he would return to Mackenzie the gray pacer he had run out of our camp this night.

******

The Comanches went almost over headquarters, as it was located directly under the ridge along which they rode, and where they first struck it.

When the alarm was first given, the writer frantically grabbed for his picket pin, only to see it whizzing through the air into the darkness beyond his reach, and his horse going like mad for the huddled herd of "F" troop. Following with desperate energy, knowing full well the value of his efforts in that direction, he saw the lariat catch in another; the horse jerked back; it held. His hand was upon it. He drew in hand over hand, upon the terrified animal. He felt that he had drawn a prize. The din and uproar was at its height. Getting a half hitch on his horse's nose and holding on with main strength, it was found that his hobbles—a new pair—were unbroken, and as soon as the tumult had somewhat subsided, the writer mounted him as speedily as possible and unattended—for it was impossible to find a trumpeter—started to ascertain what damage the picket posts had sustained. They had been overrun. The nearest post was about twenty yards outside of "F" troop's horses, and in charge of a Dutch corporal, who told his story in a very broken, brief, but ludicrous manner:

"I vas lying down, sir, ven I hears a shot. I shoomps up, dries to get my bicket pin as de horses roosh py, and de next ding I knows de Injuns dey ride all ofer me. I raise my carbine to my preast as he broosh py me; he stagger, almost fall, and he deesappear in de dark."

The Stampeded Horses—Attack and Chase

While the command was still saddling up, and before the dawn was beginning to streak the east, I rode out through the gloom and sage brush to the other picket posts, crossed the Fresh Fork up to the

134

saddle girth, pistol in one hand, bridle rein in the other, feeling at any moment that the Qua-ha-das might be on the outskirts of the camp to pick up loose horses. I saw the trail of the stampeded horses, but neither saw nor heard anything else until the last picket post on the bluff was reached. Their story was soon told, and the direction of the frightened horses going out. Cautioning them to give the alarm promptly, I passed on. Reaching the most remote post on the hill overlooking our camp, to gain which the river had to be recrossed, I was about to question the pickets, when I heard a shot (this shot was fired by Quartermaster Sergeant Morgan of "C troop), followed by a loud shout in the valley beyond. I galloped rapidly up.

Here, coming from different directions, also at a gallop, I met two detachments of "K" and "G" troops which had been sent out shortly before to hunt up stray horses, and to find the trail of the stampeded herds. They were commanded by Captain E. M. Heyl and Lieutenant W. C. Hemphill. All looked down the valley. A dozen or more Indians were seen rapidly making off with as many of our horses. In a moment we were dashing after them. Although still quite dark their forms were distinctly visible. The men scattered out somewhat in the chase, the best and freshest horses of "K" troop leading. We gained on them rapidly, were almost within pistol shot, and a moment later the men began to open fire, when suddenly the Indians abandoned the animals and disappeared in a ravine or arroyo, crossed it, and rode out on high ground beyond, toward a high bluff or mountain, now clearly outlined in the quickening dawn of day.

Most of the men stopped short at the break or arroyo, as there was an abrupt shelf or jump-off, quite difficult for any but the best horses to clear, but Captain Heyl and myself were close upon the Indians. We gave our horses the spurs, jumped the ledge into the ravine, scrambled out, and were again closely following them to the open prairie, now gradually ascending until it seemed to terminate in a smooth prairie ridge as we approached the mountain or butte.

Mount Blanco—"My God, We are in a Nest!"

We were now more than two miles from the camp in a direct line, and more than that by the route we had come. As we ascended the ridge, glancing quickly to the front, there at the base of the bluff or butte could be seen in the clear light of approaching day the ground fairly swarming with Indians, all mounted and galloping toward us with whoops and blood-curdling yells that, for the moment, seemed

135

to take the breath completely from our bodies. But a scant dozen of our men had followed us across that difficult arroyo in the prairie, and the first, almost paralyzing, effect it had upon that little party can never be effaced from one's memory. The picture is indelibly stamped upon the brain.

It was like an electric shock. All seemed to realise the deadly peril of the situation and to take it in at a glance. For a moment the blood seemed fairly congealed, for we realised what the ruse of the Indians had been and knew now that their purpose had been to lead us into an ambuscade. We all drew rein on the ridge as one man, each looked at the other, and then raised a simultaneous sound of surprise. Captain Heyl was the first to speak: "Heavens, but we are in a nest! Just look at the Indians!" Although I echoed this sentiment, in my heart I could not speak it. No words could express it. No act could convey what we felt at that moment. The Indian's attack started without delay and they advanced upon us in open order.

The well delivered fire of our little handful of men, covering now a considerable line, caused the savages to scatter out still more, to falter and hesitate, and to commence their curious custom of circling. They were naked to the waist; were arrayed in all their war paint and trinkets, with head dresses or war bonnets of fur or feathers fantastically ornamented. Their ponies, especially the white, cream, dun, and clay-banks, were striped and otherwise artistically painted and decorated with gaudy stripes of flannel and coloured calico. Bells were jingling, feathers waving, and with jubilant, discordant yells that would have put to blush any Confederate brigade of the Civil War, and uttering taunting shouts, they pressed on to what they surely considered to be their legitimate prey.

Mingled with the shouts, whoops, and yells of the warriors could be distinctly heard the strident screeching and higher-keyed piercing screams of the squaws, far in rear of the moving circles, which rose above the general din and hubbub now rending the air. In the midst of the circling ponies we could see what appeared to be two standard bearers, but upon their nearer approach we discovered them to be two scalp poles gaily decorated with long scalp locks, probably of women, with feathers and pieces of bright metal attached which flashed in the morning light. There were also other flashes seen along their line which I afterwards ascertained were small pieces of mirrors held in the hand and used as signals in the alternate advances and retreats, deployments and concentrations, in place of tactical commands. These were carried by the principal warriors or sub-chiefs, acting, I supposed, as file closers, squad leaders, etc. They had no squad, platoon, or company line formations, and no two, three, or four Indians were seen at any time to come together or bunch.

While a general line was maintained at all times, it was always a line of circling, individual warriors with varying radii, expanding and contracting into longer or shorter lines, advancing or retreating during these tactical manoeuvres. The scalp-pole bearers I took to be chiefs, or big medicine men, for they were arrayed in all the gorgeous trappings that savage barbarity is capable of displaying. It was a most terrifying spectacle to our little band, yet wild, grand, and novel (to look back upon) in the extreme. No shouts or cheers from our men were given in response to the diabolical yelling and din of screeches of the Indians. They maintained a stolid, grim silence, one of determination to do or die to the last.

Unfortunately Heyl's men were nearly all new recruits who had just joined us on this expedition. They had never been in a fight before; were all well mounted on comparatively fresh horses, and as with him (Heyl), who was mounted, as has been already stated, on a large, powerful, black horse, full of fine spirit and strength, the excitement of the chase having partially subsided, everything thus far having gone their way, their fighting ardour had as rapidly cooled, and, seeing the ultimatum of being surrounded and massacred, unless assistance arrived very soon, chose to trust to their horses' heels in an endeavour to escape, rather than to face longer the ferocious Qua-ha-das, whose wild yells, whoops, screams, and screeches now sounded so unpleasantly close to their ears.

This is just precisely what they did do. To my utter surprise and consternation, on my attention being called by one of my men—"Lieutenant, look over there, quick; they are running out!"—I saw Captain Heyl and his men "bunch," and with spurs in their horses' flanks, ride out of the fight at full speed.

Shouts, commands, threats, curses were of no avail. The moral effect of that wild, fancifully dressed, shrieking band of half-naked Comanches, drawing about our flanks and now beginning to close in with their arrows and pistols, was too much for raw men who had never been "tried out" under fire. To my utter dismay I was left a long distance in rear with these five men of "G" troop, a gallant, brave squad of men. We were still some hundreds of yards from the ravine toward which we had been slowly but gradually drawing when we first realized our critical dilemma. This was all done without any notice or warning being given to me by Captain Heyl. He had given no orders or instructions since we had first arrived on the ground.

At this movement by Heyl and his men, the Comanches gave an extra yell of supreme satisfaction, began bunching for a charge, and, making a sudden dash at us with some of the leading warriors, the bullets and arrows began coming in quickly, and to brush uncomfortably near us from every direction.

Knowing that it would be certain death should he turn, try to join the panic-stricken, retreating party, and make a run for the shelter of the arroyo, the writer mounted his men, cautioned them to keep well deployed, cut off the magazines of their Spencer carbines, reserving them until the last moment, to commence falling back—using single shots—turning to fire, but on no account to turn and run until they got the word. The order was carried out to the letter. The Indians were poorly armed with muzzle-loading rifles and pistols and bows. We commenced moving to the rear, bending low on our horses, several of which were struck with arrows. We faced about as often as possible to fire and check them, hoping every moment to see the head of Mackenzie's column come out of the adjacent valley of the Fresh Fork. When we finally faced the leading warriors, a bullet struck Downey in the hand, cutting two fingers, as he was in the act of working the lever of his carbine. With his hand streaming blood, his efforts seemed useless. The shell would not eject. "Lieutenant, what shall I do?"

I shouted, "Use your hunting knife, and eject the shell with it!"

The brave man did it with his wounded hand, and firing a moment later, almost in their faces, dropped an Indian out of the saddle. They were still afraid of our carbines. Using them up to the last moment as single shooters, I shouted, as we neared the arroyo: "Now unlock your magazines, bunch your shots, pump it into them, and make a dash for your lives! It is all we can do!" The Indians recoiled as we delivered this volley, and several going off their ponies caused some confusion, as we made the run. Thank God for those Spencers! My affection for them has never changed. It was not necessary that they should carry one thousand or twelve hundred yards, but kill at from five hundred down to twenty or thirty yards, in what almost became a mix-up. The situation had been desperate from the first.

It now seemed to be absolutely hopeless. I never expected we would reach the arroyo. I felt that our time to die had come, and many thoughts rushed unbidden to the mind. Gregg was about ten or fifteen yards to my right and rear, after we gave them our magazines and turned, riding then on my right flank. He said: "Lieutenant, my horse is giving out!" I glanced partly over my shoulder, and saw that it was too true. He was on an old flea-bitten gray, and the horse was beginning to sway in that peculiar manner always seen in an exhausted horse. The Comanches, almost by intuition, also knew that he was in their grasp, and the leading Indians, having partially recovered from the blizzard we had pumped into them, and seeing the animal stagger and falter, rushed in to dispatch the unfortunate man.

A large and powerfully built chief led the bunch, on a coal-black racing pony. Leaning forward upon his mane, his heels nervously working in the animal's side, with six-shooter poised in air, he seemed the incarnation of savage brutal joy. His face was smeared with war paint, which gave his features a satanic look. A large, cruel mouth added to his ferocious appearance. A full-length headdress or war bonnet of eagle's feathers, spreading out as he rode, and descending from his forehead, over head and back, to his pony's tail, almost swept the ground. Large brass hoops were in his ears; he was naked to his waist, wearing simply leggings, *moccasins* and a breech-clout. A necklace of bear's claws hung about his neck. His scalp lock was carefully braided in with otter fur, and tied with bright red flannel. His horse's bridle was profusely ornamented with bits of silver, and red flannel was also braided in his mane and tail, but, being black, he was not painted. Bells jingled as he rode at headlong speed, followed by the leading warriors, all eager to outstrip him in the race. It was Quanah, head war chief of the wild Qua-ha-das.

★★★★★★

It had been the writer's belief for some years after this action that the chief who led the advance warriors was either Mow-wi or Para-a-coom, but Quanah told General Frank Baldwin, U. S. A. (then a Captain Fifth Infantry), while acting as Indian agent at Fort Sill, Indian Territory, also Colonel J. F. Randlett, U. S. A. (then a Captain Eighth Cavalry), while acting as Indian agent at Anadarko, Indian Territory, that he not only led his Indians the night of the stampede, but also in the attack upon Heyl and the writer on the morning of October 10, 1871.

★★★★★★

In vain did we try to save the life of the doomed man. I turned, checked up my horse, shouting for the men to do the same. With a Smith & Wesson pistol I fired several shots at a distance of not more than thirty feet, but the wily chief was on the other side of Gregg, and guiding his pony by rapid zigzagging so as to make a shield of him, his (Gregg's) life was in danger from our shots. Melville, at just this moment, was hit in the arm.

We dared not close with them, as that would, in a *mêlée*, be almost certain death. In vain did I shout for him to use his carbine. Alas! he did try, but, through nervous strain or excitement, his pull on the lever was too weak, and—the cartridge stuck.

Again I shouted, "Pull your six-shooter!" He reached for it. Too late! A flash! A report from the chief's pistol, now at Gregg's head—a fall—a thud—a tragic death—and his horse, now relieved of his rider, turned and ran into the Indian lines. *This was tragedy number one of Cañon Blanco.*

✶✶✶✶✶✶

Lieutenant John A. McKinney, of the Fourth Cavalry (killed in the fight with Dull Knife's band of Northern Cheyennes in a cañon of the Big Horn Mountains, Nov. 25, 1876), told the writer that when he was at Fort Sill in 1872 the Comanches brought in a buffalo robe with a pictograph on it representing this scene. It was at the moment of Gregg's fall from his horse, and the latter running into the Indian lines. The writer was shown, firing at Quanah. Five Indians were shown dead on the ground, just the number they admitted they lost. The writer endeavoured, later, to secure this robe, but could get no trace of it either through the two interpreters or the Indian agent.

✶✶✶✶✶✶

It seemed almost an age since we had first discovered the Indians, and they had charged out for us. But this had all occurred in a very brief space of time, much less than it has taken the writer to record it. It seemed as though General Mackenzie must have heard the firing and even then be coming out of the valley to our rescue.

Without stopping to scalp the fallen man or to finish us, as we naturally expected might now be done almost any moment, the Quaha-da suddenly whirled, and followed by his warriors—more than forty of whom were within a few yards of us—he rode rapidly toward the mountains.

We were saved! With a loss of one man killed and two men wounded, almost at the edge of the ravine, into which a few moments before the recruits of "K" troop had so ingloriously fled in a headlong demoralised flight.

What had proved our salvation? What had caused this sudden turning of the band? Did the wily chief suspect a decoy to the ravine, there to be met by the command, cut off, and his warriors massacred? Did he suddenly discover the dust of the column coming out of the adjacent valley by the Fresh Fork? Or did he consider his vengeance satisfied, blood for blood, for the warrior killed by the corporal at the picket post during the stampede?

A loud shout, and I turned quickly. Looking to my left in the direction toward our camp, I saw in a moment the true cause for our rescue, and the mysterious conduct of the now retreating Comanches. For, over the little hill or knoll which separated this prairie from the valley down which we had chased the Indians who were running off our stampeded horses, only in a shorter and more direct line to our camp, came all of our Ton-ka-way Indians, with Texas, the squaw, fantastically arrayed in all their finery, mounted on their war ponies, their carbines cracking, yelling with all their lungs, and kicking up such a dust that to the keen eyes of the wary Qua-ha-da chief indicated the rapid and close approach of the main column, which, coming up in his rear, would have pressed him between the ravine and the mountains, with a poor chance for escape.

★★★★★★

Mackenzie had given positive orders that none of the Ton-ka-way squaws should accompany the expedition Notwithstanding this, Texas, a young squaw, had, in some unaccountable manner, smuggled herself on Lawton's train, and, mounted on a clay-bank pony which she had striped with paint so that it closely resembled a zebra, and decorated with feathers and red flannel, was now in the midst of the bucks, full of fight, yelling and screaming like a demon—a veritable virago.

★★★★★★

Lieutenant Boehm had heard the firing; had rushed out in its direction; met the flying recruits, and, brandishing a carbine, compelled them to return, together with many stragglers from our chase belonging to the two troops; also Captain H—— and Lieutenant Hemphill, and, in another moment, waving on his "Tonks," the entire force, amounting now to not over forty men, but, with the heavy dust of a galloping column of over five hundred troopers close behind, were pressing the flying Comanches. Captain Heyl did not assume command, neither did Hemphill utter a word. Boehm said, "Bob, you take the left and I will take the right of the line! Let's push them now. Mackenzie is right in our rear." With our skirmish line well deployed we moved forward steadily toward the butte of the Cañon Blanco. A novel battle now ensued.

★★★★★★

"Peter" Boehm, as he was affectionately known in the old army, enlisted as private, general mounted service, and bugler. Company B, Second Cavalry, July, 1858, discharged March 1, 1865. During the Civil War he was, for a long time, brigade orderly trumpeter for General Custer. At the Battle of Gettysburg, during Custer's great charge with the Michigan Brigade ("Wolverines") on the right flank, he sabred and captured General Wade Hampton's trumpeter, at the time General Hampton was cut across the face with a sabre. For this act Custer had him (Boehm) commissioned second lieutenant, Fifteenth New York Cavalry, and took him on his staff as one of his aides.

At the Battle of Dinwiddie C. H. he rallied the brigade and drove the enemy back several miles and was awarded the Cong. Medal of Honour. At the Battle of Five Forks he was desperately wounded in the arm and leg while charging over the breastworks. His horse was killed, and falling pinned Boehm to the ground, where he was picked up for dead. Appointed second lieutenant. Fourth Cavalry, May 1 1866; first lieutenant, September 27, 1866; captain. May 1, 1873; retired, March 1, 1876; Major, April 23, 1904. He died in 1914. The writer had his remains transferred from Chicago to the Arlington National Cemetery, and on each Memorial Day he plants a flag over his grave in loving remembrance of this gallant soul and generous, faithful companion.

★★★★★★

In the rear of the Indian lines could be seen the squaws now bringing up led ponies, keeping up their shrill, discordant screeching and screaming, and at the base of the butte, or low mountain, the savages were spread out, and circling here and there, looked like a swarm of angry bees, so that it was almost impossible to estimate the number of the moving mass with any accuracy, although we judged that there might have been from three hundred to four hundred—including the squaws.

They were heartily responding to the shouts and war whoops of our scouts, sometimes interlarded with most emphatic and regular old-fashioned, round cursing. Here the real excitement and fascinating charm, so peculiar to an Indian fight, began. It was one grand, but rather dangerous, circus. As before stated, an irregular line of battle, or front, was kept up, always, however, in continual motion, every individual warrior fighting for himself—each, as he came around on the front arc of his circle, which he described with ever-varying radius, firing, whooping, or yelling, and brandishing his arms. This yell can hardly be described, but it approached a *Yah-hoo! Y-a-a-h-h-o-o-o-o!* and with the high keyed-up pitch.

At no time did our lines approach close rifle distance. Occasionally a Ton-ka-way would leave his circle, and, dashing straight to the front, would be imitated by a Comanche, both apparently bent upon meeting in personal combat, or a duel; but, as we breathlessly watched, expecting every moment to see the collision, they whirled, and delivering their fire, strongly reinforced by untranslatable Indian language—which we took to be serious name-calling—they darted back to their places in the ever-changing battle line.

This went on for some time. Occasionally a warrior could be seen to stagger as though about to fall; again, a pony was shot and fell, but instantly the wounded savage was hurried to the rear to be cared for by the squaws, who also brought up an extra pony, to remount the one whose animal had been shot, not forgetting to keep up their ear-splitting screaming, horrible screeching, and noisy exhibition of courage.

Upon the sides of the mountain, or high butte, the Indians could be seen gliding from rock to rock, and the puffs of smoke, from time to time, accompanied by the uncomfortable *ping-p-i-n-g-g* of the bullets close to our ears, told us that they had a lot of old target rifles in the hands of skilful marksmen on the summit. Their line was falling back rapidly, even before our small numbers.

This was easily accounted for, as the dust of our main column was approaching nearer and nearer. The breaks or deep arroyos and numerous ravines in the prairie were full of Indians, hastening to the level ground beyond, to guard against surprise, there to keep up the rapid circling, firing, and falling back as before. They had no idea of being caught in any traps, and the rapid movement of the galloping column hastened their steps.

CHARGE UP THE BUTTE—THE SHATTERED LEG—TRAGEDY
NUMBER TWO

Upon a suggestion to Boehm that we rout out the Indian sharpshooters from the butte, we took about a dozen men from the line and started up. Captain Heyl remained below. Our route was up the sides, and finally along a narrow, steep, zigzag path, either a buffalo trail or one used by the Indians. We hardly knew but at any moment we might be picked off by a bullet. Urging my horse to his utmost speed by voice and spur to lessen their chance, I came suddenly upon a sharp, projecting boulder, jutting over the narrow trail. I turned my horse's head quickly, thinking to avoid it. Too late!

Just at that moment he stepped upon either a rolling stone, or slipped and stumbled, and my left leg struck the boulder with a crash that almost sounded like the crack of a pistol, and I was almost lifted out of my saddle by its force. I grasped the pommel, for it made me sick, and all was dark and swimming before my blurred eyes. I felt myself sway and stagger, then apparently fall down an interminable distance. The cold sweat came from every pore, and I became unconscious, but dropped myself forward upon the horse's neck as I lurched. It has always been a puzzle how I got up the side of the butte. My horse had carried my dead weight, and my arms were still tightly clasped about his neck, with the reins loosely dangling.

Luckily, the Indians, upon our nearing them, had hastily galloped off, abandoning the position, and scattering in every direction. I remember the cheering, seeing the big column come up, with Mackenzie at its head, knew that we were saved—and then all is blank. The cool air at the top of the bluff, a dash of water in the face by one of the men, and a drink of water from his canteen revived me somewhat. The pain was intense, but, looking about me, I could see the Indians still falling back; could hear the cracking of the carbines, and shouts below, as the entire command deployed into lines and rode through the broken gullies and over the plain beyond.

The Indians were being continually mounted on fresh horses, while our own were jaded and worn out by long and continuous marches, the stampede, and the hard run of the morning. I traversed the length of the butte slowly with my men and joined the column where it shelved off, it having arrived just in time to see the last Qua-ha-das rapidly disappear in the hills and bushy ravines that ascend to and clearly define the plateau of the "Staked Plains" or Llano Estacado. *This was tragedy number two of Cañon Blanco.*

Slowly we turned, further pursuit at that time being useless, and sadly retraced our march back over the ground just fought over to where the body of Gregg lay just as he had fallen when shot through the head by Quanah. We hastily buried him under the shadow of the butte (Mount Blanco) at its southeast foot, with the simplest form of a soldier's funeral, no chaplain being with us, and after heavy stones had been placed over the mound to protect it from the big wolves that swarmed all over this country, without unsaddling, we went into a temporary bivouac, and awaited further developments. Pickets were thrown out to guard against surprise, and the horses were allowed to graze under strong guard.

We remained here until about 2.30 p. m., the "Tonks" in the meantime coming in and reporting a broad and fresh trail leading up from the mouth of the canon, which they said undoubtedly led to Quanah's village. Up to this time, in the excitement since the night before, I had neglected to attend to my wounded leg, but now that the nerves had somewhat relaxed, an intense pain warned me that, perhaps, it was more serious than I had supposed. It was now badly swollen and stiff, and growing more so. I called our contract doctor, A. A. Surgeon Rufus Choate, and consulted him. The boot had to be cut off. Slitting the boot leg down and removing all covering, it really presented a dreadful appearance. It was covered with clotted blood, black and blue, terribly swollen, with much laceration.

The doctor, after a hasty examination, for the trumpeters were then sounding "boots and saddles," decided that the leg was not broken, but it might be a fracture, and considered it wise to put my leg in splints, which he did, using my boot leg and what material he happened to have on hand for that purpose.

We had no ambulance or stretchers with the column, and there was no material at that place with which to construct a horse litter or a "travois," nor was there sufficient time. I mounted my horse; the command "Forward!" was given, and soon the column was moving around the base of the mountain and up the canon to take the freshly discovered trail. It was impossible for me to go back forty miles of more to Lawton's supply camp on Duck Creek. Taking charge again of the pack train and rear guard, with instructions to afford whatever assistance to Lieutenant Vernou, now in command of the dismounted men, who had lost their horses, we moved out on the trail for the Comanche village.

The Pursuit—The Qua-ha-da Village and Ruse

These men were somewhat demoralised at the prospect of following afoot over many weary miles of plain, and through canon, in search of our wily enemy, which had but a few moments before disappeared from our view on the horizon of the Staked Plains, and up the trail we were now on. A dismounted cavalry trooper is a much more demoralised man than a tired-out, straggling infantry soldier, since, from force of habit, he has learned to rely almost wholly upon the strength and brute courage of his faithful horse rather than in his own powers of endurance, thus subtracting to an important degree that factor of initiative so necessary in any soldier there in that country where our resources were so limited.

The saddles of our stampeded animals had all been concealed, or "*cached*," in some of the many small, bush-lined ravines, or "pockets," with which the country abounded. It was a hard march. Animals and men were very weary from the continuous strain of the previous forty-eight hours. By dint of hard talking, sharp commands, and even threats, accompanied by strong appeals to their pride, etc., we succeeded in getting the miscellaneous assemblage of foot-sore, chafed, blistered, mad, and disgruntled grumblers, grouchers and kickers, and the sore-backed horses and mules into camp, but it was at the expense of about every atom of our patience, strength, and nerves, and only after these "tag-ends" had all been urged and shamed into their last ounce of energy and patriotic ardour. We so informed Mackenzie that night. We bivouacked without shelter, "cross side lined" our animals, picketed the camp, and, with strong sleeping parties among the horse herds, we "turned in"—an almost exhausted command.

★★★★★★

The writer never saw this method of a "cross side line" used by any other cavalry command. It is extremely doubtful if there are many officers living today who know the full meaning of this term. The two leather hobbles are fastened, one on the nigh fore, the other on the off hind leg, well below the knee and hock, at the joint, connected by a light chain, with toggle or swivel to prevent kinking or knotting, and a ring midway the connection, through which is passed the lariat. While it shortens the grazing radius of the animal, on a thirty-foot lariat, the fulcrum of the lever operates to throw the horse upon his nose or side whenever he lunges, plunges, or jumps back, without injuring him or pulling the picket pin. When not in use it was carried with the coiled lariat on the left side of the pommel of the saddle.

★★★★★★

Mackenzie must have diligently chewed the matter over during the night (he rarely slept much anyway during an Indian campaign), regarding my plight, and the condition of these dismounted men, for early the next morning he sent for me. I was asked if I wanted to go ahead with the column, then moving out, or conduct these horseless troopers by slow and painful marches back to Duck Creek. He said, "I am told that your leg is badly injured, and the doctor has put your leg in splints. These dismounted men can go no farther with the column; they will only impede our march in pursuit. An officer will have to conduct them back, and this seems to be the only way in which you can, by taking charge of them, get good care and treatment at Lawton's camp. While it is true that I want you with me, I am looking out for your interest and safety. There is no ambulance with us to carry you should you become more disabled so that you can not march, and you had better go back. That is my advice and judgment."

"Is it an order, sir?"

"No, sir, it is not an order, but, I repeat, I am considering your comfort and safety."

"Then, sir, if it is left to me, I go forward with the command!"

He added, "Another thing—I have been told that Captain Heyl did not behave well in that action yesterday morning. I had him transferred to this regiment because of his ability, efficiency, and reported gallantry in action. What do you care to say about it? You were a close witness of his conduct."

I hesitated. At that period I could not feel like making any statement that would absolutely destroy the future reputation and permanent career of any officer who had stood sufficiently high in the estimation of Mackenzie to warrant his transfer to the Fourth Cavalry. So I quietly replied, "Well, General, if you have had him transferred on account of his previous good reputation as a gallant officer, I shall say nothing that might injure or destroy that reputation. I will merely say that under all of the circumstances of that affair, in my opinion he committed a *very grave error of judgment*, and you can draw your own conclusions!" He never took any action in the matter. I never referred to it again to him. Captain Heyl never made any statement, or spoke of it, either to Boehm or myself, and it passed into regimental "*innocuous desuetude.*" Some time later, however, a most amazing event occurred—never fully solved—which caused all of the officers of the Fourth Cavalry who had full knowledge of the two tragedies already described to sit up and almost gasp with astonishment, as will be shortly shown. In the National Cemetery of Arlington there is a memorial over Heyl's grave. On it is a full-length bronze tablet reciting most minutely the details of every event of his military career—*except that one incident.*

It is not recorded. He could never allow himself to figure or to be included in that tragedy—the death of Gregg, and my almost certain destruction in Cañon Blanco through that act. This is conclusive evidence that whatever Mackenzie, in his deliberations, decided to do or not to do, Heyl himself knew and felt what that act was, and that he could have no justification in perpetuating it in bronze at Arlington, unless he perjured his own soul or perpetrated a fraud upon the two men then living who were witnesses of that event. The writer left Mackenzie to draw his own conclusions forty-eight years ago. The reader can draw his own now in view of this omission on the bronze tablet. Many years after this affair, Captain Heyl told General H. W. Lawton, when both were Majors and Assistant Inspectors General:

> Lawton, that day was the bluest moment of my military life. I was so dazed when I faced up to that horde of yelling, rushing Indians, with almost certain death staring me in the eye, that I simply lost my head and went in to a state of blue 'funk,' and the worst of it was, I could not help it!

This Lawton frankly told the writer, with no reservations of confidential secrecy, in the winter of 1888-9, while a guest for eight months in his house in Washington during that season.

Lieutenant C. A. Vernou went back with the dismounted men. The two columns separated, and were soon lost to sight as they moved in opposite directions. Everywhere, as we advanced up the canon with its abrupt bluff faces, we saw evidences of its having been occupied by Indians, and scattered all along were many of the small "wickey-ups," still intact, put up for the use of the Indian herders, usually half-grown boys and girls. Every few miles the canon widened out into more or less broad valleys bounded by almost impassable bluffs. We also saw numerous ravines and sand hills, as well as many small herds of buffalo.

Here and there the creek (Catfish) widened out, sometimes presenting a succession of small, but beautiful, ponds or lagoons, clear as crystal, out of which swarmed immense flocks of wild ducks and curlew, and occasionally a majestic swan, whose trumpet notes sounded strange to our hunters who had rarely, if ever, seen such game. All the following day we marched steadily along, without catching even a

148

glimpse of Indians, although they were undoubtedly spying on our every movement from their secret hiding places. The stillness and utter solitude of this lovely valley was only disturbed by the constant tramp of our horses' hoofs, until late in the afternoon when our trailers suddenly discovered the long sought for village, or where it had been—for what apparently was a large buffalo lodge village had suddenly vanished.

They had "folded their tents and silently stolen away," everything indicating a hasty departure. A broad lodge-pole and stock trail showed plainly out of the village, leading up the canon. Our halt was brief, stopping only long enough to ascertain what was inside of the freshly heaped mounds of earth all about, which looked like small graves, and debris of every description. The "Tonks" laughed at this, and said it was done as a "blind" to detain us—to "*pull wool over our eyes.*" Continuing, we soon came to where the trail divided; it was confused, crossing and re-crossing in every direction, and for the first time our sharp-eyed scouts seemed "at fault." After much parleying and time lost, they concluded that the wily enemy had "doubled" on us and gone back upon the same trail.

Countermarching and moving down the open valley again, we found, much to our chagrin, that it was even so, and after marching on the "back trail" until dark we were compelled to bivouac not far from where we had first discovered the abandoned village. The following morning, soon after we were in motion, the "Tonks" signalled from the edge of the bluff on the plains above us that they had " picked up" the lost trail leading over the seemingly impassable barrier.

There was a long delay in scaling with horses the steep ascent, but, at length, after toiling over high, rocky bluffs and floundering around in the "breaks" and "arroyos," all were over and out of the canon upon what appeared to be a vast, almost illimitable expanse of prairie. As far as the eye could reach, not a bush or tree, a twig or stone, not an object of any kind or a living thing, was in sight. It stretched out before us—one uninterrupted plain, only to be compared to the ocean in its vastness.

This was the beginning of the "Staked Plains," or "*Llano Estacdo,*" which we had been seeking, and over which we would now be compelled to trail Quanah's moving village.

It was October 12, and a cold, overcast, gray morning. Our elevation was over three thousand feet. The air grew sharp and penetrating. We were all clothed for a summer campaign on the low plains of

Texas. A severe "norther," peculiar to Texas at this season of the year, was beginning to strike us upon this barren waste, which, by contrast with the warm, bright sunshine of the previous day in the sheltered *cañon*, chilled us to the very marrow.

A short, dry, buffalo grass grew upon this immense plateau, over which our keenest-eyed "Tonk" trailers, now dismounted, were endeavouring to follow the slightest "signs." We moved along cautiously, marching slowly until about noon. Fresh signs of the Indian ponies in the large "*caviard*," or herd of horses which the enemy was driving, were the only indications of the course to be taken. Lodge poles on the dry, stiff stubble gave no trail.

Suddenly, however, the trail turned, and again went over the bluff into the *cañon*. This was unexpected; but, dismounting again, we led out "by file," slipping and sliding down the dangerous descent, until all were once more at the bottom, and again there was a confused lot of fresh trails—some leading up, others down, while still others led straight across the valley, directly at right angles.

Again, in our supreme disgust, we felt that we had been completely foiled. The "Tonks" scattered and rode rapidly all over the valley, and before the rear of the column had got fairly down into the *cañon* and closed up, they were waving us on. It had been found going out again over the bluff, this time, however, on the opposite side of the *cañon*. We were soon ascending for the second time that day the steep, precipitous sides of the rocky barriers. It was a singularly sharp trick, even for Indians, done, of course, to blind us and to gain time in moving their families of women and children as far as possible out of our reach. Without our own Indian scouts to beat the Comanches at their own native shrewdness, we would have undoubtedly lost the trail and hopelessly abandoned the task.

But now we found ourselves on a very broad and distinct lodge-pole and stock trail, leading in but one direction, and that to the west and northwest. We carefully estimated that they had from two to three thousand head of stock, and that the entire "outfit" was moving along with them, with all the plunder incident to a stampeding village. Could we overtake it, its capture was almost certain.

THE "NORTHER"—"HOT TRAIL"—NIGHT ATTACK—A BITTER STORM

The bitter cold increased, and on this high tableland, with no shelter, the wind from the northwest swept through our thin uniforms.

Many had no overcoats or gloves, and the suffering grew intense. But we consoled ourselves with the though that if Indians with their women and children could endure it, we certainly must.

The trail grew fresher and "warmer." We now stretched out and moved more rapidly. We crossed numerous "*carreta*," or cart trails, made by the Mexicans in trading with the Comanches. They were well defined and headed toward the Pecos River. As we "rose" or "lifted" a slight ridge in the almost level prairie, we observed, in the far distance, moving figures, silhouetted against the sky line, as of mounted men galloping along the horizon, here as distinct as the sea line that limits the boundless ocean. First, two or three, then a dozen or more, until finally, on both sides of our now swiftly speeding column, there seemed to be hundreds. The "Tonks" said they were the Comanches, and we knew ourselves that at last we were on the right track!

We now had them! Or, at least, we thought we did. Everybody was elated. The writer had not thought of his smashed leg, with its pain and uncomfortable splinter, for hours, so keen had become the excitement of this most absorbing chase, as the Comanches began to swarm on the right and left of the trail, like angry bees, circling here and there, in an effort to divert us from their women and children. Every preparation was made for a fight, for we firmly believed that, failing to throw us off the lodge-pole trail of their fleeing village, the red scoundrels had gathered all of their warriors for a determined resistance and a supreme effort should we overtake their families. We knew that it is then that an Indian will fight with all the ferocity of a wild animal, blind to everything except the preservation of his squaws and *papooses*.

Their efforts were therefore now all concentrated in an endeavour to throw us off the lodge-pole trail in order to gain time for the squaws. But Mackenzie determined, upon the advice of the Ton-ka-way chief and our best Indian campaigners, to disregard this wily bait, and keep steadily on, knowing that we must now be very close to them or the Qua-ha-das would not make such warlike demonstrations in the face of our superior force. We also fully realised that by keeping after the lodges, the warriors would soon close in and fight to the last Indian for the rescue of the ones they held most dear. Our object was, therefore, twofold. We could secure the ponies later.

The Qua-ha-das now began to get excited when it was found that we did not chase out after them, and, as we hoped, they began to swarm in toward us. The command was closed up in columns of fours, the men "counted off" again, and were directed to fill their blouse pockets with both carbine and pistol ammunition, of which we had taken along an ample supply. Cautionary commands were given for squadron and platoon formation, deployment to the front, right, and left, fighting on foot, etc. The pack mules, always a source of anxiety in the emergency of a battle, so far away from our base (nearly 100 miles), as they carried all of our precious food in this far-off wild, were closed in and placed in herd formation; a squadron was detached to surround them and guard them from stampede while still rapidly in motion—a, sort of hollow square. A strong line of mounted skirmishers were thrown out to the front while flankers rode far out on the sides of the now threatening Comanches.

The Ton-ka-ways—McCord, the head chief; Simoon, "One-armed Charlie," Jesse, Lincoln, Grant, "Old Henry," Anderson, Job, William, Buffalo (the "Beau Brummel" of the "Tonks"), Black Bill, John Guy, and many others whose names can not now be recalled—slipped from their riding animals, caught up, from their pony herd being driven on the flank, their favourite war ponies, until then unused, stripped all superfluous loads from their saddles, and quickly began, in their rude, inartistic way, to paint and adorn their persons for the coming battle, which we now surely considered was impending. A small piece of looking glass, a puddle of saliva in the hollow of the hand, much red, green, yellow, and black paint (ochre), quickly applied in reeking daubs. The cream, clay-bank, dim or white pony was plentifully striped. Head dresses, horns, much red flannel, and bright-coloured feathers completed the "Tonk" ensemble.

The whole operation did not exceed five minutes, but sufficiently long to excite the laughter of the entire column of brave troopers even at that critical moment, when all were expecting a battle. Our gallant allies then pranced alongside the column, posturing, moving their heads from side to side, brandishing their carbines, and evidently feeling all the pride of conquering monarchs, so self-conscious were they of the dignity which all this display of paint, feathers, *gewgaws*, etc., gave them.

The afternoon was now on the wane. We began to see ahead of us, although indistinctly, the dark, moving mass of the fleeing village. The Comanches still swarmed about our flanks. We came upon their fires, still burning, which they had hastily abandoned upon our approach. Then we struck a large lagoon of fresh water in a depression or "sink" in the prairie, where we hastily watered. Pushing rapidly on, we came upon lodge-poles scattered in large numbers on the trail in their sudden flight, also many iron and stone hammers, mortars, pestles, and all sorts of strange tools of the rudest description.

Puppy dogs of the Indian half-wolf breed had been dropped by the squaws. The men picked up several and carried them on the pommels of their saddles. Great chunks of mulberry wood, and mesquite roots, used for cooking purposes when crossing this treeless desert, were also to be seen all along, and occasionally—what they never throw away unless hard pressed—the dried buffalo skins of their "*tepee*" or lodges. The chase had now grown "hot." The dark cloud of fleeing Indians loomed up closer. Still the Qua-ha-das dashed and circled about watching for a chance or vulnerable point for attack in our compact fighting column. Several times we thought that they were bunching for a charge, and our skirmishers and flankers grew more alert and drew in closer.

It grew darker and colder. The wind whistled. The air grew thicker and more hazy, and soon a cold rain, mingled with snow and sleet, began to drive into our faces, through our bodies, and into the very marrow. This was the supreme moment—a crisis. This was the time to have speeded up, made a sharp dash by a part of our command among the huddled, frightened, and demoralized women and children guarded for the most part only by old men and boys, while the other and larger half could have engaged and easily defeated the warriors. Nothing worse could have happened than a few men killed or wounded, but we surely would have got the entire "outfit," stock, women and children with all of their plunder, and made a "clean sweep up." Everybody was looking for Mackenzie to give the order to "Trot!" "Gallop!!" and "Charge!!!" It never came.

This time he leaned, it seemed, on the side of extreme caution, and lost, what the writer believed at the moment, the best opportunity the Fourth Cavalry ever had for capturing practically Quanah's entire village and "lay-out." Or, it may be (for we never asked him the reason) that he was guided by feelings of humanity, and the big risk which we all ran, so far away from our supply camp, had our losses been heavy in a fight with a band that had always been noted for its bravery and hard-fighting qualities. Personally, it is the writer's belief that the snow and rain squall, driven by a howling northwest gale, was the determining factor that influenced, to a greater extent than any other, Mackenzie's judgment at that moment. Let us see what occurred.

The village, which seemed but a mile or more away, was at once shut from our view, and to our utter dismay the inky blackness of night was instantly upon us. It seemed as though a great black curtain or pall had suddenly dropped in front of our eyes, shutting off every object. We could hardly distinguish forms about us even a foot or two away. Had the trot and gallop been taken half an hour earlier, there is little doubt that we would have captured the entire village and pony herd, but the menacing attitude of the warriors just as the storm was about to strike us, partly, if not wholly, diverted the general from his true objective.

The horses were very thin and much worn. We had no fresh mounts to draw from as the Indians possessed. The men were terribly fagged and tired; but the *moral, fighting spirit,* and *confidence was intact,* and all they needed at that moment was the word to "turn loose" and finish those Indians then and there—what they had come for, marched so many weary miles for, and sacrificed so much to accomplish.

Perhaps Mackenzie's judgment and wisdom was best, and we might have met with a calamity or dire disaster. "*Quien Sabe!*" But, looking back through that long *vista* of years it seems improbable, almost impossible, that we would not have achieved a complete success had we been given the command at the crucial moment before that black curtain fell and forever shut out the fleeing village and the "norther" that saved them. In discussing this campaign later, it was with the keenest regret and bitter disappointment that the driving of this half-breed Qua-ha-da into the Fort Sill reservation to become, later, a "good Indian" could not have been accomplished then by the Fourth Cavalry, instead of its being delayed until more than three years from that date, and then by converging columns operating in four different directions.

We were at once dismounted. Mackenzie seemed to be deliberating whether further pursuit was practicable, when the storm, which had been gathering all day and had already begun, burst upon us with renewed fury, cutting man and beast to the very vitals. It raged, sleeting and raining alternately, freezing as it fell and coating us with ice, which soon stiffened our clothes, and, as we could not see an arm's length before us, all hope of striking the trail was out of the question. The wind increased to a gale, and whistled and moaned incessantly. We formed a large ring, or defensive circle, with a radius of about one hundred and fifty yards, with the pack mules in the centre. The men held their horses.

While in this position, and awaiting further developments, a shot, then several, followed by a loud volley, greeted us, and the entire band of Comanches dashed almost over our close circle and instantly swept off into the impenetrable darkness that enveloped us, their taunting whoops and shrill yells sounding strangely to our gallant troopers as though to mock them in their helplessness. The Qua-ha-das had evidently seen the command halt before the storm broke upon us. The gloom of night had suddenly shut us from their view, and riding at breakneck speed in the direction where they had last seen us, to ascertain just our position, if possible, had accidentally stumbled upon us. All crouched down; the volley was returned; nobody was hurt, and the intense excitement this episode furnished us was soon over. Other difficulties confronted us.

A squadron under Captain Wirt Davis was hastily pushed out after their retreating forms, guided only by sound, and for a few moments the lurid flashes and loud banging of our skirmishers, rising high above the howling storm, indicated quite a lively fight, but, as the Indians fled, it soon ceased, and our men came in, having been lost at a distance of less than five hundred yards, and only guided back to the circle by a peculiar yell, rarely used by Indians except when lost, and now made by our scouts accompanying it and answered by those scouts who had been left inside the circle.

Every precaution was now made to shield men and horses from the piercing cold and the fury of the storm. Enormous hail stones had began to fall, pelting the animals so that they could only be held with the greatest difficulty, and bruising the men's bodies. "Tarpaulins" (canvas) were dragged from the mule packs; robes and blankets were fished out in the darkness and spread inside the circle, where they would do the most good, and keep all from perishing, and, half lying and squatting beneath these improvised shelters, we wore out the livelong night, one long remembered by every officer and man in that gallant command of the Fourth Cavalry.

Pack mules and horses trampled, in their fright, near our heads and feet, and their continued moving and stamping, snorting, and wee-haw-ing made sleep out of the question among the men, who took turns by detail in holding on to the suffering animals. It was a bare existence, with nothing to eat since morning, and a bitter night to wear out. Mackenzie had no overcoat, and somebody wrapped his shivering form in a buffalo robe. Several wounds received during the Civil War had disabled and rendered him incapable of enduring such dreadful exposure.

It was with many misgivings that we thrust our heads out from under the close, heavy, lead-coloured (painted) "paulins" in the sharp morning air. A beautiful day was ushered in. The frightful storm had spent itself, and was giving place to genial warmth and balmy sunshine. Without breakfast, we broke our "charmed circle," and, by early light, were soon on the trail, still plain and leading in the same general direction. There was little or no enthusiasm, however. The spirits of the column "flagged," for no living creature was in sight on that vast expanse. We knew, or felt, that the village had been moving all night, and it would prove a hopeless, stem chase—a long march, fruitless of results.

Soon a spy or two occasionally showed themselves on the horizon to watch our movements. A little later that wonderful phenomenon of the mirage was perfectly shown—

Clear shining through the swimming air,
Across a stretch of summer skies.

THE RETURN MARCH—DEAD COMANCHES—MACKENZIE WOUNDED—TRAGEDY NUMBER THREE

Mackenzie soon found from our maps that in a direct west course the Pecos River was far away. The nearest post (Fort Sumner) was in New Mexico. The animals were now suffering for water, and some were beginning to show clearly signs of giving out. Our "chow" or rations were growing slim. The Comanches, by that lucky storm—for them—still had a night's march ahead of us, so he prudently, but most reluctantly, turned back. There was nothing to cook our food with but buffalo chips (*bois de vache*), and with scarcely water enough to wet our lips. We made a dry camp at our impromptu bivouac of the night before; the next day, in a sort of melancholy procession, reaching the lagoon, where it was decided to fill up with fresh rain water, and rest the command.

The men on this day's march had picked up hundreds of smooth, well-worn cedar lodge-poles which the Comanches had dropped in their headlong flight, to be used for fuel at our bivouac supper. It was a most singular sight to see a long column of five hundred troopers, each with two or three fourteen-foot poles raised high in air over their shoulders. Mackenzie, who, at the head of the column, when his attention was first called to it, suspecting a joke, or that they were being carried along as relics, was about to seriously order them to be thrown away, when somebody suggested their possible utility for fuel instead of buffalo chips, which scented our bacon and coffee. They re-

156

minded one of a travelling circus, rather than a well drilled, disciplined body of cavalry.

The writer had been riding all this time with his battered leg in splints and closely bandaged. Upon Dr. Choate's inspection this day, after removing the bandages, it was found that it was not only not broken or even fractured, but was terribly bruised, and the flesh badly crushed and frightfully lacerated. Bathing it freely in the soft water of the lagoon, carefully cleansing and re-bandaging it.

I experienced little stiffness or pain. This lagoon we found to be full of countless numbers of curlew and many white swan, but none were killed.

Taking up the old route again the next day, there was absolutely nothing to relieve the voiceless march, so singular had become the effect of this mysterious silence of the Staked Plains upon the men. We leisurely dropped down again into Cañon Blanco, drinking in the quiet solitude and natural beauties of this Indian paradise. The "Tonks" were leading. The men and horses, who had been resting all day, now half asleep, were suddenly startled by the cry of "Indians! Indians!!" which brought every trooper erect in his saddle. All was soon organized activity. A healthy excitement ran through the bronzed column. Striking a trot, lope and gallop, all carefully closed up, and horses well in hand, we soon saw our advance scouts running at breakneck speed toward some small ravines, followed by the leading troop.

The excitement grew intense. Two Comanches had been discovered following our old trail up the canon, dismounted and leading their ponies. When discovered by our "Tonks" they abandoned their animals and ran into some bushy ravines, our scouts closely pursuing. As soon as we arrived, all entrances were closed. The "Tonks" went up over the bluff, thus cutting off their escape in that direction. Mackenzie directed the leading troop to open fire, while our Indians, by their fire from above, tried to drive them out into our command. The Comanches were game. They would not come out. Mackenzie ordered Boehm to take fifteen dismounted men and drive them out. There were several openings into the ravines. Boehm divided his men, and worked several paths. Mackenzie, becoming impatient, dismounted and got in behind Boehm to direct him, the two Comanches firing all the time.

Just then something happened. A sharp swish, a thud, and a spiked arrow buried itself in the upper, fleshy part of Mackenzie's leg. He hurried back to the rear and had the spike cut out and the wound dressed. Soon all firing ceased, and we knew that the two Comanches were dead. The "Tonks" came down from their high perches on the bluff overhead, where they had given the entire command one of the finest circus acts (with several rings) of lofty tumbling, somersaults, vaulting, standing on their heads, etc., it had ever been our good fortune to see in an Indian country, and, upon parting the bushes, found both Qua-ha-das. One was shot several times through the body, the other through the head. One had been shot in the hand while firing his pistol. The bullet had shattered the pistol butt. A bloody bow-string showed that he had used his bow later. With the strength necessary to draw the string, it must have proved very painful, and a clear test of the Indian's wonderful courage, tenacity, and stoical nature under certain circumstances. One of our men, a farrier of Troop "H," had been shot through the bowels, and, in turning, was shot in the hand. This *was the third tragedy of Cañon Blanco.*

As it was getting late, we bivouacked near the spot. The "Tonks" entered the ravine, shot a few bullets into the Comanches' bodies, as was their custom, scalped them, ears and all, and then cut a small piece of skin from each breast, for good luck, or rather "good medicine"— such was the peculiar superstition of the Indian. This, dried in the sun, and placed in a bag, or attached to a string and worn next to the person of the warrior, acts as a safe guard against danger or sickness in any form. It was their "medicine" or "mascot." At night Dr. Rufus Choate, Lieutenant Wentz C. Miller, and two negro boys, field cooks, went up the ravine, decapitated the dead Qua-ha-das, and placing the heads in some gunny sacks, brought them back to be boiled out for future scientific knowledge.

THE BOILING HEADS—AND WOUNDED FARRIER

Shortly after midnight we heard the wolves, which had sniffed the flesh from afar in the keen night air, fighting, snarling, and howling like incarnate fiends over this horrible human feast.

A barbarous and tragical end to a barbarous band, who, while mutilating and heaping red-hot coals upon the nude forms of their writhing victims (as the writer had seen the preceding May at the massacre on Salt Creek prairie) in the peaceful settlements of Texas, dining their numerous blood-thirsty raids, had danced for joy at the savage torture inflicted.

Before starting the next morning, a horse litter had to be constructed upon which to carry our wounded man. The poles were lashed to the pack saddles of two mules travelling tandem. Cross-pieces were lashed to them in rear of the croup of one mule and in front of the breast of the other. A head covering was made of a framework of boughs, over which a blanket or shelter tent was thrown. He was thus carried one hundred miles, and by the personal nursing and unremitting attention of our faithful and efficient doctor, Rufus Choate, he lived, although his bowels had been perforated.

On this day we had but just gone into camp, and were about to eat our dinner, when Miller shouted to Major Mauck and myself, from a short distance up the canon, "Come up, we have something good!"

"What is it?"

Miller replied, "Soup!"

We had observed two camp kettles strung on a pole over the fire. Seizing our cups, never suspecting a joke, we reached the spot. When to our horror we saw the two Comanche scalped heads, with the stripes of paint still on their faces, and with eyes partly opened, bobbing up and down, and rising above the mess kettles, mingled with the bubbling, bloody broth. It was a gruesome spectacle.

★★★★★★

One of these skulls proved to be of no value, as it had a bullet hole in it. The other the writer saw in October, 1885, in the Smithsonian Institute. Later he saw it in the National Museum to which it had been transferred. In 1890, he saw it again in the Medical Museum, where it had again been transferred. It bore the following inscription: "Skull of Indian chief, Texas. W. R. Choate" (nephew of Dr. Rufus Choate). Smithsonian No. 42911; National Museum No. 3051. It was in the southeast corner of the gallery among the "Unknown Indian Skulls." In 1912, it had been again transferred to the Ethnological Bureau of the New National Museum. It has travelled some. It is hard to say when or where this Qua-ha-da Comanche skull will find its last resting place. As the word Qua-ha-da signifies "Wanderer" he may, like Tennyson's "Brook," "go on forever."

★★★★★★

With hands on our stomachs, we fled, directing "Bob," our valuable sable cook to transfer our dinner and all of our personal belongings farther down the canon, out of sight and reach of our esteemed ethnological head-hunters and skull boilers. A more sickening sight it would be difficult to conceive of. We were no longer hungry that night.

There was a night alarm about midnight. Some Indians who had followed our trail tried to creep by our pickets, which, as officer-of-the-day, the writer had charge of, and stampede our horses. They were soon driven off with the assistance of "F" troop (Wirt Davis). We moved slowly down the canon, the animals getting weaker and weaker. Lieutenant Warrington was sent in to Lawton's camp on Duck Creek to direct him (Lawton) to move his train and meet us at the Fresh Fork. Here we camped near the scene of our tragedy of October 10. Many of our hardships for the time being were forgotten in complete rest, good food, and calmness of mind and body.

We visited the scene of our action. Armfulls of arrows were brought in, and all shuddered who had participated in the narrow escape, and loudly praised the prompt action and bravery of our noble, gallant "Peter" Boehm and the conduct of our faithful friends and rescuers, the Ton-ka-way scout allies. Upon going to Gregg's grave, it was found the earth had been dug up by wolves so that it was nearly uncovered. The region was scoured for larger stones with which to cover and anchor it down.

The wounded farrier of Troop "D" who had been shot through the bowels, and whom we had brought down the *cañon* on the horse litter, was very low. The ball had passed completely through him, cutting the intestines, which, with the faecal matter, exuded from the hole in his back. Gas was also being emitted from the wound. No one believed he could recover. Our efficient, tireless, ever-persevering A. A. Surgeon, Dr. Rufus Choate, never left him for a moment. He not only devoted his professional skill to saving the man's life, but, as a nurse, his tireless care and attention, notwithstanding the long period of jolting over very rough ground, placed him on the road to a quick recovery and permanent cure. He could only retain liquid food, nourishment taking place by absorption. It was Dr. Choate's object, therefore, to afford this with the least possible strain upon his physical and nervous system. Buffalo meat, devoid of all fat or gristle, was converted into a strong beef tea by quick methods. Liebig's condensed beef was added to this hot "*bouillon*," and poured into him as often as possible, at least without nauseating.

His wound thus closed, while his strength was conserved, and in this manner his life was saved. It was one of the most marvellous recoveries—due to perseverance, skill, and devotion to duty by an unselfish medical officer—known to us who had seen many deaths from culpable neglect both during the Civil War and afterwards. Two years later the writer saw this man, who had been discharged, working in the Quartermasters Corral at San Antonio, Texas.

"Camp Misery"—The Doctor's Practical Joke on Mackenzie

Several horses died here. Others, too weak to move, had to be shot, and still more were broken down. Lawton arrived with forage and rations for the horses and men. Mackenzie, feeling confident that Quanah, finding that on account of the storm we had abandoned further pursuit, would turn back from the Pecos River and move to one of their old, well-known haunts on Pease River, determined to send a part of the command in further search of him, taking command himself, sending all disabled, dismounted men, and weak, sick animals into Duck Creek. On October 24 the two commands separated. After reaching Duck Creek, Mackenzie's wound proved too painful and he was compelled to come in, and joined us on the 29th.

From this camp we moved to another, in a frightful storm of rain and hail. The "pull" through the sand and "shin oak" killed off more animals. The general was irritable, irascible, mean and "ornery." Nobody seemed to want to go near him even for sociability. Our esteemed A. A. Surgeon, Dr. Gregory, who had remained with the infantry at the supply camp, incubated a scheme or practical joke, however, which he confided to Lawton and the rest of us, by which he was going to "put one over" on the "old man." He would go and tell him that it was necessary for the preservation of his life for him to keep quiet and calm, etc. Otherwise he would be compelled to *amputate his leg*. He went to Mackenzie's tent. We watched him disappear. Shortly after we saw the doctor shoot out of the tent and make for his own, his face a deep scarlet.

We could only guess at the result. We ascertained later, however, from him that with the conscious importance of professional skill, he took off the bandages, examined the wound, and with the utmost gravity told General Mackenzie that it was very much inflamed, and unless he controlled his irritability, he would be compelled to amputate the limb. He got as far as amputate when the general seized a crutch or big cane, and making for the doctor caused him to jump out from under the tent flap to save his own head from amputation. He did not repeat that advice. The joke fell flat.

From this camp the writer was directed to take command of all the dismounted and disabled men, sore-backed horses and mules, all

161

the "tag ends," and proceed to Cottonwood Springs on the Double Mountain Fork, put them in camp and await the return of Major Mauck with his column from Pease River, while Lawton was ordered to take the supply train into Fort Griffin, load with half forage of com, and return to our camp. This was carried out. The writer spent a lonely five days in the new camp. Thousands of buffalo darkened the prairie about us.

BESIEGED BY WOLVES—A DOSE OF STRYCHNINE

Frequently on the march we came suddenly upon many packs of wolves of from eight to ten in number, dashing ahead of the column through the numerous breaks which cut our trail. They were hanging on the outskirts of the immense herds, waiting patiently for some young calf, or sick, or wounded buffalo left to die, which they soon feasted on. Many a bleached skull remote from the herds attested the untiring patience of these savage hangers-on to the interests of their ever-craving appetites. It was not so easy, however, to get the calves at all times, for the cow buffalo, unaided, was no weak fighter and defender of her young, and, when aided, as was generally the case, by a circle of young bulls, the cowardly sneak thieves were frequently tossed and trampled out of all shape. It was rarely the case, therefore, that a pack of wolves would go into a buffalo herd and made a desperate fight for a calf or a distressed cow. It was only when the helpless animals were abandoned that the wolves banqueted.

We gathered all the disabled animals and sick and wounded men, made a small enclosure, or breastwork, on three sides of a square, out of boxes, barrels, bags filled with earth, etc., pitched our tents, placed everything inside and prepared for a defensive stay—a period of "watchful waiting"—until the return of the Pease River column.

We had every reason to believe that the hostiles, eluding the column sent there, might seek and follow our trail with a large body; if so, our little handful of men would, it was feared, have made a feeble resistance if attacked. At night the wolves came out of the "bottoms" and numerous coulees, arroyos, and ravines, in countless numbers and besieged this camp. The sick and wounded became very nervous, for in their boldness the ravenous animals advanced to within a few feet of our tents in their eagerness for the meat which we had hung all about us in large quantities for immediate use, besides the carcasses scattered here and there had attracted their scent, and in the glare of the campfire their long, white teeth could be distinctly seen, as they

162

tumbled, fought, and howled over their canine feast.

It came as an unpleasant episode in our enforced imprisonment. No such number of wolves had ever been seen or heard by us in that country. If some came nearer than others, we charged them with large fire brands, throwing them in their midst, whereupon the brutes scattered in every direction. They dreaded fire. About the third or fourth night, however, during which it had been impossible to sleep, their number seemed to increase and double up. They became bolder than ever, for now, outside the camp, they had but a few bones to quarrel over, having picked them white, while our fresh meat was still a very great temptation. The little A. A. Surgeon, Dr. Culver, who had been with the infantry column, and Lieutenant Speer of the Eleventh Infantry, became perceptibly nervous, if not actually alarmed. We played cards to divert our minds, but still the wolves gathered and crowded in upon us. We did not dare to open a rifle fire upon them for fear our shots might attract any Indian scouts that might, perhaps, be lurking about our trail.

The doctor had a quantity of strychnine among his medical stores, and, at the suggestion of the writer, we used it all in poisoning a quantity of meat and scattering it here and there. We soon had the satisfaction of hearing their blood-curdling yells and howls while fighting for the poison. When morning came, we found them stretched out in every direction; some were dead, others were *wanting to die,* being in their last agonies after having gone to the stream to "water up," where we found their already bloated bodies. It was only a temporary cessation of hostilities. On the last night, not daring to sacrifice any more of our meat, which we might need, for we had no serviceable horses with which to run the buffalo, still in large numbers all about us, we tried the experiment of poisoning some of the wolf meat. They again congregated by thousands, coming out of the river bottom at dusk and remaining until the first streak of dawn. They sat upon the bluffs, gathered about the carcases, and again set up noises hideous enough to cause the hair to stand upon end, but they would not touch the meat.

They will not banquet upon their own kind unless driven to it by desperation, no matter how much the meat might be disguised. This lobo fraternity had been pretty well fed up. Again we could get no sleep, and once more resorted to firebrands. If one could control their nerves, the tumbling and stampeding of this vast throng would have been most laughable. But their terrifying yells had somewhat the same effect upon the doctor and Lieutenant Speer as the Germans in their campaign of frightfulness in the world's war. *The more noise, the greater the effect.* The writer had heard this noisy yelling in many battles of the Civil War. Thus we spent five days and nights in this wolf-besieged camp, with nothing to do, and nothing to see but that vast expanse of solitude and wilderness, the horizon of which was a constant mirage, except the immense buffalo herds which we could no longer reach except by still-hunting.

THE MARCH IN—SNOW, SLEET, ABANDONED ANIMALS—"HOME AGAIN!"

On November 6, the command from Pease River under Major Mauck arrived in the midst of a dense, driving snow storm and "norther," it having snowed the night before to the depth of five inches and grown colder, and many animals had died at the picket line, their backs crusted with snow and ice. Many of his command were riding pack mules. They had been unsuccessful in their search for the Comanches. The animals, many of them, were mere shadows. They needed some corn for feed and fuel so that we might save those that remained and get them in by short and slow marches. Lawton rolled in the next morning (8th) with his corn train. Both outfits had had a rough time. We commenced to feed full forage. The poor brutes could hardly stand up. With great caution, and amidst intense cold and much suffering among men and animals, we made our may in across California and Paint Creeks and the Clear Fork of the Brazos, and slowly into Fort Griffin, which we reached on November 12, singing the same old song with which we had started more than a month before: "Come home, John, don't stay long; come home soon to your own Mary Ann!"

The writer left thirty wolf skins under five inches of snow in that wolf camp on the Double Mountain Fork—enough to make eight large, fine robes—which he never saw again.

On the night of the 13th the "Tonks" gave us a scalp dance in their village on the flat below the post. They had divided the two scalps into 8 equal parts. We did not stay long. It proved to be too warm in their small "*tepees*," and too "smelly," as they had stripped off in the dance down to their breech clouts, and later, when they discarded them, *was the time when we departed.*

On the 17th we were slowly marching across Salt Creek prairie toward Fort Richardson; when about halfway across, near the scene of the massacre in May, a storm of rain and sleet, which had been brewing all day, broke upon us. It blew a gale and toward night had changed to a driving sleet, hail, and snow storm, compelling us to go into camp. The men were much exposed all night trying to save the animals from perishing by using their saddle blankets for covers. Many died, however, during the night, and more men were mounted on the pack mules. Major Mauck, who was in command, decided, if we were to save the remainder, we must make a desperate effort to negotiate the remaining twenty miles, and that without delay.

Breaking camp early, therefore, in the midst of the raging storm, the snow from six to eight inches deep, we "led out," the men dismounted, and the entire command floundered and staggered into the protection of the post-oak timber near Rock Station, fourteen miles from Fort Richardson, where we were somewhat sheltered from the pitiless hail and sleet which cut our faces like glass, and, after a short halt, pushed on, arriving at the post at three p. m., tired out, cold, hungry, and dirty. We had at last arrived "home," for that was what it seemed to us, after most of the regiment had been in the field since May 1. All were delighted to greet their wanderers, and, like all soldiers' hardships and sacrifices, they were all soon forgotten in hot baths, change of clothing, good grub, complete rest, and the warm congratulations of our friends and the love of anxious, devoted wives and families.

MACKENZIE'S AMAZING REPORT—THE FOURTH CAVALRY'S VERDICT

Owing to the writer's hesitation and unwillingness to characterize Heyl's conduct, place it in its proper light, or to reflect in any way upon his conduct as an officer, because of Mackenzie's strongly avowed personal liking and attachment for him, together with the statement he made to me on the morning of October 11 in Cañon Blanco when about to send back the dismounted men to Duck Creek, as to his reasons for desiring Heyl's transfer from the Ninth to the Fourth Cavalry, and my sudden resolve, in view of such frank reasons, to say or do nothing to blast that officer's reputation among his brother officers in the regiment, or at that time in the army, a most amazing event occurred which, in its far-reaching effects, caused the officers of the Fourth Cavalry, who had full knowledge of the two tragedies already described to sit up and almost gasp with astonishment.

Mackenzie made a report! The reaction which followed such a report is difficult to contemplate or clearly analyze even after the lapse of nearly half a century. They were simply confounded. It was then and will always be most difficult to explain, except upon the fact, which developed later, that he was even at that period, already showing unmistakable indications of dementia or mental aberration.

Mackenzie came in from that campaign a sick and very much disappointed man. Circumstances, entirely beyond his control, worked against his entire success, as he had so optimistically hoped for. He was, therefore, incapable, or in no condition, to make a clear, concise, and dispassionate report of this affair in the Texas Panhandle. This is clearly shown, not only by his inaccurate statements, some of the days of movement even being wrong, but it is a mere skeleton. By this report it will be seen that no mention whatever had been made either of Boehm's generous and gallant act or of the writer and his almost fatal injury. *We were both absolutely ignored.*

It will also be observed that he does not even report himself as wounded, but that he returned "on account of sickness." The officers were all amazed that he made no such mention, when it was so well known, even among the men, that Heyl and Hemphill figured only in a most unfortunate incident, since no orders were given by either of them at any time, except his (Heyl's) order to "mount" and "run out." Boehm and myself, besides the few men with us, were the only witnesses of that act, and had a full report been called from either of us, his (Heyl's) hopes would have been blasted forever. The writer saw Boehm and his Ton-ka-way Indian scouts, with other men whom he had gathered in his gallant run to my rescue, driving Heyl and his panic-stricken men back to our line at the point of his (Boehm's) carbine.

Mackenzie's report follows. In no sense does it cover the scope or period of our active operations, and but few, if any, of the important, vital details or recurring incidents of the campaign, and is otherwise incomplete in every respect as well as badly misleading. As a report it was absolutely valueless. It could not have been taken from any note book, itinerary, diary or memorandum of any kind, because the initial dates are wrong. It shows an *absolute lapse of memory.*

Headquarters,
Fort Richardson, Texas, November 17, 1871.
The Assistant Adjutant General,
Department of Texas.
Sir:
I have the honour to state that I reached this post on the 8th

instant, having been obliged to leave the command on the 28th of September (?), *en route* to the head of Pease River, on account of sickness.

A part of the command had a skirmish with the Indians on the 11th of September (?) (Note—We left Camp Cooper October 3) near the Freshwater Fork of the Brazos River, in which one soldier was killed, the loss of the Indians, if any, not being known. The Indians were followed until the 14th, when the trail was left at a point about forty miles west of the Freshwater Fork of the Brazos, and supposed by me to be about eighty miles east of Fort Sumner, New Mexico. Returning, two Indians were killed near the Fresh Fork of the Brazos, one soldier was wounded. A very bad stampede was effected by the Indians on the hills near our camp—firing, etc. This took place on the night of the 10th(?), and by it sixty-five horses were lost. This interfered very much with subsequent movements. A full report with map and itinerary will be sent as soon as the command returns.

I have the honour to be.

Very respectfully, your obedient servant,

(Signed Ranald S. Mackenzie,
Colonel Fourth U. S. Cavalry.

Official copy.

(Signed) H. Clay Wood,
Assistant Adjutant General.

No further report could ever be found at Headquarters, Department of Texas.

Headquarters,
Fort Richardson, Texas, February 5, 1872.

The Assistant Adjutant General,
    Department of Texas,
    San Antonio, Texas.

Sir:

I have the honour to transmit herewith maps of two scouts under my direction during the past year, one to the headwaters of the North Fork of the Red River, and one to the head of the Freshwater Fork of the Brazos.

Very respectfully, your obedient servant,

(Signed) R. S. Mackenzie,
Colonel Fourth Cavalry, Commanding Post.

Itinerary of scout of Companies A, B, D, F, G, H, K, and L, of the Fourth Cavalry, and Companies F and I, Eleventh Infantry; Colonel Ranald S. Mackenzie, Fourth Cavalry, commanding:

From October 3 to October 10, 1871, marched (west by northwest) one hundred and forty-six miles, camped on Freshwater Fork of the Brazos.

October 11, 1871, about 1 a. m., Indians attacked the camp. The horses were frightened and sixty-six stampeded. At daylight the command was ordered to saddle up. Shortly afterwards, a small party of Indians were seen off on the hills, when Captain Heyl with a small portion of Company K, and Lieutenant Hemphill with a detachment of Company G, gave chase. After running the Indians for two or three miles they came upon a very large party of them; had a skirmish in which one man of Company G was killed.

The command chased the Indians about eight miles, but could not get near enough to engage them. The Indians scattered and went off in small parties. Captain Heyl and Lieutenant Hemphill together had about fifteen men. Found large Indian trail and marched on it north by northwest fifteen miles, and camped on some ponds on the Freshwater Fork of the Brazos. October 12, 1871, marched north by northwest and camped on the river. October 13, 1871, marched twenty-one miles west by north, and camped on Staked Plains.

Saw several parties of Indians, but could not get near them. Several attempts were made to overtake them. About seven p. m. one of the pickets reported a large body of Indians preparing to charge the camp, when two or three companies were ordered out to meet them. Upon arriving at the ground where the Indians were seen, it was quite dark. The Indians fired several pistol shots and then went off. Nothing more was seen of them. October 14, 1871, marched eighteen miles (west); found Indian trail so scattered that it was impossible to follow it farther. The command turned around and marched twelve miles east.

October 15 and 16, 1871, marched thirty-six miles east by south. October 17, 1871, marched nine miles (east by south) when two Indians were seen in the valley of the river. They were pursued and killed. One man of Company H was wounded in the skirmish. October 18 to November 8, 1871, marched two hundred and forty-seven miles (east by northeast) and arrived at Fort Richardson, Texas.

(Signature not included in copy.)
Official extract and copy.
(Signed) J. B. Martin,
Assistant Adjutant General,

While it is not charged that he (Heyl) was directly responsible for the injury which the writer sustained on that morning, because he did not cause his horse to fall, nor did he place the boulder on the buffalo trail against which the leg was smashed, it is, nevertheless, just as certain that he was indirectly responsible, from the fact that, as the ranking officer of the other two, who had placed themselves under his command just as soon as they had joined the chase, he led them into an ambuscade or trap which the Indians had prepared for us, and which by the freshness and speed of his horse and those of his men enabled him to do, and then, when he found that we were all liable to be cut off and massacred, by that same agency or resource, and with the full responsibility of command upon him, he not only did not exercise his authority as commanding officer, or give us any warning, but, finding that he could save himself and the lives of his men by fresh and fleet horses, he ran out and left us to be sacrificed.

This was the first Indian action in which the writer had been engaged, and he naturally looked to one who had been a captain of volunteer cavalry, and a captain of a regiment with such a reputation as the Ninth United States Cavalry then had, and who had come to our regiment upon Mackenzie's recommendation, for guidance and decisive action.

Fighting Spirit and Efficiency *vs.* Criminal Neglect— Capture, Mutiny, and Fighting Paralysis

During the Civil War, Heyl had been an officer of the Third Pennsylvania Volunteer Cavalry. On November 28, 1862, that regiment was posted at the most vital point in the outer picket line of the Army of the Potomac, one squadron, with a picket outpost and its reserve, being near Hartwood Church, Virginia, under a Captain George Johnson. Heyl was in this command. They had been specially warned and directed to remain saddled up during tile night and to exercise more than the usual precautions, as an attack was expected in force that morning. At sunrise a picked column of Stuart's Confederate Cavalry completely surprised this picket outfit, overran it, and captured the entire body, with all of their horses and arms, except five outposts who escaped into the woods, but left their horses.

No fight seems to have been "put up." There were captured, according to Confederate reports, eighty-seven men, two captains, three lieutenants, two colours, one hundred horses, carbines, etc. It was one of the most shameful and humiliating affairs that every occurred in the history of that war. General Hooker characterized it as "a disgraceful affair," and called a court of inquiry "to fix the responsibility upon the culpable, and have them brought to trial and punishment." The "greatest vigilance and care" was enjoined upon this command. General Averill, the division commander, in commenting upon it, said, "He permitted his command to be surprised and a great portion of it captured, bringing disgrace and shame upon his regiment and the brigade to which it belonged, and our cavalry service into disrepute," and he requested that Johnson be dropped from the rolls!

By order of the President he was "summarily dismissed." Captain Johnson was, of course, as ranking officer, and therefore responsible, made the scapegoat. But the other officers were also equally culpable. Heyl was either with the picket outpost, or with the reserve, and was captured in this shameful manner. That fact alone probably saved him from the same fate as Johnson. Such a surprise in time of war, at the most vital point in our lines, and wholesale capture and "sweep up" of a cavalry picket supposed to be guarding the safety of the army, could only have been the result of the culpable carelessness and criminal neglect of the five officers, including Heyl, who were captured with all of their men, and without apparently much resistance, four men only being wounded, with no loss to the enemy. It was a subject for comment by Generals Lee and Wade Hampton.

Had Stuart been backed up by a large force of infantry, it would have afforded Lee an opportunity, which he had not before enjoyed, to have seriously menaced the entire Union Anny. Heyl told the writer that he had been a prisoner during the Civil War, but he never related the details. These can be found with a circumstantial narrative, correspondence, etc., in the *Rebellion Records*, Volume 21, Series 1, pages 13-17. There is no other instance known in the history of the Civil War where a squadron of cavalry on outpost picket duty was surprised and absolutely overrun and captured in a body through the criminal neglect and cowardice of its officers.

Heyl was appointed a first lieutenant. Ninth Cavalry, July 23, 1866, and captain July 21, 1867.

About 1868 or 1869 he was in command of a troop of that regiment, and in camp near San Antonio, Texas. A mutiny broke out among his men. He shot his first sergeant dead. It was all he could do. A court of inquiry exonerated him for the act. It was all *they* could do. But, the query in the army always was: Why this mutiny if the discipline in that troop, or the loyalty of his men for him, was what it should have been?

Let us stop to ponder for a moment.

Here we have cited three disgraceful affairs in which Heyl had prominently figured or been involved during a certain period of his military career:

1. The disgraceful and shameful picket affair of the Third Pennsylvania Cavalry near Hartwood Church, Virginia, by which, through his own culpable neglect or criminal carelessness, he was taken prisoner.

2. The unnecessary killing of the First Sergeant of his troop near San Antonio, Texas, of which, although it is true he was exonerated, there is almost always a suggestion, if not conclusive evidence, that a mutiny is generally caused by harsh treatment and brutality, or criminal neglect of the true interests of one's men. In nearly every such instance during the Civil War it was found to be true.

3. Rank, white-livered cowardice in the affair with Quanah Parker's band of Indians, when he became panic stricken, showed the "white feather," and ran out of the fight, leaving his comrades to be killed. And yet he "carried on," being appointed, either through political pull, War Department favouritism, or theatrical self-advertising, in the Inspector General's Corps, gaining one promotion after another until he attained the grade of Colonel and Assistant Inspector General at the time of his death.

COMMENDATORY LETTERS CONFIRM STATEMENT

Following are letters from the late Major (then Lieutenant) P. M. Boehm, the late Major (then Lieutenant) W. A. Thompson, the late Lieutenant, Colonel (then Captain) John A. Wilcox, and others, voluntarily given in support of the writer's statement:

Boehm says:

I was present at the time the Indians made the charge, and I can vouch for the brave conduct and skill of Lieutenant Carter.

I can not express in too great a sense the ability shown by this officer in covering the retreat, and holding his men in such a position as held the Indians back.

Thompson says:

Had it not been for your coolness, good judgment, and great gallantry that morning, the chances are ten to one the whole command would have been killed before we could have reached them. . . . .*Prompt and decisive action and bravery held the men to their work and saved the day.* . . . .The Qua-ha-da Indians are noted for their great bravery and close fighting. I can add that the part taken in this Indian fight by Captain Heyl (late Fourth Cavalry) left the impression that all the credit was due solely to Captain P. M. Boehm and Lieutenant R. G. Carter (at which time both were Lieutenants of Fourth Cavalry, now retired.

Wilcox says:

Your personal bravery in the fight near the Brazos River when the Indians partially cut off your little detachment, and killed your sergeant, is well known to all the old officers of the Fourth Cavalry. In regard to the occurrences incident to the fight at Re-molino, Mexico. I was present and distinctly recollect your coming up and reporting that you had but recently killed an Indian. I am familiar with your statement about the packs being cut loose from the mules. . . . . . . I distinctly recollect the 'captured Indian' you speak of being brought into camp by the Seminole scout; his efforts to shoot Captain Mauck and his being killed on the spot. Many discharged their pieces, and you among the rest. I was standing within ten steps from this Indian when he was shot. . . . . What you claim regarding yourself are undeniable facts.

Vernou (now Colonel C. A. Vernou, U. S. A.) says:

. . . . . .As soon as some of the horses which had stampeded the night before were caught and sent in from the front, we heard from the men about the man of Troop "G" being killed, and they told us of Lieutenant Carter's gallant behaviour, and said if it had not been for his action *things would have gone pretty badly.*
. . . . .

There also follows a letter from one of the oldest and best first sergeants in the Fourth Cavalry, later Ordnance Sergeant Joseph Sudsburger, U. S. A., retired, now dead:

To Whom It May Concern:

This is to certify that I was a Corporal of Troop "B," Fourth U. S. Cavalry, which Lieutenant R. G. Carter commanded (being specially detached from his own Troop "E" for that purpose) in the campaign against the Qua-ha-da Comanche Indians from October 2 to November 18, 1871. On the morning of October 10, 1871, the Indians stampeded our camp on the Freshwater Fork of the Brazos River, Texas.

While I did not participate in the action which followed later that morning, I know that the statement of Lieutenant Carter is absolutely true in every respect. I had knowledge of all the facts. It was common report among all the enlisted men in the regiment that had it not been for the great skill, cool judgment, and most conspicuous bravery of Lieutenant Carter in the action of that morning, every man of both his own and Captain E. M. Heyl's detachment would have lost their lives. Private Gregg was killed within a few feet of him, and Privates Melville and Downey of Troop "G" were wounded by his side.

I have full knowledge of all the facts connected with the serious injury which Lieutenant Carter received that morning by the falling of his horse when making a charge upon a body of Indian sharpshooters posted on a rocky bluff; of his riding five days with his leg in splints when in pursuit of this band of Indians; and of his treatment for such injury by A. A. Surgeon Rufus Choate, when the command was moving out. I have seen him often since 1887, and known of his suffering ever since.

I was with the command when it made its great raid into Mexico, May 17-19, 1873, and was present when a Lipan Indian, who was decoyed into the burning Kickapoo Village, by a Seminole Indian scout and not disarmed, tried to shoot Captain Mauck, who commanded my troop.

I saw Lieutenant Carter and a corporal of Troop "M" shoot the Indian down, the former firing first, his shot turning him around and backward so as to throw up his rifle at the moment of discharge into the air, when he fell dead. Lieutenant Carter, by his prompt action, saved the life of Captain Mauck, and the act was witnessed by many officers and men in the command who were standing around the captured prisoners in groups.

Lieutenant Carter was always regarded in the regiment as one of its hardest worked, most efficient, and bravest officers, not only by the commissioned, but by the non-commissioned officers and enlisted men. His constant and valuable services, tireless energy, and conspicuously gallant conduct during those years of continuous Indian warfare, and his uniformly firm but kind treatment of the men in his troop, afforded an example and incentive which stimulated them to their best efforts and made the Fourth Cavalry, under the leadership of General Ranald S. Mackenzie, second to none in the entire army. It was the only cavalry regiment that ever received the thanks of a State for its services in driving the Indians from its frontier counties.

And when the Army Appropriation Bill of 1877 failed in Congress, and the officers of the army were without their pay for a period of about six months, in a letter which General Sherman wrote to General Mackenzie, at Fort Hays, Kansas, which I saw, he stated that the entire Texas delegation agreed to vote for the bill, provided General Mackenzie with the Fourth Cavalry should be ordered back to the Department with headquarters at Fort Clark, Texas.

Joseph Sudsburger,
Ordnance Sergeant, U. S, Army, Retired.
Late First Sergeant, Troop "B," Fourth U. S. Cavalry.
Sworn to and subscribed before me, a Notary Public for the District of Columbia, at Washington, D. C, this 29th day of April, A. D. 1904.

Thomas J. Sullivan,
(seal.)   Notary Public, D, C.

In 1896, Col. E. B, Beaumont was Acting Inspector General of the Department of Texas. At that time he made, at the request of the writer, a search for Mackenzie's report, and wrote the following letter:

San Antonio, Texas, March 22, 1890.
My Dear Carter:
The adjutant general is having copy made of Mackenzie's report, but, as I surmised, he made no mention of you or Boehm in his report, and on the contrary Heyl is reported as having driven the Indians several miles without bringing them to a fight. Possibly if he had been up when you and Boehm were in such a tight place he would have been able to participate in a

fight. I am in exactly the same position as you and Boehm, for although I made the *entire* captures at the Palo Duro fight, having command of A and E Companies in the advance, and Boehm was with me, neither of us were mentioned in the report; in fact, it does not appear that we were there at all. . . . . I consider that to my part we owed all our successful captures. But I was never mentioned. . . . . in fact we were completely ignored. These reports have given me a view of Mackenzie's character that I never saw before. . . . . ."*De Mortuis Nil Nisi Bonum*" is the old adage, but as we all toiled and fought to advance him, it would have been a graceful act, to say the least, if he had said a pleasant word of praise for duty fairly performed. The lesson comes late in life and after we have borne the heat and toil of the day. No matter how hard we strove to do our duty and what hardships we had to undergo. You remember the fatigue of our Mexican trip. It was never known beyond our own orbit and I can now understand how little interest was expressed in us when we occasionally visited Washington.

War Department greeting:

"Ah, how are you, Jones?

"Where is your station? How long are you going to stay in the city? Good morning."

The fact is, I do not believe you can strengthen yourself by searching for commendations from Mackenzie, for he never wrote any, I think. The proper way, and only one now left, is to get the testimony of the officers who were with you, setting forth the facts of the case, and then get General Augur to recommend you. . . . . I would like the truth to be known about that fight. . . . . if the gentleman who "*skinned out*" for the ravine and left you in the lurch attempts any "Shenanigin" you must go before the Military Committee and tell the truth about the fight. I have always considered that you and Boehm, and I believe "Old Tone Henry," were the heroes of the fight and that you had a mighty close call. . . . .

Keep the greenest spot in your heart for me.

    Most truly your friend,

                            (Signed) E. B. Beaumont.

R. G. Carter,

    U. S. Army.

A true copy.

Letter of Brigadier-General Wirt Davis, U. S. A. (then Captain Fourth Cavalry), now dead, follows. His reputation throughout the entire army was that of being one of the bravest and most efficient officers in the cavalry service.

Baltimore, Md., December 6, 1904.

To Whom It May Concern:

This is to set forth that Troop "F," Fourth U. S. Cavalry, of which I was then the captain, was one of the six troops of that regiment, Colonel R. S. Mackenzie, Brevet Brigadier General, U. S. A., commanding, that took part in the expedition in October and November, 1871, against the hostile Qua-ha-da band (Quoina's) of Comanche Indians, and that I was present during the whole campaign.

About sunset on the 9th of October, 1871, the command encamped on the Freshwater Fork of the Brazos River, Texas. About 1 o'clock a.m. on the 10th of October, 1871, as the moon was setting, a considerable number of mounted Comanches, yelling and firing pistols, charged past our camp and succeeded in stampeding some horses and mules. At daylight several officers with detachments of men were sent out by Colonel Mackenzie to search for and recover the stampeded animals. . . . . A large party of Comanches suddenly attacked Captain Heyl's troop while hunting for the loose horses, killed one of his men, but were assailed and driven off by Lieutenants Carter and Boehm, who, with their detachments, promptly and gallantly rushed to Heyl's relief.

Colonel Mackenzie, when the firing was heard, ordered me to mount my troop (the horses were already saddled), and with him I proceeded at a gallop toward the scene of conflict. When we arrived there, however, the Indians had scattered and had fled up the Freshwater Fork of the Brazos toward the Staked Plains. Lieutenant Carter, while pursuing the Indians who had attacked Captain Heyl's troop, was badly injured by his horse falling and jamming his leg against a rock. The injury was a serious one, and it was so pronounced to be by Acting Assistant Surgeon Rufus Choate, U. S. A., who attended him.

Although I was not an eyewitness of the mishap that befell Lieutenant Carter in the affair with hostile Comanches on October 10, 1871, yet I know that he was injured as described herein. Lieutenant Boehm, who was first lieutenant of my Troop "F," but who on that expedition was chief of scouts for Colonel Mackenzie, related all the facts and circumstances in the case to me in camp on the following day and subsequently often referred to the matter in conversation with me. It may not be irrelevant for me to state that Lieutenant Carter was known in the Fourth Cavalry as a *very energetic and gallant officer*, and his involuntary and reluctant retirement from the service on account of disability in the line of duty was regarded by *many officers as a decided loss to the regiment.*

Wirt Davis,
Brigadier General, U, S. Army, Retired,
In 1871— Captain, Troop "F," Fourth U. S. Cavalry.

In a personal letter to Captain Carter, General Wirt Davis adds the following:

Dear Carter:
Enclosed with this is a statement concerning the affair on the Freshwater Fork of the Brazos River, Texas, and although *it is not as strong as I would like to make it*, still I hope it may help you in securing favourable action on your petition. I have read the brief very carefully, and it is a lucid and forcible statement of reasons why an enabling act of Congress should be passed authorizing the President to appoint you a Colonel, U. S. Army, mounted, to date from January 30, 1903. You certainly deserve consideration for your service in the War of the Rebellion and in the arduous Indian campaigns after that memorable war. I sincerely hope that you may be successful in obtaining special legislation for your relief.

The foregoing letters are from every officer of the Fourth U. S. Cavalry now living, (1919), who was with Captain Carter in the Indian campaign of 1871.

Life is full of "ifs." They are the turning points in our career. "If" is a little word, but is a big factor. "If" the writer had realised what that report of Mackenzie's was to have been and what it would mean to him, his answer to the question put to him in Cañon Blanco would have been of a far different nature. In his generosity to avoid smirching or blasting a brother officer's career, an injustice was done to him and his truly brave, generous rescuer, which now, after a lapse of 48 years, is just being set right. It is this little word "if" that makes life, after all, a gamble.

"If" it should be said that this is a case of the "*donkey kicking the fallen lion*," the answer might be "*see yourself in the mirror*," or, read Charles Reade's *Put Yourself in His Place*.

Some men are like counterfeit or spurious coins. But, by self-advertising or the undue influence of sycophantic friends, they sometimes manage to retain their purchasing power, and remain at their face value, even though oftentimes they have been known to be failures or to achieve success in any way. This has been accomplished by the P. T. Barnum process of everlasting talk, newspaper twaddle, and red and yellow posters. There is, it seems necessary to repeat, a great deal of hypocrisy, cant, Barnum humbuggery and hysteria in this country, and in no place is it more in evidence than in the Capital. The writer has gained this knowledge by a close observation of more than 30 years directly in contact with the machinery by which this government is supposed to function. No close observing man, with ample time on his hands, could remain in Washington during both the Spanish-American and this World War just closing without gaining this knowledge—almost at first hand—or being fully impressed with the startling truth of the psychological developments of both of these war periods, with their excitement, "endless chain" methods, emotional frenzy, and hero worship.

MEDAL OF HOMER: "MOST DISTINGUISHED GALLANTRY"—

BREVET: "SPECIALLY GALLANT CONDUCT"

The writer, many years after this affair, was accorded partial justice by being awarded the Congressional medal of honour, the officers of the Fourth Cavalry practically uniting in an endorsement on the following application made by Major P. M. Boehm, then Captain U. S. A., retired.

Washington, D. C, December 13, 1893,
To the Assistant Secretary of War,
Washington, D. C. Sir:
I have the honour to recommend and to request that First Lieutenant and Brevet Captain R. G. Carter, U. S. A., retired, may be awarded a medal of honour for conspicuous gallantry and bravery in action with Qua-ha-da Comanche Indians on the Freshwater Fork of the Brazos River, Texas, on the morning of October 10, 1871.

I have read Lieutenant Carter's statement and it is correct in every respect. I was present at the time the Indians made their last charge upon him and his little command, and can vouch for the *conspicuously brave conduct, skill, and good judgm*ent shown by Lieutenant Carter.. . .

If any distinguished honour is to be bestowed upon any officer engaged at the time herein mentioned. Lieutenant R. G. Carter is clearly entitled to it, as his act was entirely voluntary, he being officer of the day at the time, and on a tour of the pickets when he first sighted the Indians which he and the other officers chased with their commands until they met the main body. I have the honour to be, sir.

Very respectfully, your obedient servant,

(Signed) P. M. Boehm,

Captain, U. S. A., Retired.

This medal of honour was awarded the writer for *Most Distinguished Gallantry* in action against Indians on Brazos (Freshwater Fork) River, Texas, October 10, 1871, in holding the left of the line with a few men during the charge of a large body of Indians, after the right of the line had retreated, and by delivering a rapid fire, succeeded in checking the Indians until other troops came to the rescue, while serving as Second Lieutenant, Fourth Cavalry."

Under the act of Congress of February 27, 1890, granting Indian brevets for gallantry, the writer was given the brevet of First Lieutenant, U. S. Army, for "*Specially Gallant Conduct* in action against Indians on the Brazos (Freshwater Fork) River, Texas, October 10, 1871," and later the brevet of Captain, U. S. Army, for "*Gallant Services* in action against Kickapoo, Lipan, and Mescalero Apache Indians at Remolino, Mexico, May 18, 1873."

QUANAH SURRENDERS—ADOBE WALLS—PALO DURO

The expedition into the Texas Panhandle in 1874 of four columns, operating from the north, south, east, and west, and resulting in the actions near Red River on September 27-28, and at Las Lagunas Quatro and at the Palo Duro on November 5, 1874, and Quanah's disastrous defeat by the destruction of his villages and the wholesale killing of nearly two thousand ponies, which had been captured from him, a whole day being devoted by Lawton to shooting them, one troop being detailed for that purpose—the pile of bones being still there, according to reports of the inhabitants of that region to the writer—

179

forced Quanah to come in and surrender early in 1875. Just prior to these fights, however, Quanah made one last desperate effort to hold his Indians together, and through his influence and wily diplomacy succeeded in persuading all of the bands of the Comanche and Cheyenne tribes with about half of the Kiowas and other Indians to affiliate with him and make an attack upon an organised company of white buffalo hunters whom he claimed were depredating upon the well recognised Indian lands over which the immense herds of buffalo grazed, and upon which the Indians then relied for almost their very existence in lodge-skins, clothing, food, etc.

He mustered about seven hundred warriors, and the campaign began June 24, 1874, with an attack led by Quanah in person with his confederated Indians, against the buffalo hunters, who were strongly entrenched in a rude fort known as the Adobe Walls, on the South Canadian in the Texas Panhandle. In addition to the thick walls, the hunters had a small field piece which they used with such good effect that after a siege lasting all day the Indians were obliged to withdraw with considerable loss. Most of the hostiles then surrendered, but Quanah, implacable to the last, kept the Qua-ha-das (Kwahadi band) out till the last, when these four converging columns finally administered the death blow to him and his Indians, "the *Vanishing Race*."

QUANAH AS A "GOOD INDIAN"—HIS REWARD—ANOTHER RO- MANCE—HIS DEATH—LAST RITES

Quanah lived, after "coming in," at the Fort Sill Reservation. To placate him, and keep him on the "good road," so that he might follow the white man and be a useful member of society, he was given land, horses, mules, and cattle, and a substantial two-storied house to live in. This house had a large star on the roof, to distinguish it, presumably, from the other houses, and was about twelve or fifteen miles from the town of Lawton. He leased his land to cattlemen for grazing purposes, and, in this way accumulated a large fortune for an Indian. He rode in state (four-mule ambulance) with his squaws—of whom he had, it was reported, at one time seven—and twenty-two children. He came to Washington many times, and at Theodore Roosevelt's second inauguration, in 1905, the writer saw him ride up Pennsylvania Avenue in the inaugural column with other "good Indians," most of whom had dipped their hands in many a white settler's blood on the once far off borderland of the West.

On February 10, 1908, Hon. John H. Stephens, Member of Congress from Texas, offered a bill appropriating one thousand dollars for a memorial to Cynthia Ann Parker in Texas, offering the following as his reason: "In view of the *public service* rendered by this Indian (Quanah) to the white people on the Texas frontier, in *causing his tribe* to quit the war path and live on their reservation, and the further fact of the suffering of his mother for so many years as a white captive among the savages." This was done at the request of Quanah, then in Washington, in behalf of his mother, who had died about 1864, and his infant sister, Prairie Flower, both of whom had been buried in the Fosterville cemetery, near Poyner Station in Henderson County, Texas. This bill was passed on the Indian Appropriation Bill on the same day. Quanah then had ample means to erect this memorial.

The Texas authorities having refused Quanah permission to remove the bodies of his mother and sister to his new home, he, accompanied by C. W. Birdsong, Indian agent, and son-in-law of Quanah, on November 29, 1910, smuggled the bodies from their graves, and brought them to Cache, about twelve or fifteen miles west of Lawton, near Fort Sill, Oklahoma.

Quanah died February 22, 1911, of an attack of asthma and rheumatism, leaving three wives and fifteen children. He was reputed to be the wealthiest Indian in the United States, through the generosity of the government. He was buried at Post Oak Mission Cemetery, near Lawton, on February 24, 1911. The reburial of his mother had been postponed for the following Sunday, and it had been planned that Quanah should perform the ceremony, but his sudden death interrupted these plans. At sunrise on the morning of his death, the real Indian burial ceremony began. Three times dining the night, "Toonicey," the favourite of Quanah's remaining three squaws, arose and loudly called to the Great Spirit for her chief. At five o'clock, crying loudly, "This is the time I always build a fire for him," she waked all the family. At six o'clock, Marcus Poco, Chief Medicine Man of the tribe and preacher, conducted the "sunrise funeral," crying to the Great Spirit and to the white man's God to accept the spirit of the dead chief. The Indians chanted weird dirges. More than one thousand attended, including hundreds of Indians.

The body of Quanah was dressed in his buckskin suit of former days. At noon the funeral party wended its way among the hills of the Parker ranch to the little Indian cemetery, and the funeral service began. A. J. Breaker (or Becker), Mennonite missionary, conducted it after the manner of the whites. Following this, the Indians sang the

"Swan Song," the Medicine Man again cried to the Great Spirit, and the body was lowered to the side of his white mother. In the coffin were placed a buckskin bag containing Quanah's favourite feathers, his war bonnet, trinkets, and jewellery. Among the latter was a diamond brooch, valued at $450, the present of cattlemen who had grazed their stock on the Comanche ranges fifteen years before, and became rich.

Nacona, a town named after Quanah's father, is on the M. K. & T. R. R., in Montague County, a few miles south of Old Spanish Fort on the Red River.

Quanah, a town in the Texas Panhandle, some miles east of Canon Blanco, the county seat of Hardeman County, not far from the town of Vernon on Pease River, is named for him, the latter town being near where Peta Nacona, his father, was killed, and where his mother was recaptured by Captain Ross' rangers. Has anybody ever heard or known of other county seats in the Texas Panhandle being named for any officers of the Fourth United States Cavalry, who risked their lives and sacrificed their health and future happiness here on earth in more than one effort to drive out that savage Qua-ha-da Comanche band and open up that wild and desolate region to settlement, civilization, wealth, and all the material prosperity it now enjoys, (1919), and which that wily Indian was seeking to prevent by bloody incursions, burning, plundering, and savage orgies?

A Retrospect

It has been said by wise men, great writers, sages, and ancient philosophers that one should never regard the past, or look or turn backward, but always live in the present, and look forward to one's future life, the past being forever dead and buried. That is excellent advice and philosophy for youth. Few young people do look backward, for their interest centres in their present work and ambitions, and their future lies before them full of gilded hopes and promises. But this chunk of wisdom does not always hold true with the aged for, while they are compelled to adjust themselves to the present, there are few, if any, rosy promises held out to them for a future—unless, with full faith, it is the one after life—especially if some event in that past life has been largely responsible for much of the sorrow, bitter disappointments, and blasted hopes in their selected career and life profession, or, for past and present danger, physical pain and daily suffering.

These same historical writers and wise men frequently quote that old Latin adage, "*de mortuis nil nisi bonum*" (say nothing but good of the dead). That is also a good philosophy if not carried too far, and provided it does not work too much injustice to the living. We have been living for years in a crazy age of grotesque humbuggery, of fraud, of sham, and "faking." It has smacked strongly of the P. T. Barnum age, that great showman, who once wrote a book on how to "fool" and "humbug" the great American people. It has been the age of false pretension, of "hypnotism," of "fads," and "mind reading," "absent treatment," "theosophy," "spiritualism," and the "occult," etc. An age of "cure alls."

Some years since the writer called attention in a book which he had published, *Four Brothers in Blue*, to the Battle of Chancellorsville, in which he was engaged, where a drunken commanding general imperilled the lives of his entire army by his conduct. He held eighty thousand men's lives in the hollow of his hand, and for more than two days that magnificent old Army of the Potomac was without a commander or a leader. The latter was lying *spineless, inactive*, and *inert* in his tent, while the gallant men in that army, ready to do and dare, were humiliated by being held in an almost paralyzed condition for lack of that leadership. If anybody dared to speak or come out in print and give, from their own knowledge, the true cause for such a woeful condition, he was immediately assailed, and this old Latin saying was sprung on him, "*Say nothing but good of the dead*," in an effort to "whitewash" and stifle criticism of the one man who was really responsible for such an act, and the never-to-be-forgotten and disgraceful disaster which followed as a result, and for which we all had to suffer indescribable hardships as well as unnecessary humiliation through *his* failure to achieve success either through criminal carelessness and neglect, or *his* weakness and moral and mental unfitness to assume such responsibilities.

While there are probably none who would not gladly subscribe to the ethics of the wise adage just quoted, because it is a truth which few would or could seek to disregard, yet there is something beyond and greater than this in its practical application, and that is a living force. It is *justice*, without which life is a travesty, a farce, and a hollow sham. *Justice to the living*; for there were, and are today, many real victims of the acts of the dead, and it is worse than folly to feign blindness or knowledge of the truth. It is a crime!

There are men living today, (1919), who saw the author of that disgrace lying impotent and nerveless in his tent by the side of the little white house (Bullock's) near the intersection of the Ely's Ford and the

183

United States Ford roads, and have lived to see an equestrian statue in bronze erected in commemoration of his deeds near the State House in Boston. But no soldier who was in the battle line at Chancellorsville and near enough to this self-exalted commanding general of the old Army of the Potomac to see his condition, will ever forget what took place there during those fateful hours (May 2-6, 1863) with nobody in command, or, now the "grotesque humbuggery" of perpetuating this man's memory, or such a deed, in the face of what we knew then, and what we had to endure on account of the same. Even his adjutant general, who was for years in one of the Departments in Washington, admitted the urgent need of stimulating him when it was seen that he had "lost his grip" on the situation, but, in doing so, realised that they had, unfortunately, exceeded the limit and rendered him *hors de combat*. Upon being asked by General Doubleday sometime after the battle what was the matter with him during that crisis. Hooker's reply was:

The shock I received by shell concussion at the Chancellor House did not injure me, I was not drunk, but I was not, on that day, 'fighting Joe Hooker."

And everybody was free to draw their own conclusions, except those alone who knew the facts, having seen all with their own eyes, and there were many who did see and know.

The case, given in illustration, can be applied with full force, and in all its meaning, to the writer's case in connection with the tragedy of Cañon Blanco. He has been urged many times to tell the true story, even if necessary to the committees of Congress, before the medal of honour was awarded him, and especially in view of Mackenzie's most amazing report, which was not known of for a number of years. Nobody can fully analyze, not even a soldier, another man's thoughts, his feelings, or sensations at a moment of extreme danger, a sudden crisis, or his mental, physical, and moral attitude.

Much less is he able to control them. But he can analyze that man's acts who, being impelled by some sudden impulse or force has lost control of himself, so far as it may affect another's life, his hopes, ambitions, and future prospects. Is one always to live a life of suffering and injustice when it has been brought about by the wrong-doing and deliberate acts of the dead, who, when living, never by word or deed gave expression of regret for such act, except to an intimate friend in a moment of confidence and, perhaps, of remorse? In this case the commanding officer was *not drunk*. He simply lost his head—went off in a blue "funk"—became panic stricken—fled the field and left the writer not only to suffer the consequences of such an act at the moment, but to be punished and be the victim for the balance of his life, with no remedy except through the generosity of his brother officers in securing him the medal of honour and a brevet as a matter of justice, after all the facts had been known, verified, and sworn to by them.

Then why this cry of "*de mortuis nil nisi bonum?*" What about the living, especially when they have had to suffer for the mental, physical, and moral attitude of the dead—their lapses and lack of decisive action? Is something not due to them if their lives have been so closely interwoven with the acts of the dead as to make it practically impossible to separate or dissociate their present and past, is not their future, lives from those acts? Forty-eight years have passed, (as in 1919), but the human mind is utterly incapable of assuming the task of forgetting under all the circumstances this tragedy of Cañon Blanco.

The world moves in cycles or periods, psychological periods or eras of "farces," "shams," "isms," "cults," "endless chains," etc. Every such recurring cycle or period has its insincere, two-faced hypocrites—some humbug, like a Barnum—to make the world pay for its humbuggery; some idealist or dreamer who pleads for an Eutopia or the millennium; some prophet who predicts the approaching end of the world; or a Bolshevist or Anarchist who preaches anarchy, destruction, and chaos. Wars have been a most prolific source of such a worldwide craze, of frenzied hysteria, of license, camouflaging under the mask of liberty, of hero worship, and of personal adulation to a sickening extent, *ad nauseam*.

In every age, and in the cycles and periods of that age there have been charlatans, frauds, shams, fakes, and humbugs, and the people have been "fooled," "flimflammed," "hoodooed," or "buncoed" ever since the world begun, and still there are among them some wise sages and philosophers who still cry out "*de mortuis nil nisi bonum*," and the world moves on—stumbling, blundering, bungling along toward its ultimate mission, the mystery of which we mortals, poor little ants, know not of. We had these conditions during the Civil War, during the Indian wars, the Spanish-American war. It was present in the campaign after Quanah's band, and in the action at Canon Blanco. The word "camouflage" had not then come into use as a military term. All of these strange conditions were "camouflaged" under another name which even Barnum himself would never have recognised as "humbug." When Mackenzie made that strange and meagre report of

185

the expedition of 1871, he had, perhaps unconsciously, come under the influence of this camouflage. We might as well call it by its right name. He had either been completely humbugged, or had come under a spell of "hypnotism," or else his star had even then begun to set in the overshadowing darkness of a clouded night, and later, when the mental and physical strain had been too great, the "silver chord was loosed," the "golden bowl was broken."

To the Memory of Gen. R. S. Mackenzie.

Mackenzie, thy warfare is o'er—
Thy bold, loyal heart is at rest.
Thy noble soul suffers earth's sorrows no more,
For thy bark sailing seaward has reached the lone shore
Of that far-away land of the blest.

Brave hero, we mourn not for thee.
Thou hast gone from life's troubles and care;
Thy stern, soldier spirit forever is free;
It has joined the Grand Army encamped by the Sea
In the bivouac realms over there!

And yet since by love thou wert slain,
In pity we bow o'er thy bier,
And we sigh when we think of thy story of pain,
Of that proud, loyal love that thou lavished in vain.
And in secret we shed the sad tear.

But we feel that affection like thine
Is not lost 'neath the gloom of the sod.
That beyond the dark valley where love is divine,
It will glow evermore and eternally shine
In the balm-breathing Edens of God.

Mackenzie, true soldier, goodbye;
The wind wails thy long reveille.
And tonight on the plains where the weird coyotes cry.
Far away o'er thy trail 'neath the tents of the sky,
I breathe this slight tribute to thee.

The incidents and events of that period are all indelibly stamped and photographed upon the brain. Can any occult science, or hypnotic influence, or the lapse of time remove these impressions? Is it possible for the writer to relegate to obscurity, oblivion, or to " innocuous desuetude" that which has dwelt there during all of his younger days, of his middle life, and now, during the rapid approach of old age? It can not be! Human nature is poor indeed that will seek to befog or shield the act of any man, who himself acknowledged that he was in a state of "blue funk," when that act had so much to do with the life of another man who has so grievously suffered thereby. It seems to admit of no argument, no matter how much the victim may deplore that act or hesitate during almost a lifetime to set it forth in its true light, with all of its dreadful consequences.

While these conditions, past and present, and the strange psychological periods of sham, farces, humbugs, etc., already referred to, might not seem to the average reader to be in any way relevant to the subject-matter—a tragedy in Cañon Blanco, in the Texas Panhandle—they all have a bearing upon this sham and shameful farce of an official report which credited two officers with an act which they not only did not perform, as has been shown by letters and affidavits of all the surviving officers of the Fourth Cavalry, but, by the only two eyewitnesses of that act, they reflected nothing but discredit to themselves, upon their regiment, and the entire army, and had these officers not repudiated such a report, which must have been initiated under a disguise of sham, fraud, fake, and a frame-up, Heyl, upon a strict interpretation of that same report, had he not died, might have been awarded the medal of honour. The writer has seen almost as strange a case of official hypnotism and psychological flimflam as this dining his military career, as he actually knew of an amputation of the wrong limb dining the Civil War, the victim of this sham operation never recovering his lost member or receiving any satisfaction for such loss.

It is hardly necessary to cite to the present generation the case of an extremely obese officer of our Regular Army, weighing over three hundred pounds—who had been unable to mount a horse for years— selected to actively (?) command our Army at Santiago during the Spanish-American war, or of all the distressing and painful complications arising therefrom, some of which have never been satisfactorily explained since. It was a clear case of P. T. Barnum's red and yellow poster advertising, of hypnotic camouflage, and official propaganda.

So much for "*de mortuis nil nisi bonum!*"

That affair in Cañon Blanco, the fight with the Comanche chief and his horde of wild savages, the misconduct of a brother officer, and the wreckage resulting therefrom was indeed the great tragedy of the writer's past life.

As a result of that terrible injury, and because surgical science at that period could not come to his relief, he was, after struggling along for several years, compelled to be retired at an age when most men are or should be most actively enjoying the prime and fullness of life. It has been a hard struggle ever since, because he was too sick to be able to take up the business activities which friends had opened up for him. Most of the expense of this sickness he bore out of his meagre pay as first lieutenant, retired, while endeavouring, although in extremely wretched health, to support a wife and four children, eking out that same pay by doing school and college work, which, physically, he was unable to do without great risk to his life, although compelled to perform it by force of circumstances.

One hospital operation after another, while they saved his life, which for years was constantly in danger, never fully relieved him from the great handicap that hung like a great shadow over his life.

The leg was badly lacerated and bruised, thereby injuring the superficial veins, which shortly after began to enlarge and varicose. Subsequent hard service caused an extension of this enlargement above the knee and to the abdomen, and caused the valves of the large internal saphenous vein to break down, forcing it to perform the duties of an artery. There was a constant tendency to rupture—it was similar to an aneurism of a large artery. While it was not a gunshot wound, its progressive effects were worse, far more reaching, from the fact that it not only caused him very great pain daily, and frequently endangered his life, but it seriously impaired his general health, and could not be checked nor relieved by the ordinary methods employed in skilful surgery, at that time, or for more than twenty-five years after, notwithstanding his frequent application for special treatment and such medical or surgical relief as the Surgeon-General's Office might afford, as is shown by his papers filed with the President.

The writer, by advice of Mackenzie, consulted the best medical and surgical authority at the Massachusetts General Hospital in Boston. He was examined by all the surgeons there (6), including Dr. Henry J. Bigelow, then at the head of his profession, and professor of surgery, etc., at Harvard University. On their united certificate, each having examined him separately, declaring that no radical operation would relieve him, and that any would be at too great a risk to his life, upon going before an Army Retiring Board, he was retired. One of these surgeons who signed that certificate, Doctor Porter, years later performed the first operation for the excision of the saphenous vein by the Trendelenburg method, which the writer, after consultation with Major W. A. Borden, of the U. S. Medical Corps, had performed at the Washington Barracks General Hospital in March, 1901, after nearly thirty years of pain and constant danger almost unprecedented in the medical history of our army. In addition to enlargement of the saphenous vein, breaking down of the valves, etc., forcing the column of blood downward instead of its return to the heart, many other alarming symptoms had set in, such as neurasthenia, nervous indigestion, chronic insomnia, etc., the effects of which are still apparent. His case was demonstrated at the Washington Barracks Hospital before the class of officer medical students by Major W. C. Borden, Surgeon U. S. Army, January 22, 1903, who then declared that had these operations, by which Lieutenant Carter was relieved of his disability, been known in 1876, "*he need not have been retired*," So successful had this operation been, however, that Colonel Borden gave the writer the following certificate:

(Copy.)
U. S. Army General Hospital,
Washington Barracks,
Washington, D. C, February 10, 1903.
To Whom It May Concern:
I hereby certify that I operated upon Captain R. G. Carter, U. S. Army, retired, at the U. S. Army General Hospital, Washington Barracks, in March and June, 1901, for extensive varicose veins of the left leg, using the Trendelenburg and Schede operations, in the belief, as expressed at the time, that he would be greatly benefited if not permanently relieved, of his disability, but that it might be a year or more before the result would become fully apparent. I have recently examined Captain Carter and it is now my belief that he has been relieved of this disability.
(Signed) W. C. Borden,
Major and Surgeon, U, S. Army, Commanding Hospital.
A true copy; original filed with papers to the President.

The following statements of Dr. Rufus Choate are added to clearly indicate the serious nature of the injury received, its gradual progression, and efforts made to save the writer's life:

Washington, D. C, 310 Indiana Ave., May 3, 1890.
This certifies that I attended R. G. Carter, First Lieutenant, U.S.A., an officer of the Fourth U. S, Cavalry, while engaged in the pursuit of Comanche Indians in the campaign of 1871-72,

under General Mackenzie, and especially on the morning of October 10, 1871, and for several days thereafter, for a severely injured leg.

I clearly remember the circumstance of the first examination. The command was in hot pursuit of Indians when Mr. Carter was injured. The leg was contused and greatly swollen, and the pain was so severe that I instructed the officer to remain on his horse while I examined the injured limb. I dismounted and found a condition that caused me more anxiety that I was disposed to exhibit. I expressed the opinion that probably a bone had been fractured, and I enclosed the leg then and there in a bandage, using the boot-leg as splints; believing that firmer splints would subsequently have to be applied.

I expressed the opinion that he would always suffer from the injury. The case has frequently recurred to my mind as one of more than ordinary importance.

This officer was always a close applicant to duty. In the severe service required at that time by every one I may have given him attendance without carrying him on the sick list, but surely I must have made an entry of the case in my report to the Surgeon General.

Very respectfully,

Rufus Choate, M. D.,
Late Acting Assistant Surgeon, U. S, A.

Dr. Rufus Choate.   The Farragut,
Washington, D. C, February 18, 1903.

Having again read the statement made by me in the case of Mr. R. G. Carter, Lieutenant, U. S. Army, at the date of May 3, 1890, I reaffirm what is therein stated.

The gentleman has for many years been under my personal observation. The disability that began October 10, 1871 (in pursuit of Indians), had increased to an extent that was growing dangerous to life by beginning to varicose the veins within the abdomen, until the wonderfully skilful operation of Dr. W. C. Borden, Surgeon, U. S. Army, performed in March and June, 1901, has intervened, to which I believe Mr. Carter owes his life.

Very respectfully,

Rufus Choate, M. D.,
Late Acting Assistant Surgeon, U. S. A.

Subscribed and sworn to before me this 25th day of February,

1903.

M. LeRoy Gough,

(seal.)   Notary Public.

If that operation was a success, and had restored him to a normal condition so that he could perform duty, why should he not have applied for restoration to the active list for duty which he not only knew he could perform, but in which he was sustained by one of the best medical officers of the army? This, as a simple act of long-delayed justice, and as a reward for his past services? He did so, going with that certificate personally to the President, Theodore Roosevelt.

He would have been a captain June 30, 1883; a major July 5, 1898; a lieutenant-colonel February 17, 1901, and a colonel January 30, 1903, and by operation of law, could then have retired as a brigadier-general. In February, 1903, upon presenting a petition to the President setting forth all the facts in his case, citing all the precedents and asking for executive relief, and to be appointed to the grade he would have attained had he not been unfortunately retired, and alternatively expressing a desire for active duty in the field, the President assured him that: "any officer with such an exceptionally brilliant record, who had served during the Civil and Indian Wars, a graduate of West Point, who wore the medal of honour, was certainly entitled to *consideration*," and while he could not promise him the relief asked for, he would certainly go over his papers carefully, which he did, and discovering that he did not possess the executive power to grant the relief, without an enabling act of Congress, he so informed the writer, and urged him to take that action.

What "*consideration*" could the President have had in mind, were it not that for which he had just asked—a restoration to active duty? He practically said that any bill looking to that end would receive his hearty approval. And that is just exactly what he meant, for Theodore Roosevelt was no "four-flusher."

Then began the opposition, largely stimulated by greed, jealousy, and "*sour grapes*"; a rather hazy misunderstanding of the case; the underlying motives, etc. Through the do-nothing policy of a cold-blooded, discourteous, overrated, and obtuse militia chairman of the sub-committee on restorations, retirements, etc., of the Military Committee of the House of Representatives—the so-called guardian of the key to such bills—and an over-cautious Secretary of War, looking to the dollars and cents sacrificed (?) by a wealthy Nation in rewarding its Civil War and Indian fighters, this last act of injustice was finally perpetrated. When this effort was made for Congressional action to restore the writer to the active list as an extra number colonel for active duty he could then have well performed, the Secretary of War, Elihu Root, in reporting adversely, made the astounding declaration that while:

> This officer had a very enviable and most gallant record (with the M. H. and two brevets, etc.), a most generous government had liberally provided for him by placing him on a retired list and rewarding him with the sum (computed down to the last cent by some pay expert designated for the purpose in the Pay Department) of ——— dollars, and he greatly feared that it would be establishing a bad precedent to advance him to the grade he would have attained could surgical aid have been secured sooner, etc.

The Chief of Staff, General Chaffee, while strong in his praise of the writer's "gallant record," said practically the same thing, but to salve the writer's feelings, he was given a most munificent (?), but most strenuous, recruiting detail in the State of Alabama for two years, but with no increased rank. It was too strong a combination. Restoration of officers under the circumstances of a complete recovery for duty had been given in many instances, and numerous cases were cited, some with arms and legs off, in a brief, where such a restoration had been to the advantage of both army and navy. The writer would have had six of eight more years to his credit, and could then have retired at the age of sixty-four as a brigadier general.

While it is believed to be true (and the contrary is challenged) that the writer then had the best fighting record among the graduates of West Point, either on the active or retired lists of the army, and perhaps has it now, in view of this world war just terminating, these "medals," "badges," "brevet commissions," "grateful thanks," "letters of congratulation," "letters of commendation," "personal thanks," etc., "butter no parsnips," nor can they now compensate him for all the mental and physical anguish he has endured during this long period of years, through the many sacrifices he had made for his country, in view of his arriving at the age of seventy-four, and still on the list as a captain (about the only one at that age), and daily in contact with men of high rank—some of them made almost overnight—who, through no fault of theirs, of course, have—some of them—never seen an Indian except a wooden image in front of a tobacco store, and who, even in this great world war, have never even been under rifle or shell fire, the battle statistics of that war showing that not one general officer in the A. E. F. was ever killed, wounded, shell-shocked, or scratched; while one hundred and twenty-three (123) general officers were killed or died of wounds in our Civil War. This is sad to contemplate, even as a retrospect, aside from hunger, thirst, hardships, privations, including the tragedy in that campaign.

This record of the writer's was earned in just two years and seven months of the most active field service which ever fell to the lot any cavalry officer—even in those days of strenuous duty—to perform. There are many officers on the active list of the army to-day, all of whom have come in since the Civil War, and most of them since the Indian Wars—who, after from 30 to 40 years, have no distinguished service record to their credit; merely the performance of perfunctory duty in garrison or in a swivel chair, and with almost phenomenal promotion. In this respect, therefore, length of service, with a mere performance of nominal duties, none of which disables or shortens one's life—will not compare with, nor will it bear the add test of, severity of field service within a prescribed limited period.

That any officer of the army should, at seventy-four years of age, be on the retired list as a captain, with such a record, would, in any other country in the world, as we have seen in the cases of the German generals, Ludendorff, Hindenberg, and Von Mackensen, be almost an absolute impossibility, and in ours seems almost incomprehensible. At least it is pitiful in the extreme, especially when that captain is one of the last surviving few veterans of both the Civil and Indian Wars, the youngest of four brothers, who, starting in at Bull Run, terminated their services at Appomattox Court House, in their fight for the preservation of the American Union, and who aided in the defeat and surrender of this wily savage who never came in voluntarily to be such "a friend to the people of Texas and the Southwest" (as Mr. Stephens states) or to take up the "white man's burden," or camouflage under the hypocrisy of a suddenly acquired Christianity.

Not until his band was driven from the fastnesses of the Palo Duro Cañon in 1874, his villages were destroyed, and his ponies were captured and shot, did he submit, relent, or repent. Then, seeing his ultimate fate, he "came in" and became a "good Indian." Generous Government, indeed! Could a generous government afford to do less for a "gallant officer" of the army who had almost sacrificed his life in an effort to promote the settlement of that wild, uninhabited, savage-infested territory, and to advance civilization in that now richest of rich countries, than it could later do for this murderous savage, so suddenly become converted to the white man's ways, but whose entire previous career had been devoted, not, as Mr. Stephens declared when asking for a $1,000 memorial to Quanah's mother, in "public service rendered by this Indian chief on the Texas frontier in causing his tribe to quit the warpath and live on their reservation," but in burning, pillaging, plundering, ravaging, and murdering every man, woman, or child who attempted to settle there.

Did he (Mr, Stephens) ever dream that munificently rewarding an Indian chief on the ground of a sentimental gush, the brotherhood of man, or humanitarianism, who had murdered and scalped helpless women and children, was a worse precedent than in doing justice, although long delayed, to the officer who helped make him a "good Indian?" The two cases, the one considered by a Secretary of War, the other by the Member of Congress from Texas, are absolutely irreconcilable with the case of the writer, under any form of government, paternal or otherwise.★

★★★★★★

Could Mr. Stephens have seen the Fourth Cavalry in the action at Palo Duro in 1874, he would have witnessed their method of "inducing" Quanah and his Indians to go into Fort Sill, and thereafter follow the "white man's road." It would certainly, in these days of a maudlin sentiment, have been a revelation to the average settler of the Texas panhandle.

★★★★★★

The writer did not ask for, or want to receive, "something for nothing," or to be a useless incubus upon the army. He wanted to perform duty, only in a grade which he believed his years and experience entitled him to, even offering to go to the Philippines. If Congress, through such a sentiment for a so-called civilized (?) Indian, whose career had been marked by an orgy of blood and rapine, some of the foulest, darkest deeds ever recorded in the annals of Indian warfare, leaving always a trail of fire in his path, could bestow a $1,000 monument to honour the white mother who bore this implacable half-breed Comanche, and give him a Christian burial with imposing ceremonies (the writer has erected his own memorial in Arlington from the amount which Mr. Elihu Root declared a most generous government had paid him for his wreckage), it could certainly have

194

done a simple justice to the one officer who was so ready, for the sake of peace and civilization in that far-off Texas Panhandle, to risk his life in what has, indeed, proved to be something more than a mere story, a chronicle of events, or a calm retrospect. It has become the supreme sacrifice, an almost life-long heritage of a real and truly great tragedy of Cañon Blanco.

A Second Account of the Fall of Parker's Fort

James T. De Shields

Settlers at Parker's fort participated in the "runaway scrap" in the spring of 1836, and went as far east as the Trinity which they were unable to cross, as the river was so swollen by heavy rains. While encamped on its western bank, they were informed of the victory of San Jacinto, and at once started back to the fort, which they reached without unusual incident.

Parker's Fort was located! near the headwaters of the Navasota, one half miles northwest of the site of the town of Groesbeck, in Limestone County, in the heart of what was then a wilderness, but now a fruited and thickly populated region divided into farmsteads and dotted with villages and towns.

Fort Houston, situated a mile or two west of the site of Palestine, on land now included in the John H. Reagan farm two miles west of Palestine, in Anderson County, was the nearest white settlement. Others were distant sixty miles or more.

Parker's fort consisted of cabins surrounded by a stockade. A large double gate afforded access to the enclosure. The outer walls of the log cabins formed part of the walls of the stockade. Their roofs sloped inward. At one or more corners of the stockade were block houses. The walls around the entire quadrangle were perforated with loop holes. The fortification was bullet proof, and, like others of the kind, could not be taken by Indians if defended by a few well-armed and determined men. It was built for the purpose of being occupied by the families living in the vicinity, when there was danger of attack by Indians. Most of the farms—some of them nearby and others a mile or so away—were provided with cabins where the tired colonists occasionally spent the night.

The patriarch of the settlement was Elder John Parker, seventy-nine years of age. His aged wife, "Granny" Parker, was, perhaps, a few years younger. He was a Virginian by birth; resided for a time in Elbert County, Ga.; chiefly reared his family in Bedford County, Tenn.; afterwards lived for several years in Cole county, Ill.; and then moved, in 1833, to Texas where Parker's fort was erected in the following year. Some of the family came to Texas prior, and others subsequent, to that time.

The little group consisted of the following persona: Elder John Parker and wife (Granny Parker); James W. Parker (son of Elder John), (wife, four single children, married daughter, Mrs. Rachel Plummer, and her husband, L. T. M. Plummer, and fifteen months old son, James Pratt Plummer, and one daughter, Mrs. Sarah Nixon, and her husband, L. D. Nixon; Silas M. Parker (son of Elder John) and his wife, and four children; Benjamin F. Parker (an unmarried son of Elder John); Mrs. Nixon, Sr., (mother of Mrs. James. W. Parker); Mrs. Elizabeth Kellogg (daughter of Mrs. Nixon, Sr.); Mrs. Duty; Samuel M. Frost and his wife and children; Robert Frost; G. E. Dwight and his wife and children; David Faulkenberry and his son, Evan; Seth Bates and his son, Silas H.; Elisha Anglin and his nineteen year old son, Abram, and old man Lunn—in all thirty eight persons.

On returning to Parker's Fort from the Trinity, the little band busied itself with gathering together its scattered stock and in preparing the fields for putting in crops, all unconscious of the fearful massacre that was to extinguish, so soon, the bright hopes they entertained of the future, and the lives of many of their number; and an unspeakable mental anguish and physical sufferings upon others of the survivors.

Early on the morning of May 19, 1836, James W. Parker, Nixon and Plummer left the fort, and repaired to a farm a mile from there, and David Faulkenberry and his son Evan, Silas H. Bates and Abram Anglin went from the fort to their fields a mile farther away.

Seth Bates, Elisha Anglin, and old man Lunn either slept at their cabins the night before, or left the fort prior to 9 o'clock the morning of the 19th.

At that hour from five hundred to seven hundred Indians (Comanches and Kiowas) appeared on the prairie two or three hundred yards from the fort, displayed a white flag, and sent forward one of their number, who said that they had no hostile intentions, and merely wanted someone to come out from the fort and direct them to a spring which they understood was nearby, and to be furnished a beef.

Subsequent events justify the belief that this Indian acted as a spy, noticed that nearly all the men were absent, end reported the practically defenceless condition of the occupants of the fort. Benjamin F. Parker went out to the Indians and, after returning, stated that it was his belief they were hostile and intended to attack the fort. He said that he would go to them again and try to dissuade them.. His brother, Silas M. Parker, urged him net to go, but her went, nevertheless, and was immediately surrounded and killed.

While this tragedy was in progress, Elder John Parker, "Granny" Parker and Mrs. Kellogg, fled from the fort in one party, and Mrs. James W. Parker and children by themselves; Silas M. Parker and Mrs. Plummer ran outside the stockade. Everyone tried to escape.

As soon as the Indians appeared, Mrs. Sarah Nixon left for the farm where her father, husband and Plummer were at work, to tell them of the imminent peril the occupants of the fort were in.

The savages kept up terrific shouting and yelling while they were murdering Benjamin F. Parker—the peculiar blood-curdling Comanche scream (once heard, never forgotten) rising above the less distinctive cries of the Kiowas. Most of them rushed upon the fort, the gate of which was open; the remainder went in pursuit of the parties of refugees that were still in sight.

The main body of Indians first encountered and killed Silas M. Parker just outside the fort, where he fought to the last, trying to protect Mrs. Plummer. This opposition necessitated the attention of some of the Indians, who, killed and scalped Silas M. Parker, knocked unconscious with a hoe and captured Mrs. Plummer, after fierce resistance on her part, and then poured into the fort, where they joined their companion fiends, and helped to murder Samuel M. and Robert Frost, who fought and fell as true men should. Mrs. Nixon, Sr., Mrs. Duty and all the other women and children, managed to get out of the fort before and during the *mêlée*.

Shrieks of victims rent the air. Hundreds of brazen throated savages shouted and screamed war-whoops, curses, and taunts. The thud of blows delivered with war-clubs and tomahawks, and the sharp reports of firearms resounded. Blood and death were everywhere. Murder, with bat-like wings, brooded over the scene infernal, and drank in the babel of piteous and fierce sounds that rose from it

Elder John Parker, "Granny" Parker, and Mrs. Kellogg were captured when they had gone three-fourths of a mile. They were brought back to a spot near the fort, where Elder John Parker was stripped, speared and killed, and "Granny" Parker was stripped of everything except her underclothing, speared, outraged, and left for dead. The Indians kept Mrs. Kellogg as a prisoner.

When Mrs. Sarah Nixon reached the field to tell of the coming of the Indians, she found her father, James W. Parker, and Plummer. Her husband had gone down to the other farm. Plummer at once hastened to the latter place to convey information of the danger. James W. Parker started immediately for the fort. *En route* he met his wife and children, and others.

Plummer reached Nixon first and told him that the fort was surrounded by Indians. Without waiting for the other men to come up, Nixon, though unarmed, ran toward the fort. In a few moments he met Mrs. Lucy Parker (wife of Silas M. Parker) and her four children, just as they were overtaken by Indians. They compelled her to lift behind two mounted warriors, her nine-year-old daughter Cynthia Ann, and little boy, John. The foot Indians then took her and her two younger children back to the fort, Nixon following. She passed around, and Nixon through the fort.

At the moment the Indians were about to kill Nixon, David Faulkenberry appeared with his rifle and levelling it, caused them to fall back. Thereupon Nixon left in search of his wife and overtook Dwight and family, and Frost's family, and with them, met James W. Parker and family and his own wife, Mrs. Sarah Nixon. This group hastened to the Navasota bottom and hid in a thicket.

Faulkenberry ordered Mrs. Lucy Parker to follow him, which she did, carrying her infant in her arms and holding her other child by the hand. The Indians made several dashes toward them, but were brought up standing each time by Faulkenberry turning upon them and presenting his rifle. One warrior, bolder than the rest, rode up so close that Mrs. Parker's faithful dog seized his horse by the nose, whereupon horse and rider somersaulted into a gully. At this time Silas H. Bates, Abram Anglin and Evan Faulkenberry, armed with rifles, and Plummer, unarmed, came up, and the pursuing Indians, after making further hostile demonstrations, retired. While this party of refugees were passing through Silas M. Parker's field, Plummer, as if awakened from a dream, asked where his wife and child were, and taking the butcher knife of Abram Anglin, went in search of them. Seth Bates and old man Lunn were met a little farther on, and the party proceeded to a hiding place in the creek bottom.

1. Isaac Parker 2. I. D. Parker
3. Cynthia Ann Parker 4. Quanah Parker

1. JOHN NEELY BRYAN. FATHER OF DALLAS. 2. CAPT GEO B. ERATH
3. CAPT. RANDAL JONES. 4. CAPT. ROBT. M. COLEMAN

1. Capt. Shapley P. Ross 2. Capt. Henry S. Brown
3 Capt. Henry Stout 4. Capt. Sam Highsmith

At twilight Abram Anglin and Evan Faulkenberry started back to the fort. On reaching Seth Anglin's cabin, three-fourths of a mile from their destination, they found " Granny" Parker. She had feigned death until the Indians left and then crawled there, more dead than alive. When Anglin beheld her, he thought he was looking at a ghost. In his account of the incident he says:

> It was dressed in white, with long white hair streaming down its back. I admit that I was worse scared at this moment than when the Indians were yelling, and charging us. Seeing me hesitate, my ghost now beckoned me to come on. Approaching the object, it proved to be old "Granny" Parker.
>
> I took some bed-clothing and carrying her some distance from the house, made her a bed, covered her up, and left her until we should return from the fort. On arriving at the fort we cattle lowing, the horses neighing, and the hogs squealing.
>
> Mrs. Parker had told me where she had left some silver, $106.50. This I found under a hickory bush, by moonlight. Finding no one at the fort, we returned to where I had hidden "Granny' Parker. On taking her up behind me, We made our way back to our hiding place in the bottom, where we found Nixon.

Next morning Silas H. Bates, Abram Anglin and Evan Faulkenberry went back to the fort, where they secured five or six horses, a few saddles and bridles and some meal, bacon and honey; but, fearing that the Indians might return, did not tarry to bring the dead.

With the aid of the horses and provisions, the party with David Faulkenberry made its way to Fort Houston. They did not then know what had become of James W. Parker and those with him.

The people with James W. Parker, consisting of G. E. Dwight and nineteen women and children, reached, after travelling six days, Tinnin's, at the old San Antonio and Nacogdoches crossing of the Navasota, emaciated by starvation, with nearly all their clothing torn off of them by thorns, and that which remained reduced to shreds, their bodies and limbs lacerated and their feet swollen and bleeding. Messrs. Carter and Courting learned of their approach, went out to meet them with five horses, and brought them in.

The settlers at Tinnin's, themselves but recently returned from the "runaway scrape" and poorly supplied with necessaries, divided their little all of food and clothing with the sufferers, and cheered and comforted them as best they could.

There were hearts of gold in Texas in those days—of the kind of gold that is in the heavenly city, and not in the fated fane of Mammon.

A party of twelve men went up from Fort Houston and buried the dead. "Granny" Parker did not live long after reaching Fort Houston. Most of the Parker's Fort settlers later returned to that location.

Upon leaving Parker's fort after the massacre, the Comanches and Kiowas travelled together until midnight, when they halted, went into camp, tied their prisoners so tightly hand and foot that blood welled up from beneath the cruel cords, threw the prisoners on their faces, built fires, erected a pole, and engaged in a scalp dance around it that lasted until morning. The savages seemed drunk with the horrors they had perpetrated, and abandoned themselves without restraint to the frenzy of the dance.

They chanted and shouted themselves hoarse, leaped into the air, contorted their bodies, and re-enacted the murders they had committed until even the limit of their physical endurance was exceeded.

The maddened demons tramped upon the prisoners and beat them with bows, until they were covered with blood and bruises.

The orgy ended at last, leaving Mrs. Kellogg, Mrs. Plummer and the children more dead than alive.

When the Indians parted they divided the prisoners among them. Mrs. Plummer was separated from her little son, James Pratt Plummer, he being taken by one band and she by another. (Her full narrative can also be found in this book).

Mrs. Kellogg was sold to the Keechies and by them to the Delawares, who, about six months after her capture, carried her into Nacogdoches and surrendered her to Gen. Sam Houston, who paid them $150.00, the amount they had paid the Keechies, and all they demanded.

While she was being conveyed from Nacogdoches to Fort Houston by James W. Parker and others, a Mr. Smith wounded and disabled an Indian, whom she recognised as the savage who scalped Elder John Parker. As soon as she made known the fact, Parker, Smith and others of the party killed the man—riddling his carcass with bullets, and leaving it where it fell for wolves and buzzards to dispose of.

Six months after she was captured Mrs. Plummer gave birth to a boy baby. She begged an Indian woman to tell her how to save the child, but the squaw turned a deaf ear to her pleadings. One day, while she was nursing the infant, several Indians came to her and one of them tore the child from her, strangled it with his hands, tossed it in the air and let it fall on the ground until life seemed extinct, and then threw it at her feet, while the others held her, despite frantic struggling. The bucks then left her. In her printed narrative she says:

> I had been weeping incessantly whilst they were murdering my child, but now my grief was so great that the fountain of my tears was dried up. As I gazed on the bruised cheeks of my darling infant, I discovered some symptoms of returning life. I hoped that if it could be resuscitated, they would allow me to keep it. I washed the blood from its face, and after a time it began to breathe again. But a more heart-rending scene ensued. As soon as the Indians ascertained that the child was still alive, they tore it from my arms and knocked me down. They then tied a plaited rope around its neck and threw it into a bunch of prickly pears, and then pulled it backward and forward until its tender flesh was literally torn from its body. One of the Indians, who was mounted on a horse, then tied the end of the rope to his saddle and galloped around in a circle until my little innocent was not only dead, but torn to pieces. One of them then untied the rope and threw the remains of the child into my lap, and I dug a hole in the earth and buried them.

The Indians killed the child because they thought that caring for it interfered with the mother's work. Afterwards she was given to a squaw as servant. The squaw, after much cruel treatment, attempted to beat her with a club. Mrs. Plummer wrenched the club from the Indian woman's hands and knocked her down with it. The Indian men, who were at some distance, ran, yelling, to the scene. Mrs. Plummer expected nothing less than to be killed by them. Instead, they patted her on the back, exclaiming *"bueno! bueno!"*—good! good!

After that she was called the "fighting squaw," and was much better treated. After a captivity of one and a half years, she was ransomed by Mr. William Donoho, a Santa Fe merchant-trader—the same generous, tender- hearted and noble gentleman through, whose efforts the unfortunate Mrs. Horn and Mrs. Harris were rescued from savage captivity, as previously related.

The Indian camp in which she was found was so far north of Santa Fe that it took seventeen days travel to reach that place. Mr. and Mrs. Doncho took her with them to Independence, Missouri. There she met her brother-in-law, L. D. Nixon, who brought her to Texas, where she crossed the door sill of her father's home February 19, 1838. She wrote, or had written, an account of her Indian captivity. Her death occurred February 19, 1839. The 19th day of months seems to have had an occult significance for her. She was born on the 19th, was married on the 19th, was captured on the 19th, was ransomed en the 19th, reached Independence on the 19th, arrived at home on the 19th and died on the 19th.

She died without knowing what had become of her son, James Pratt Plummer. He was ransomed late in 1842 find taken to Fort Gibson, and reached home in February, 1843, in charge of his grandfather, and became a highly esteemed citizen of Anderson County.

CYNTHIA ANN PARKER—JOHN PARKER—CHIEF QUANAH PARKER.

Many efforts were made by their relatives to trace and recover Cynthia Ann and John Parker, and Texan and United States government expeditions kept a sharp lookout for them; but without avail, until Cynthia Ann was unexpectedly captured at the Battle of Pease River, in 1860.

There is a fairly authenticated story to the following effect: In 1840 (four years after her capture at Parker's Fort) Col. Len Williams, Stoal (a trader) and a Delaware Indian guide, named "Jack Henry" found her with Pa-ha-u-ka's band of Comanche Indians on the Canadian River. Col. Williams offered to ransom her, but the Indian into whose family she had been adopted said that all the goods the colonel had were not sufficient to get her, that she would not be surrendered for any consideration. Col. Williams requested the privilege of talking with her, and she was permitted to come into his presence. She walked quietly to him and seated herself at the foot of a tree, but could not be induced to utter a word, or make a gesture that showed whether she did or did not understand what he said to her. She was then thirteen years old. Some years later she became the squaw of the noted Comanche chief, Peta Nocona, and bore him several children.

Victor M. Rose says:

Fifteen years after her capture a party of white hunters, including some friends of her family, visited the Comanche encampment on the upper Canadian, and recognising Cynthia Ann, probably through the medium of her name alone, sounded her in a secret manner as to the desirableness of a return to her people and the haunts of civilization. She shock her head in a sorrowful negative, and pointed to her little naked barbarians sporting at her feet, and to the great, lazy buck sleeping in the shade near at hand, the locks of a score of scalps dangling at his belt, and whose first utterance upon arousing would he a stern command to his meek, pale faced wife. Though, in truth, exposure to sun and air had browned the complexion of Cynthia Ann almost as intensely as that of the native daughters of the plain and forest. She said:

> I am happily wedded. I love my husband, who is good and kind, and my little ones, too, are his, and I cannot forsake them.

If, indeed the entire account given by Rose is not apocryphal, it is certain that Cynthia Ann did not employ, in her reply, the set of words attributed to her, and that she did not speak in her mother tongue.

When recaptured, the veneer of savagery that covered her was so thick that it took time and unremitting, loving care to remove it.

Young Lawrence Sullivan Ross, then a dashing ranger Captain; in after years to win much renown as a Confederate Brigadier-General; Governor of Texas, and later. President of the A. and M. college of Texas till his untimely death, in command of a company of Texas rangers, a sergeant and twenty United States dragoons, and seventy citizens from Palo Pinto county under Capt. Jack Curington, came upon an Indian village at the headwaters of Pease River. Most of his men were some distance in his rear, their horses being much jaded by travel and want of food. With him were the dragoons and twenty of his own men. With these, he charged immediately.

The Indians, although surprised, fought with more than usual bravery, their women and children and all of their possessions being with them. They could not hold their ground against such an attacking force, however, and, after many had been killed, the survivors tried to escape to the mountains, about six miles distant. Lieut. Thomas Kellihuir pursued one, and Capt. Ross and Lieut. Somerville another. Somerville was a heavy man, and his horse fell behind. Ross dashed on and overtook the Indian he was after. A fierce combat followed, resulting in the death of the Indian, who proved to be Peta Nocona, chief of the band.

Kellihuir captured the supposed Indian he was after, and who proved to be Cynthia Ann Parker. She had in her arms a girl child about two and a half years of age, Topasannah—"Prairie Flower." It was not known at the time who the captured woman was. She spoke no word that tended to clear the mystery. Lieut. Sublett picked up a

Comanche boy. Capt. Ross took charge of him, named him Pease, and reared him at Waco.

On returning to the settlements, Capt. Ross sent for Isaac Parker, thinking it possible that the woman might be Cynthia Ann Parker. Thrall says:

> The venerable Isaac Parker, still in hopes of hearing of his long lost niece, went to the camp. Her age and general appearance suited the object of his search, but she had lost every word of her native tongue. Col. Parker was about to give up in despair, when he turned to the interpreters sand said very distinctly that the woman he was seeking was named 'Cynthia Ann.' The sound of the name by which her mother had called her, awakened in the bosom of the poor captive emotions that had long lain dormant. In a letter to us Col. Parker says: 'The moment I mentioned the name, she straightened herself in her seat and, patting herself on the breast, said, 'Cynthia Ann, Cynthia Ann.' A ray of recollection sprang up in her mind, that had been obliterated for twenty-five years. Her very countenance changed, and a pleasant smile took the place of a sullen gloom.' Returning with her uncle, she soon regained her native tongue. It was during the war, and she learned to spin and weave and make herself useful about the house.

Her uncle took her to his home in Tarrant county. Soon thereafter she was carried to Austin and was there conducted by a party of ladies and gentlemen into the hall where the State Secession Convention was being held in Austin, in 1861. She appeared to be greatly distressed. Inquiry revealed the fact that she thought the assemblage was a meeting of war chiefs, convened for the purpose of deciding her fate, and was apprehensive that they would condemn her to death.

An act of the Texas Legislature, approved April 8, 1861, granted Cynthia Ann Parker a pension of $100 a year for five years, dating from January 1, 1861, and required the county court of Tarrant county to appoint a guardian for her, the guardian to give a bond, "conditioned for the faithful application of the pension, and for the support and education of her child." Another act of the Legislature, in the same year, donated to her a league of land.

An act of the Legislature, approved January 8, 1862, contained the following:

Silas M. Parker, of Van Zandt County, is hereby constituted as agent of Cynthia Ann Parker, formerly of Tarrant and now of Van Zandt County, and, on his giving bond in the sum of $400 to the Chief Justice of Van Zandt County, for the faithful application of said pension to the support of said Cynthia Ann Parker, and for the support and education of her child, Topasannah, the State Treasurer shall pay said pension to the said agent, or his order.

The last appropriations to pay the pension were for the years 1864 and 1865, and are contained in the general appropriation act parsed by the Tenth Legislature, approved December 16, 1863.

Topasannah (little Prairie Flower) died in, 1864, and during the same year the soul of the mother winged its way to the spirit land. Cynthia Ann was buried in the Foster graveyard, Henderson County, Texas where her remains reposed for forty-six years—till late in December, 1910 through) the efforts of the adoring son, Chief Quanah Parker, they were exhumed, conveyed to Lawton, Okla.; and, after much ceremony, re-interred in the Indian family cemetery at Post Oak, in the Wichita mountains. And thus briefly traced, closes the history of this unfortunate woman, far famed in the border annals of Texas.

Cynthia Ann Parker had two other children, besides "Prairie Flower"—both sons, and both with the Comanches. One of the boys died not long after her own demise; the other, Quanah by name, who long survived and acquired renown as the head chief of all the Comanches. Aged, and beloved by both the red and white man, the famous chief died at his tribal home, on Thursday, February 23, 1911, and was buried as he had so desired to be, by the side of his mother, "Preloch,"—Cynthia Ann Parker.

The death of Quanah Parker marked the passing of the last of the great Indian chiefs—Sitting Bull, Red Cloud, Crazy Horse, Chief Joseph and Geronimo having preceded him some years to the "happy hunting grounds."

John Parker, brother of Cynthia Ann, grew to manhood among the Comanches, and participated in their forays as a Comanche brave. During a raid into Mexico, a Mexican girl was captured. Shortly thereafter be was stricken with smallpox. The tribe fled from him in consternation, and left him to die without attention. The Mexican girl remained with and nursed him back to health. Disgusted with his former comrades, he followed the girl's advice, and went with her to

her people beyond the Rio Grande. He served in a Mexican company in the Confederate Army during the war between the states, but
would not leave the soil of Texas, refusing even to cross the line into
Louisiana. The last heard of him, he was living on a ranch in Mexico.
He, too, has long since gone to his reward.

LEONAUR

ALSO FROM LEONAUR
AVAILABLE IN SOFTCOVER OR HARDCOVER WITH DUST JACKET

THE FALL OF THE MOGHUL EMPIRE OF HINDUSTAN *by H. G. Keene*—By the beginning of the nineteenth century, as British and Indian armies under Lake and Wellesley dominated the scene, a little over half a century of conflict brought the Moghul Empire to its knees.

LADY SALE'S AFGHANISTAN *by Florentia Sale*—An Indomitable Victorian Lady's Account of the Retreat from Kabul During the First Afghan War.

THE CAMPAIGN OF MAGENTA AND SOLFERINO 1859 *by Harold Carmichael Wylly*—The Decisive Conflict for the Unification of Italy.

FRENCH'S CAVALRY CAMPAIGN *by J. G. Maydon*—A Special Correspondent's View of British Army Mounted Troops During the Boer War.

CAVALRY AT WATERLOO *by Sir Evelyn Wood*—British Mounted Troops During the Campaign of 1815.

THE SUBALTERN *by George Robert Gleig*—The Experiences of an Officer of the 85th Light Infantry During the Peninsular War.

NAPOLEON AT BAY, 1814 *by F. Loraine Petre*—The Campaigns to the Fall of the First Empire.

NAPOLEON AND THE CAMPAIGN OF 1806 *by Colonel Vachée*—The Napoleonic Method of Organisation and Command to the Battles of Jena & Auerstädt.

THE COMPLETE ADVENTURES IN THE CONNAUGHT RANGERS *by William Grattan*—The 88th Regiment during the Napoleonic Wars by a Serving Officer.

BUGLER AND OFFICER OF THE RIFLES *by William Green & Harry Smith*—With the 95th (Rifles) during the Peninsular & Waterloo Campaigns of the Napoleonic Wars.

NAPOLEONIC WAR STORIES *by Sir Arthur Quiller-Couch*—Tales of soldiers, spies, battles & sieges from the Peninsular & Waterloo campaingns.

CAPTAIN OF THE 95TH (RIFLES) *by Jonathan Leach*—An officer of Wellington's sharpshooters during the Peninsular, South of France and Waterloo campaigns of the Napoleonic wars.

RIFLEMAN COSTELLO *by Edward Costello*—The adventures of a soldier of the 95th (Rifles) in the Peninsular & Waterloo Campaigns of the Napoleonic wars.

LEONAUR

ALSO FROM LEONAUR
AVAILABLE IN SOFTCOVER OR HARDCOVER WITH DUST JACKET

THE 9TH—THE KING'S (LIVERPOOL REGIMENT) IN THE GREAT WAR 1914 - 1918 *by Enos H. G. Roberts*—Mersey to mud—war and Liverpool men.

THE GAMBARDIER *by Mark Severn*—The experiences of a battery of Heavy artillery on the Western Front during the First World War.

FROM MESSINES TO THIRD YPRES *by Thomas Floyd*—A personal account of the First World War on the Western front by a 2/5th Lancashire Fusilier.

THE IRISH GUARDS IN THE GREAT WAR - VOLUME 1 *by Rudyard Kipling*—Edited and Compiled from Their Diaries and Papers—The First Battalion.

THE IRISH GUARDS IN THE GREAT WAR - VOLUME 1 *by Rudyard Kipling*—Edited and Compiled from Their Diaries and Papers—The Second Battalion.

ARMOURED CARS IN EDEN *by K. Roosevelt*—An American President's son serving in Rolls Royce armoured cars with the British in Mesopatamia & with the American Artillery in France during the First World War.

CHASSEUR OF 1914 *by Marcel Dupont*—Experiences of the twilight of the French Light Cavalry by a young officer during the early battles of the great war in Europe.

TROOP HORSE & TRENCH *by R.A. Lloyd*—The experiences of a British Life-guardsman of the household cavalry fighting on the western front during the First World War 1914-18.

THE EAST AFRICAN MOUNTED RIFLES *by C.J. Wilson*—Experiences of the campaign in the East African bush during the First World War.

THE LONG PATROL *by George Berrie*—A Novel of Light Horsemen from Gallipoli to the Palestine campaign of the First World War.

THE FIGHTING CAMELIERS *by Frank Reid*—The exploits of the Imperial Camel Corps in the desert and Palestine campaigns of the First World War.

STEEL CHARIOTS IN THE DESERT *by S. C. Rolls*—The first world war experiences of a Rolls Royce armoured car driver with the Duke of Westminster in Libya and in Arabia with T.E. Lawrence.

WITH THE IMPERIAL CAMEL CORPS IN THE GREAT WAR *by Geoffrey Inchbald*—The story of a serving officer with the British 2nd battalion against the Senussi and during the Palestine campaign.

LEONAUR

ALSO FROM LEONAUR
AVAILABLE IN SOFTCOVER OR HARDCOVER WITH DUST JACKET

ESCAPE FROM THE FRENCH by Edward Boys—A Young Royal Navy Midshipman's Adventures During the Napoleonic War.

THE VOYAGE OF H.M.S. PANDORA by Edward Edwards R. N. & George Hamilton, edited by Basil Thomson—In Pursuit of the Mutineers of the Bounty in the South Seas—1790-1791.

MEDUSA by J. B. Henry Savigny and Alexander Correard and Charlotte-Adélaïde Dard —Narrative of a Voyage to Senegal in 1816 & The Sufferings of the Picard Family After the Shipwreck of the Medusa.

THE SEA WAR OF 1812 VOLUME 1 by A. T. Mahan—A History of the Maritime Conflict.

THE SEA WAR OF 1812 VOLUME 2 by A. T. Mahan—A History of the Maritime Conflict.

WETHERELL OF H. M. S. HUSSAR by John Wetherell—The Recollections of an Ordinary Seaman of the Royal Navy During the Napoleonic Wars.

THE NAVAL BRIGADE IN NATAL by C. R. N. Burne—With the Guns of H. M. S. Terrible & H. M. S. Tartar during the Boer War 1899-1900.

THE VOYAGE OF H. M. S. BOUNTY by William Bligh—The True Story of an 18th Century Voyage of Exploration and Mutiny.

SHIPWRECK! by William Gilly—The Royal Navy's Disasters at Sea 1793-1849.

KING'S CUTTERS AND SMUGGLERS: 1700-1855 by E. Keble Chatterton—A unique period of maritime history-from the beginning of the eighteenth to the middle of the nineteenth century when British seamen risked all to smuggle valuable goods from wool to tea and spirits from and to the Continent.

CONFEDERATE BLOCKADE RUNNER by John Wilkinson—The Personal Recollections of an Officer of the Confederate Navy.

NAVAL BATTLES OF THE NAPOLEONIC WARS by W. H. Fitchett—Cape St. Vincent, the Nile, Cadiz, Copenhagen, Trafalgar & Others.

PRISONERS OF THE RED DESERT by R. S. Gwatkin-Williams—The Adventures of the Crew of the Tara During the First World War.

U-BOAT WAR 1914-1918 by James B. Connolly/Karl von Schenk—Two Contrasting Accounts from Both Sides of the Conflict at Sea D uring the Great War.